Praise for Dr. Alison Plaut

Be More Happy is unique and beautiful book with powerful, easy-to-use tools for transformation. Dr. Alison Plaut shows a simple path to greater fulfillment in life. I highly recommend it!"

-Marci Shimoff, #1 New York Times bestselling author, Happy for No Reason and Chicken Soup for the Woman's Soul

Derived from the wisdom of Maharishi Mahesh Yogi's teachings of the science of creative intelligence, this book provides in simple and clear words the roadmap to a blissful life. I heartily recommend it.

-Suzy Camelia-Römer, former prime minister of the Netherlands Antilles

THREADS OF WISDOM ON THE PATH OF BECOMING

BE MORE

*18 practical steps
for more peace, success,
and happiness
in YOUR life
beginning today!*

DR. ALISON PLAUT

Red Penguin
BOOKS

To Guru Dev and to Maharishi Mahesh Yogi, for the wisdom of the fullness of life and the path to achieve it. The knowledge of this book comes from Maharishi, whose goal was to bring happiness and enlightenment to every individual, and peace to the world.

And, to all the seekers of "something more" in life. May we join hands to be more each day, and create the beautiful world we imagine.

Contents

Introduction

Have you ever dreamed that there was something more to life? Something beyond the possible allures of wealth, fame, success, adventure, security, or family? Have you ever felt this empty longing inside, like a vacuum of air, wondering, "Is this it?"

I seem to have been born with that feeling. I remember the disappointment and sadness when, after opening the generous gifts that my upper-middle-class family had given me on Christmas morning, I realized that none of the gifts were permanent joy. Of course, I knew this intellectually. It wasn't a surprise. And yet, somehow it was the end of the world.

I learned on those Christmas mornings something that can take a lifetime to learn: the anticipation of something special is, in many cases, better than the actual item. When a gift is wrapped, it can be anything—keys to a new car, keys to the kingdom, or even eternal happiness. But once a gift is open, that sense of all possibilities collapses into one very real, and not always charming, reality. Because gifts are, almost invariably, stuff. Sometimes it's really useful, beautiful, expensive, or fun stuff. But it's still just stuff.

I probably like stuff as much as you do, and yet there was a part of me that always wondered, "Is this it?" Because all stuff, sooner or later, becomes old stuff that is no longer interesting or special.

I'm sure you have a list to match mine. My treasured dolls are in a plastic bin in the garage of my childhood home. I sold my beloved horse before leaving for college. The latest and greatest iPhone of six years ago is in a bottom drawer with a cracked screen and a grimy case. And so it goes, with carpets and furniture, cars and condos, computers and TVs, and even, in some cases, relationships. While all these things may bring us temporary happiness, they do not bring permanent joy.

And so, just as some people are born to be football stars or astronauts, business coaches, or political luminaries, I was born asking the question, "Is this it?" And then proceeded to answer my own question with, "No! I want more."

The Beginning

I was born into a family of spiritual seekers living in a community of spiritual seekers. My parents had learned Transcendental Meditation (TM) in high school and college and had later become teachers of Transcendental Meditation. In 1979, instead of moving to San Francisco for an accounting job my father had accepted at a large firm, my parents decided—in a day—to move to Fairfield, Iowa, to a community that Maharishi Mahesh Yogi, the founder of Transcendental Meditation, was creating there.

People from across the country came to join the community and university being founded there, increasing the town's population by about 10%. The university, still growing and thriving today, is called Maharishi International University and emphasizes the development of consciousness as the foundation of its curriculum.

It was an idyllic place to grow up with rolling corn fields meeting large houses. As children, we could roam town freely by bike, rollerblade, skateboard, or any other means. I could stop at the local natural foods market and sign for a cookie on my parents' account. Summers were filled with days at the pool and slip-and-slides in front yards. In winter, there was sledding, holiday lights, and hot cocoa. We knew everyone, and everyone knew us.

It is the most cosmopolitan small town you will find in the Midwest. They like to boast that there are more restaurants per capita than in San Francisco. There are world-class artists, world-class scientists, and both brilliant and average people from all over the world. It also has the unique flavor that the community we joined was full of people looking for something more. It was a gathering of minds and hearts hoping to create a better world.

My parents' generation, disenchanted with the world they saw around them, took to meditation as a healthier outlet to the hippie movement. In those early years, Maharishi appeared on many US talk shows, and people signed up to learn TM by the thousands. It was a booming time for meditation, and TM specifically. Fairfield was, in some ways, a natural evolution of that generation's enthusiasm to create a better world.

While Maharishi was first my parents' teacher, even as a small child I developed a sense of reverence and awe for him. I could tell you it was his message, but it was more than that. Even from a photo, Maharishi radiated a presence of something more. I sensed he had the answer to my questions of, "Is this it?" and saw those other layers of life I so much wanted to understand. For me, it felt like certainty from a young age that, whatever I did, my life would be connected to Maharishi.

My generation, on the other hand, was born into the community and regarded it with the mix of disdain and intolerance that so often marks young people's vision of their parents' ideals. I was an exception in that way. Maharishi School, the K-12 private school founded to provide an ideal education for my generation, was a regular school in many ways, with sports, drama, field trips, and homework. But Fairfield was still a unique community.

When I was growing up, there was a sharp divide between the original town residents and the meditation community. Meditation, at the time, was considered strange. Yoga and meditation were not yet popular or mainstream, so we were teased, taunted, and ostracized for being weird. In retrospect, I think everyone who grew up practicing TM still can't believe how popular meditation is now. *You mean people think what we do is cool?*

Fairfield was both my inspiration for spirituality and my inspiration to ask, "Is this it?" To this day, there is something about Fairfield that will always feel like home, despite not living there for 25 years. But there is also something in Fairfield that makes me want to do and be more. That restless quality inspired by my hometown threw me into seeking—and finding. You could say I was born into meditation, but I made it my own gradually, over many years.

Seeking

The feeling of searching and wondering, "Is this it?" reached a crescendo in my teenage years. I was attending a school that was named—and I can't make this stuff up—the Ideal Girls' School. All 15 students were referred to as "Ideal Girls." It was a school that focused on the total development of the student and included classes in yoga, Vedic dance, self-pulse reading, Ayurveda, Sanskrit, and daily group meditations.

I loved the community of my school and the kindness of the other girls. I loved the discussions we had about human potential and the idea that we could "know, do, and achieve anything."

But by my sophomore year, that same familiar feeling started to creep in. "Is this it?" I was studying calculus and physics at the time, along with English literature, history, and those hour-long sessions of Sanskrit recitation. Even by the high standards of this "ideal" school, I was searching for more. I knew that more would come from Maharishi.

I loved to learn. But I reached the most horrid point for any student: the realization that no matter how much I learned, there was always going to be a lot more. I could never know it all at the rate I was going. While some may have found this motivating, I found it discouraging.

Because I had been taught that "Total Knowledge" led to fulfill-ment or happiness, I wanted to see the end-point of happiness. When would I be really fulfilled? When would the sudden euphoria of Knowing all and Being all dawn? Seeing that I had a long and futile path through math and physics to this ultimate happiness, I began to consider my options.

Having learned about the idea of developing full human potential to be able to know, do, and achieve anything, I wondered, *Why not do that first?* Why not achieve my highest potential, and along with it permanent happiness, before going for all the other things? Why wait for happiness?

And so, in a moment of teenage chutzpah, I wrote a letter to my spiritual teacher, His Holiness Maharishi Mahesh Yogi, saying just that.

Let me give you a brief introduction that puts into context my idea of writing Maharishi a letter. Entire books are written on the contributions Maharishi has made to society, so this is just a taste. Maharishi Mahesh Yogi first brought Transcendental Meditation to the west in 1959. Maharishi is credited with popularizing medi-tation, yoga,[1] and Ayurveda in the western world and in promoting scientific research on these modalities. Maharishi revived and reformulated the scattered, ancient Vedic literature into a complete science of consciousness.

Maharishi's depth and breadth of Vedic knowledge, and his daily living of it, is unparalleled. He is widely regarded by the great saints of the world as one of the greatest of the great. Those who understand true Vedic knowledge will say that Maharishi single-handedly restored and revitalized the entire Vedic wisdom.

But when he started, Maharishi was a monk who left India with a simple message that *"life is bliss."* When Maharishi first landed in San Francisco in 1959, a couple of dozen people came to his lectures. By the 1970s, he was holding six-month in-residence TM Teacher Training courses with thousands in attendance.

By the late 1990s, his teaching had been expanded and system-atized. There were thousands of trained TM teachers, as well as specialized teachers for the advanced programs. There were also tens or hundreds of thousands of hours of taped lectures of Maharishi available for all types of courses and presentations.

What had started with one person had multiplied. Most people could attend regular courses and learn all the advanced programs without ever speaking to Maharishi directly. Maharishi's vision to make this knowledge available to the world was coming to fruition.

By the 90s, it was considered a privilege to be on a call with a thousand or so others and Maharishi. To get into a room with Maharishi and a couple of hundred other people was even rarer. You either had to be a Nobel Laureate, a large benefactor of the Transcendental Meditation organization, the president of a nation, or extremely lucky. I was none of the above.

Millions of people had learned TM, and Maharishi was working around the clock with political, religious, and spiritual leaders throughout the world to, among other things, create Heaven on Earth and reconstruct the entire world.

To write a letter to Maharishi and have him see it was then almost unheard of. And to think I'd get a reply? Who did I think I was? But with all the optimism and naivety of youth, I wrote Maharishi a letter and asked the principal of my school to send it to him.

In the letter, I explained that I felt I should have a completely Vedic education. Veda or Vedic means Total Knowledge—complete understanding. Just as I realized I would never be able to learn everything through the traditional academic routes of study, I realized that if I could experience Veda—Total Knowledge—I would have a shortcut to knowing everything.

To me, a Vedic education was the fastest path to happiness and the end of my questioning "Is this it?" I saw it as a way to full spiritual realization—enlightenment—and along with it, unbounded happiness. The promise of realizing Total Knowledge, Veda, described by Maharishi, is the ability to know, do, and achieve anything. Who wouldn't want to be able to know, do, and achieve anything?

So instead of taking the long path to gain wisdom, I wanted the shortcut. To me, the study of Veda was the shortcut to permanent happiness. I saw it as a path not only to my own happiness but also to help others realize the same happiness. My goal was never that only I would find permanent happiness. My goal was to spread this same easy path of happiness to the world. I felt that everything else was a waste of time.

My letter also mentioned that I felt that my progressive school was not Vedic enough. My principal, to her credit, sent the letter with just a small note at the bottom saying that not all the students felt the same, and many were quite happy with their academic course.

Three months later, on graduation day, I received a reply from Maharishi. The message came that I could have a completely Vedic education, even if I was the only one. Maharishi said one line I will hold in my heart forever: *"Even if there is only one, one is good enough to change the world."*

I don't know whether he was talking about himself, me, or everyone in the world. It could be all of the above. This is a book about how one—each one of us—can be enough to change the whole world.

Maharishi also said I could skip a grade, since I'd already completed most of the academic requirements, and have one year on the "Vedic track" of high school before going into a deeper course of Vedic study. That meant I could focus on the deep principles and inner experiences that help one on the path to happiness and enlightenment. I was ecstatic.

So began my quest in earnest for enlightenment. Before, I had liked the idea, but now I had Maharishi's blessing to go for it. I began with all the fervor of a total neophyte and, at least initially, had about as much success. I'll tell you about how even failures built and shaped my vision of the path to perfection.

Gradually, like a very rough stone tumbled in water, my sharp edges began to soften. The impossible became more possible, and what I can only call miracles, happened in my life. As I learned from Maharishi, *"It is a pathless path."* Maharishi meant that we are all already at the goal, only we haven't yet realized it.

This book is a collection of some of the most important spiritual and life lessons I have learned in the last 25-plus years. They are meant to be a helping hand for those starting their own spiritual journey, or those already on their own path. Many of these lessons can be applied to all areas of life. Look and see, and you might find beautiful new possibilities open before you.

The wisdom in this book is Maharishi's wisdom. They say in the Vedic Tradition that the river of knowledge flows between two banks: that of the master and that of the student. This is the river of knowledge viewed from my bank.

These pivotal experiences not only shaped me but made me see Maharishi—and the vision of possibilities for each of us—in a whole new light. Perhaps you will find your own experiences resonating in the expressions found here.

Every part of this book is my story. It was not written with my mind but with my heart. Each sentence has been lived—both in the good and in the challenging. What may look like a lecture or dissertation is my experience. This is my story to date.

Inspired by more than two decades of treading this path, this book is meant to be a helping hand from someone walking alongside you. The path can be rocky. It is easy to take a wrong turn or get lost in the darkness. I know; I certainly have. Consider this the hand reaching to pull you up as we walk into the unknown and discover all that there is in this magical, incredible thing we call life.

Finding Something More

What was this "something more" I was searching for? I was looking for life beyond suffering, a life of eternal happiness. I believe with my whole heart and soul that such a life exists. The power of the individual and destiny can combine to create such a magical reality.

It was something I'd heard described my whole life but had only experienced in the briefest moments: inner peace and calm, vast like an ocean. I wanted more in every sense of the word: eternal happiness, unbounded creativity, and fulfillment.

No amount of money could buy what I was searching for. While glimpses could be had, I wanted it all the time. And as far as I could tell, no one—other than possibly a few saints—had that level of peace and happiness all the time.

Where did such an idea of eternal peace and happiness come from? For me, the idea came from the knowledge of His Holiness Maharishi Mahesh Yogi; and for Maharishi, it came from his master, the Shankaracharya of Jyotirmath, Swami Brahmananda Saraswati, who learned from his master, and so on.

Wise thinkers throughout the ages from nearly every culture around the world have spoken about inner peace, happiness, and calm. Buddhists call it Nirvana. Taoists call it Zen. Hindus call it Atma or Turiya Chetana. Christians know it in the Bible verse, "Be still and know that I am God." But the reality is beyond words and descriptions.

The idea that there is a level of peace that can be reached, experienced, and lived is not new. Even the ability to contact it is not new. What is new is that this level can be easily and widely available to anyone.

This knowledge of human potential is no longer isolated to a few fortunate seekers in the high Himalayas who happen to have found—often through great effort and years of searching—an enlightened master. It is the gift of this era that we don't have to leave home or give up any material comforts to seek our own highest potential.

While there are many paths and enlightened masters in the world guiding their few select disciples, there was one master who decided to formulate his teaching so that the whole world—wherever they were living and however they were living—could become disciples of supreme wisdom. Maharishi Mahesh Yogi brought to the world a simple and universally-effective form of meditation that complements all other spiritual practices.

He is the master who pioneered the idea that you are not required to sit at his feet and learn. Maharishi famously said, *"You will know me through my knowledge."* While others have a similar model, Maharishi was one of the first to create a systematic teaching method for anyone, regardless of lifestyle, religion, belief (or lack thereof), gender, education, socioeconomic background, or any other defining characteristic. It is a universal teaching.

For knowledge to be practical, you need to apply and live it. The direct, simple, and systematic means to experience the theoretical knowledge of Maharishi is through Transcendental Meditation and the advanced programs of Transcendental Meditation, including the TM-Sidhi program. With these techniques, knowledge about the unity of life and inner being are not just words, they are a living reality.

Transcendental Meditation (TM)

What makes Transcendental Meditation unique is that you can reach the depth of your self—the source of your own thinking—automatically. We often use an analogy of the ocean to describe what happens in TM. Imagine daily thinking as if your mind is swimming on the surface of the ocean. There might be big, gently rolling waves, or you might get caught in a choppy storm. Just like the surface of the ocean, our minds are always changing. You never know when the next storm might roll in—either due to outer circumstances or inner changes.

When you practice TM, the mind settles down to the source of thought. Just like the silent, peaceful bed of the deeper ocean, the source of thought is a field of infinite peace and silence. It is also unbounded happiness.

To teach this level of inner peace through TM is effortless and automatic. Anyone who can think a thought can meditate. It requires no concentration, no contemplation, and no effort.[2]

Children can learn the TM technique as young as age ten, and there is a special children's technique that they can learn from age four. The process is different from other common types of meditation, as well. Mindfulness, from the Buddhist tradition, aims to keep the mind in the present moment. In Transcendental Meditation, the mind transcends automatically - you don't have to do anything.

All the benefits experienced from TM stem from the fact that the mind can experience the source of thought systematically. This allows the body to gain deep rest and release stress. From the release of the debilitating effects of stress, life flourishes in an infinite number of ways—from better health to better memory, better relationships, greater job satisfaction, and even a better society.[3]

For more on Transcendental Meditation, see point two in the section on Practical Application.

Consciousness

Consciousness is awareness, or "that which is conscious." By that definition, to be conscious means to be awake or aware. However, consciousness can also refer to the purest, deepest state of being aware. Consciousness is another name for the settled state of the mind, the source of thought.

This definition of consciousness can be described as a universal state of Being or Am-ness. It is the underlying reality of the universe and everything that we think exists. Consciousness by this definition could also be called "orderly intelligence" or "creative intelligence" or even I-ness, Be-ing, or Is-ness. It is a state of an all-time, indestructible, eternity of awareness.

This level of consciousness is not normally experienced in day-to-day life. Most people don't describe tapping into a universal state of Being or orderly intelligence. But sometimes, some people do.

Artists describe being in the flow. Athletes describe being in the zone. Poets and philosophers describe experiences of Being and spend years or decades searching for it. Many people, if they think deeply, will find they glimpsed this at some point in their lives.

In this book, experiencing consciousness refers to this level of eternal awareness or Being, not merely to the state of individual conscious awareness. This all-powerful universal consciousness is what we contact when we practice TM. You can call it by many names, and all will be correct because this universal level is beyond any description.

How do we get there regularly? Having experienced consciousness, we can develop this reality to be an all-time experience, so peace and happiness within are never lost. This happens naturally and grows gradually. Experiencing this reality more and more is called the growth of higher states of consciousness.[4] This book is a glimpse of this reality, the infinite peace and happiness within, even in the midst of life's inevitable storms.

Something SO BIG

When I was 14, I attended a three-week summer camp at a women's retreat. This women's group would turn out to have a formative influence on me for years to come. It is a group called the Mother Divine program, founded for women who want to focus on developing their full potential to reach enlightenment. It is the ultimate personal development retreat. They offer both long and short courses for women who are focused on spiritual development as the source of highest empowerment.

The retreat facility is in the Catskill Mountains of upstate New York, set on a large, crystalline lake and surrounded by forests and wild blueberry fields. The three-week summer camp was much like a traditional summer camp: we had acting classes, sang songs, played sports, boated and swam in the lake, hiked, and picked

wild blueberries. We also did daily group meditations and practiced yoga asanas (posture or positions, simple exercise) for about
half an hour twice a day.

What happened was not in the activities, which I loved, but in my
awareness. After about two weeks, I started to feel like I was in a
giant bubble of softness. It was so big that I couldn't see the edges.
It was filled with peace and deeply-contented happiness. It felt like
silence moving, silence walking, and silence talking.

My meditations were enjoyable, but this was not an experience
solely in my meditation. It lasted day and night and changed my
perspective. What I thought of as important, suddenly seemed
unimportant. The reality of teenage worries melted away.

I felt peace, but it was not just a feeling. I was peace. Everything
around me was filled with peace.

At this moment, I saw that peace and happiness go hand in hand.
Together with so much peace, I felt deep silence along with happiness or bliss. It was this experience that convinced me I wanted to
go to school there. I never wanted the experience to end. It lasted
about a week until I felt I was unceremoniously dropped back
onto earth.

In a way, it gave me a glimpse into what the concept of "heaven on
earth" is. If so much happiness and peace are possible, then
perhaps what we think of as life on earth is just the beginning.

Prehistoric humans thought their life each day—fighting to
survive, perhaps even without fire—was life on earth. Now we
know how much more comfortable and convenient life can be.
Perhaps the new frontier of development is not in outside
advances but in inner advances.

What we thought of as "happy" or "peaceful" or "loving" is
perhaps just the beginning—less than 1% of the full reality.[5]
Until that moment, I was asking, "Is this it?" From that moment,

I knew without a doubt that there is so much more to experience, be, and become. This was one of my first lasting glimpses of higher states of consciousness and the greater possibilities that life can offer.

Embracing the Ever-changing Nature of Life

While universal consciousness is ever the same, every other level of consciousness is always changing. Perspectives in life are constantly changing with experience. What may be absolute truth to one person may feel false to another. It doesn't mean either person is wrong.

Think of a mountain: the person standing on top of the mountain will have a completely different view than a person standing at the base of the mountain. The weather, air temperature, vegetation, view, and oxygen saturation will all be different. The needs, desires, and perspectives of someone at the base of the mountain are completely different from someone at the top of the mountain. The same is true of life and evolution.

Imagine life and evolution like a chain of mountains large enough to give everyone on earth a different perspective. That perspective is not stagnant because we are always moving. We make choices, from important choices like religion, marriage, children, and career, to trivial choices like what we say or don't say, or what we eat in a day. All these choices, thoughts, and actions affect our thinking, feeling, and perspective on life.

Even if we think we are sitting still, just maintaining our life and not moving, the nature of life is to grow and progress. Even as unwilling participants, the circumstances around us will force us to move forward.

In the analogy of the mountain, even if you decide to lie down at the base of the mountain and not move, the weather will change. It may rain or get too hot in the sun. Other people will come along and ask what you are doing and if you need help. Even if you think you are not moving, life finds a way to move you forward.

What are we all moving toward? Ultimately, it is greater happiness. But it may not appear as a straight path. In fact, it will often feel like anything but a straight path. The path might appear circuitous, or that you are taking two steps forward and three steps back, or simply that you are entirely lost. The constant change of life can feel like a Ferris wheel in which we are all sometimes up and sometimes down.

But a Ferris wheel is too predictable to be an accurate analogy of life. Riding a 30-minute rollercoaster blindfolded with water elements might be a better analogy. It is long and it is unpredictable. You can go from feeling on top of the world in utter joy to sheer terror, and in between there will be times when it is a bit boring. The determination of each person to endure, persevere, and continue to hope for something better is truly amazing.

What is a person to do while riding the ultimate roller coaster called life and still asking, "Is this it?" This book will answer that question. For the skeptics, the heartbroken, the disappointed, and the disillusioned, this is my letter of empathy to you.

It is a hand reaching through the pages reminding you that you are not alone. For everyone, this is a way to reach within your own heart and find more compassion, more love, and more power than you ever thought possible.

Perspective

Experience is all about perception and perspective. It is not what others see when looking in from the outside, but what you see when looking out—or in—from the inside. This perspective is critical because, for inner exploration, the first step is to trust your perception.

We often choose to believe what the outside is telling us over what we perceive for ourselves, or we choose to belittle ourselves instead of viewing ourselves as friends. Many of us have had moments, or even decades, of incredible intuition and choose to write over it with intellectual or external pressure.

I learned as a child an expression Maharishi used in the Science of Creative Intelligence[1], *"Knowledge is gained from inside and outside."* We are all so accustomed to gaining knowledge from the outside. This book is about rediscovering the channel to gain knowledge from the inside.

Believe the one looking outside from within. Believe the one feeling. You are mighty and powerful.

The short answer to "Is this it?" is that there is so much more than any of us could ever imagine. Whatever you think of life, no matter how great you thought you could be or what you could achieve, there are worlds more possibilities than you could ever imagine in your life, and more importantly, within yourself.

Why Threads?

These threads are condensed phrases that contain within them a world of wisdom. They have come through Divine Grace, with heart-expanding, tears of despair, and a whole lot of sheer determination. These 18 threads of wisdom appear as catchy or common phrases, and yet, there are layers within them. A single phrase can be enough to change a life.

I called these lessons "Threads" because they weave through everything, but what you choose to weave, and how you put them together, is up to you. The essence is to create a beautiful new reality. You could weave a tapestry, a carpet, or sew clothing. The reality you can create with these threads of wisdom is infinite.

They are threads of wisdom I understood from Maharishi to be woven into your own understanding and experience as a unique tapestry of knowledge. The threads contained in this book are not ancient aphorisms, although many have ancient roots. They are whispers from a modern aspirant and guides to take the first step, the next step, or reach the goal.

I've also included quotes from many wise thinkers throughout the ages because truth, echoing through the corridors of time, can be spoken in many voices. These threads interweave with their wisdom, creating at once a continuity and a new beginning. You will also find that the threads are interconnected, and many themes are interwoven throughout the chapters.

Though these threads of wisdom are simple, you may find the answer to questions about eternal happiness, the nature of life, or the highest truth. I hope you also find more beauty, love, and compassion for yourself.

Each thread is self-contained, so the topics change throughout the book. They are organized to unfold, one upon the other, like new petals opening in a flower.

Many threads include stories that introduce wise and powerful figures both modern and ancient, fictional, and real. The stories are intended to be light and inspirational, but multi-faceted. Which ones speak to you?

As you read each chapter, take time to reflect on its message in your own life, in the lives of people you admire, and in nature. Once you start to look, you will be surprised at how often you find that these threads of wisdom are already there in plain sight.

They are not mine, just as sunlight is not mine; but they are gifts from nature and from a tradition of eternal knowledge that is imminently practical, and desperately needed, to bring long-sought happiness into the current age.

I offer you the tender threads of my heart and the hard-earned wisdom of my path, with the wish that it makes your days softer and brighter. And the next time you find yourself wondering, "Is this it?" you hear a whisper of "There is more; come this way."

Self-healing reveals eternal enlightenment, pure happiness,

and totality is already within each of us.

Thread 1: Always Keep Learning

"The highest education is that which does not merely give us information but makes our life in harmony with all existence."
~ Rabindranath Tagore

Tagore's words echo through time: knowledge is for action and harmony with existence. If knowledge cannot lead to lasting happiness and peace, then is there value in that knowledge? How does one acquire such a high education?

The greatest seekers are the best students. This is also true of leaders in any field of life. To become great is to become a student of the discipline and a student of life. This is not the classroom learning of multiplication tables. This is the lifetime learning which enriches and enhances the character, heart, and mind.

Knowledge is for practical application and to enrich life. One could spend weeks or months memorizing each word in the dictionary in alphabetical order. Or one could learn words and vocabulary relevant and useful to daily life. Both types of learning are valid, but the first will only interest a tiny portion of the population. Most of us prefer knowledge that is useful.

Maharishi has said that knowledge is for action. The greater the knowledge, the greater the action. Infinite, Total Knowledge is for limitless action. This level of knowledge means you can accomplish anything. It seems far away, but this level of limitless knowledge is already within each of us.

An example of knowledge for action: A student performing mathematical calculations in the classroom might not see the application. But a physicist working on a theory or an astronaut planning the trajectory of a spacecraft will immediately see the application of the fundamentals they learned in school.

This knowledge of life comes in packages large and small. These packages could be said to be what we can learn in a second, in a minute, in an hour, in a day, and in a lifetime. All these packages of knowledge provide opportunities for growth and expansion of new avenues of action.

Nearly everyone will agree that primary and secondary education is essential to develop the potential of the citizens of each country and create a productive society. But education does not stop the moment the diploma is conferred.

Humility, alertness, and openness to continue learning are some of the greatest skills a seeker can possess on the path to eternal happiness. When we learn, we grow. When we stop learning, we declare ourselves done, which is a mistake of arrogance or lack of knowledge. While on this earth, we always have opportunities to learn and grow.

Maharishi exemplified this in all his wisdom. As a great realized Rishi, he didn't need to learn from outside, he could learn from within himself. And yet, he worked with Nobel Laureates, scientists, doctors, and political leaders, listening with respect to their ideas and suggestions.

That respect and graciousness were even greater around Swamis and the spiritual leaders of India. That humility and respect were born out of fullness. When one is everything, there is no threat from the outside. Learning outside becomes learning from the inside. There is not two, only one.

One such touching story happened when Maharishi was visited by another spiritual leader, Swami Muktananda. Normally, Maharishi would sit on a couch on a stage, often with flower arrangements surrounding him. But in this case, Maharishi insisted on sitting on the floor below Swami Muktananda. This was an act of humility surprising to those familiar with Maharishi's contributions to the field of knowledge, including the revival of the Vedic wisdom for practical application in life.

Maharishi explained that Swami Muktananda was a *"Swami"* which means one who is established—realized or enlightened. Maharishi referred to himself as a *"brahmachari,"* a student. This humble proclamation was indeed a sign of Maharishi's greatness. In a simple, playful, human way, he expressed his true greatness, wrapped with love and respect for Swami Muktananda.

In other instances, Maharishi mentioned that there were a few other enlightened masters living at that time. One of them was Swami Muktananda. When both are on the highest level of life in bliss, unified within themselves, the level of respect the enlightened have for each other is without boundaries.

There is an example Maharishi used of a mango tree: when the tree is young or the fruits are green, the tree stands tall. But when the fruits are ripe, the tree bows to the ground in humility. The ability to keep learning in grace and humility is a sign of maturity and greatness.

We are all lifelong students. Whether we want to or not, we are always learning. We learn to use new technology, drive new cars, learn new words, and new ways of thinking and doing. Some of this newness we resist, but some inevitably become routine knowledge.

The wise seeker recognizes that knowledge must not only be acquired but that it should be gained in the most efficient manner for the greatest practical benefit. To gain knowledge and wisdom requires persistence, patience, and dedication. But it is not through hard work or effort that the greatest knowledge is gained. It is through uncovering the inner levels of wisdom and intelligence. As they say, it is learning to work smarter, not harder.

Knowledge Gained from Inside and Outside

In the Science of Creative Intelligence, I studied Maharishi's vision of learning with the principle that knowledge is gained from inside and outside. What does that mean? How we gain knowledge on the outside is familiar. We study, we are exposed to information, and we learn. Some knowledge is gained spontaneously while other knowledge is gained through assiduous study. Everyone, when interested in a subject, knows how to learn more about it.

Knowledge gained from the inside is more elusive and more practical. What does knowledge from the inside mean? Knowledge gained from the inside means tapping into our own human potential. From a scientific standpoint, it means using more of our full brain function.

Knowledge gained from the inside is more insightful, foresightful, and all-encompassing than basic thoughts and conclusions. It is more than ideas or conclusions derived from sensory perception. If we took knowledge on the inside to be our own rudimentary conclusions of the intellect, we would still believe the sun magically rises and sets each day or orbits around the earth.

Knowledge gained from the inside is the deep inner vision and capacity of intuition that can transcend the apparent changing reality of life to the truth. It is spontaneous knowing. When the inner ability to gain or access knowledge is awake, anything is possible.

This sounds grandiose, but it is very simple. When we are only using 10-15% of our brain's potential, we have handicapped our abilities to think, deduce, and achieve. This is not one person or a small percentage of the population—it is a limitation that humanity has been living with for centuries. If we can increase the use of our full brain potential—even double it to 20-30%—it will open unimaginable new possibilities.

For those of us prone to asking, "Is this it?" the answer is obvious. Call it intuition, a gut feeling, or even entitlement, but that little voice asking for more is right. There is so much more we can achieve through the development of full brain potential. Interestingly, this is also where the value of science and spirituality converge.

The path to gaining knowledge from the inside has been carved in ancient traditions around the world. If you investigate the deep wisdom of any religion, spiritual tradition, or ancient culture, you will find a means of connecting with higher knowledge or intuition.

The indigenous people of Colombia, the Kogis, have a special tradition to open the inner knowledge of their Shamans. The Tibetan Buddhists have their own practices to open inner vision. You will find similar traditions from the Mayans and Incans in Central and South America, the Masai and ancient Egyptians of Africa, and the Australian Aborigines. For the ancient cultures, the inner life was the first life.

For those of us not born into the Kogi tribe or on the high Tibetan plateau, inner knowledge can still be developed in a systematic manner. This is one of the most important human abilities. Anyone from any background, race, religion, socioeconomic level, or country has this birthright. We all eat, we all breathe, we all can love—and we all can develop our full potential.

When the mind opens to the source of thought, it opens to a field of all knowledge. The source of all the knowledge in creation lies within you. It sounds fantastic, whimsical, or unbelievable. And yet, this is reality. Infinite wisdom is within you.

It can be called a field of consciousness, or knowingness. This inner reality of consciousness contains pure knowledge in its seed form. And this knowledge, like all knowledge, is for action. It is as if a cosmic computer can be accessed. From that level, we can know, do, and achieve anything.

Just because we don't see it, does not mean it does not exist. The power of inner knowledge is greater than the power of outer knowledge because it is immediately relevant, applicable, and timely. Knowledge becomes available when it is needed.

All the great universities of the world have libraries filled with books. Any student will realize it takes more than a lifetime to absorb all the knowledge in even one section of one university library. The best researchers will know where to search. But if the necessary knowledge is available inside now, that is practical knowledge.

Searching in consciousness is both the same and different from searching within a library. In a library, there is a system to search for specific information. That used to be an involved process, but now anyone can search on the internet and get results on any subject of knowledge within seconds. The same is true of inner knowledge. It is like having a vast resource library inside, instead of outside in a library or on the internet.

The difference is that on the level of consciousness, you don't even need to be aware of the question to get the answer. Psychology is talking more and more about how the subconscious mind motivates so much of our lives—without our knowledge.

What if all levels of the mind and brain were working together for our goals and desires? Then, even before you want to know something, the answer comes.

Practical knowledge means not only knowing facts like the temperature on the moon or the distance in an electron orbital. It means that before you meet someone important, you have the inspiration for what to say to them. It means you have the idea to bring a coat, even though the weather is beautiful—only to find you need it later in the day. It means getting a feeling about a particular stock even though others say it's not a great pick—and finding you were right. It means sensing when to offer kindness and compassion, even when someone appears to be fine.

How much this practical knowledge is developed in your life, and how you choose to use it, depends on many factors. But one thing is certain: without the development of the brain's full potential, we make all that is easy more difficult.

Knowledge for Happiness

Making life easier for ourselves has an added benefit: we may also gain greater insight into how to solve problems for others and make the world a more beautiful, harmonious, healthy, creative, and peaceful place.

Again, in the words of Rabindranath Tagore: "*The highest education is that which does not merely give us information but makes our life in harmony with all existence.*"

When developing the brain's full potential, the level of consciousness experienced is a level of harmony, peace, and happiness. The two go hand in hand. It is not either-or. It is both at once. That means that the same experience which develops full brain potential is an experience of greater harmony, happiness, and peace. We begin to find ourselves in harmony with all existence. It is not theoretical. It is immediately practical and has been experienced by millions of people all over the world.

For me, that feeling of incredible bliss in meditation or my advanced programs taught by Maharishi Mahesh Yogi were light-bulb moments. The first time it seemed as if it was luck. The second time it seemed as if there was hope. And each time after, it feels like a gift from God, the universe, and life. No matter how hardened a heart or how limited a mind is, the ability to be unlimited—even momentarily—is like being weightless after a lifetime in a weighted suit. It is freedom and bliss.

To always keep learning is irrespective of intelligence or supposed capacity to learn. Anyone, from any level of education, can access and experience unbounded intelligence. And this unbounded intelligence is unbounded bliss. The two go hand in hand. Some will experience bliss like peacefulness, calmness, or something good that they cannot quite describe. But whatever the words, the transformation to something greater than we ever imagined is underway.

When knowledge brings fulfillment, the lifelong pursuit of "Is this it?" begins to breathe a sigh of relief. There is a light at the end of the tunnel. No matter how far away, it can be reached. And this light, this hope of happiness, is also a promise of harmony with life. It is a promise that life ceases to be a selfish pursuit and automatically brings greater harmony to the world around us.

That is an incredible comfort. How many of us worry and wonder how our actions and words will affect others? If we will unintentionally harm our children, spouse, parents, or friends? Imagine being able to lift that limitation and worry even a little bit.

What a gift to find that knowledge gained from the inside creates life in greater harmony, first with ourselves, then with the world around us and the universe. So much grace of living comes from knowledge with the greatest practical value. This knowledge is no longer about the gathering of facts and information, but about the gathering of harmony and happiness.

Whatever someone's ability or accolades, everyone, no matter how confident or content, is looking for happiness, love, and fulfillment. Inner knowledge and expansion of our full potential create the growth of happiness and harmony within ourselves and in our world. This is a direct and practical path to what we all crave most deeply. With inner knowledge comes access to inner peace, happiness, love, and a clear path to fulfillment.

In the Vedic Literature, the first verse of the Vedant sutras says,

अथातो ब्रह्मजिज्ञासा

"Now, from here, the desire to know Brahm."

This is the seeker expressing the search for the highest knowledge. It is a quest to keep learning to find fulfillment. What is this Brahm? It is the ability to know, do, and achieve anything.

From the first verse of Vedant, from the start of learning, the goal is clear. We want to know totality; we want to have limitless potential—and realize it. Now, from here, we desire to know Brahm, to know totality, to know our own greatest and highest self.

In this definition, to always keep learning means gaining the ability to accomplish any desire. Knowledge is for action—the discovery within one's self of the ability to know, do and achieve anything. No desire is beyond possibility.

As a small child, I experienced my own version of *"Now, from here, the desire to know Brahm"* as I searched for Maharishi and Maharishi's wisdom within myself. Here is the story:

In Their Intelligence Will Shine...

When I was six years old, entering the first grade, a new building was constructed for my school. It was called the Maharishi School of the Age of Enlightenment. Let's break that name down because the word "school" might be the only familiar part.

The school was named after its founder, Maharishi Mahesh Yogi. It was usually referred to as "Maharishi School." But the end part was added by Maharishi. Maharishi wanted to create what he called Heaven on Earth or the Age of Enlightenment. A simple definition of this is all good for everyone and non-good (i.e. bad) for no one. It was and is an incredible ideal.

Just before the school was to be inaugurated, an interaction between a boy and Maharishi inspired a quote that remains on the entrance of the school building still today.

The boy, called Ben, was a couple of years older than me. He heard that his family's dinner guest was going to visit Maharishi. Ben ran out into his family's driveway, collected a rock, and asked their guest to give the rock to Maharishi. Maharishi was a world spiritual luminary focused on regenerating the whole of mankind and creating Heaven on Earth. People did not give Maharishi rocks they found in their driveways.

When Maharishi heard that this little boy wanted to give him a rock, he replied with the quote that was later inscribed above the entrance to the school, *"In their intelligence will shine the world's most perfect wisdom."*

When the building was inaugurated later that year, I was entering first grade. Maharishi School had a tradition that on the first day of school all the students, faculty, and parents would gather outside the building. We would then march into the school grade by grade, youngest to oldest. That meant the first graders went first.

I vividly remember that late August day, still warm enough that we were all in short sleeves, getting sticky as we sat in clusters in the grass. When it was time to walk into the school, I marched proudly and nervously with my classmates up the new sidewalk and into the brand-new building. As I walked, I decided to practice my reading skills and read the plaque above the door.

It read: *In their intelligence will shine the world's most perfect wisdom—Maharishi.*

With my rudimentary reading skills, I took that to mean that the world's most perfect wisdom was Maharishi. I looked down at the sky-blue uniform I wore with a baby pink bow. Did I see Maharishi shining in me? I didn't.

But I knew that day would come. The world's most perfect wisdom was embodied in the person I saw as the source of the highest wisdom. I thought that one day I would see Maharishi shining in my heart.

While that day hasn't come in a literal sense, I don't think my interpretation was wrong. The reality is that knowledge shines in our hearts as well as our minds. We were learning Maharishi's knowledge, so naturally, it would shine in our thinking and intelligence. It is woven into the fabric of who we are.

Maharishi is famous for saying, *"You will know me through my knowledge."*

How precious it would be for the world's most perfect wisdom to shine all the time. To me, to always keep learning means to reach a level where the highest knowledge is integrated into the fabric of heart, soul, and personality.

This is one of the great gifts of Maharishi and other realized teachers: how to keep learning from within. We can learn outside and from the inside. The two go hand in hand. By learning to see and experience the knowledge inside, we find real wisdom shines.

Action Steps

Here are some reflections, ideas, and actions to absorb and experience this thread of wisdom:

1. Listen. Be open to learning what life presents. We don't know what we don't know. Nature knows best how to organize, and it is not always obvious what the long-term plan is. If you are presented with an opportunity to learn—take it.

2. Reflect. Take time to learn about yourself and your intuition. Listen to the finer levels of your thinking. Write in a journal. Write about your experience. Take time in nature to quietly be.

3. Reflect and Write. What have you learned that changed your life or perspective? Reflect on how continuing to learn has changed you.

4. Remember. Think of what you've learned in the last few months. How has the process of learning changed you? What has your effort to learn taught you? How has that changed the quality of your life? With this, notice how the attitude to constantly learn improves the quality of your life.

5. Notice how when you are more alert and rested, your learning ability is much higher. Notice how learning ability depends on the quality of consciousness.

Self-healing recognizes elucidating experiences, manifesting purposeful, healthy actions and thoughts.

Thread 2: Anything is Possible

"When I say anything is possible, I mean ANYTHING is possible."
~ Maharishi Mahesh Yogi

What an incredible, powerful vision of reality. If anything is possible, then truly there are no limits.

Rumi describes this in another way: *"This is love: to fly toward a secret sky, to cause a hundred veils to fall each moment. First to let go of life. Finally, to take a step without feet."*

Who wouldn't love to fly to a secret sky and step without feet? I certainly would. Who wouldn't love to make anything possible? While in later parts of this book we'll talk about how happiness, love, and attention can all transform life, this thread of wisdom is a reminder that what seems impractical could be deeply practical.

Something as seemingly poetic and whimsical as a secret sky and stepping without feet is as real as the love new parents feel when they meet their child. Changing life through love, happiness, and attention is as real as an inexplicable connection in meeting a new person. They are as real as the feeling of pride for a country, devotion to religion, or love of God. What seems impossible is, in fact, possible.

I chose the phrase "Anything is possible" because I truly believe it. I've seen it in my life as well as in the lives of others. Miracles are all around us. The impossible becomes possible in both little and big ways daily.

From the miracle of an infertile woman getting pregnant to the miracle of an unexpected recovery from illness, life is full of miracles. Even the sun rising every day, the warm breeze on your skin, and the joy you feel in seeing a loved one are little miracles of living.

The bigger miracle is that humans, with our limitations and shortcomings, can consider, and even experience, that anything is possible. The fact that we can experience the world through our senses and even go beyond our senses is a miracle. "Anything is possible" means that more than our wildest dreams are possible.

When you really desire something, there are ways and means in nature to make it happen. There is no need to plan out the why and how. Nature will have a million ways and paths to bring new possibilities and to help you fulfill the deepest desires you didn't even know you had.

This thread of wisdom is also for the moments when you want something you don't deserve or don't think you could ever achieve. "Anything is possible" is for the person in poverty who wants to be a billionaire. It is possible for the person who feels alone to find love and companionship. "Anything is possible" is a reminder that even if a person experiencing challenges or extreme sadness right now can find eternal happiness.

The Brain Can Create All Possibilities

This reality of all possibilities is seen in the brain in neuroplasticity. Every experience changes the brain. Even with trauma, stress, or PTSD, the brain, with the right tools, can enliven its full potential and become whole.

Dr. Fred Travis summarizes this in his book, *The Brain is a River, Not a Rock:*

> "The understanding that our brain changes with every experience has transformed thinking and research in neuroscience. Twenty years ago, neuroscientists thought brain circuits only changed during critical periods when children were very young. Now, it is known that experience changes the brain from birth to old age. Life can be pictured as the progressive development of brain circuits leading to the progressive transformation of how we see the world.
>
> Our whole life is the expression of changing brain connections that limit what we can experience and understand, and also are changed by each experience. Our current brain connections are the sum of all of our past experiences. The brain connections we wake up with tomorrow reflect the decisions we made today for specific experiences. It's up to us. We do create our reality; not by belief and affirmation, but by doing. We are in control. We can create whatever reality we want to have in our lives."

To say "anything is possible" is not a nice, inspirational slogan. It is a physical reality. With the right tools for transformation, and with focus, we can change our reality, day by day, year by year.

How to Make the Impossible Possible

Belief and attention, along with experience and action, make the impossible possible. Attention comes spontaneously through the experience of the inner self. Experiencing the power of conscious-ness and using that power in daily life brings about physical trans-formations that can make the impossible possible. Belief, love, and passion light the flames and open new vistas to make an impos-sible dream become a reality. One person, no matter how small or undeserving they feel, with the depth of belief, the power of love, and the experience of their own almighty level of consciousness can accomplish anything.

Of course, there are times when even with belief and passion the world seems to fall apart around us. There are accidents, tragedies, heartbreak, loss, misery, and death. This thread of wisdom is not intended to mean that if these things happen to you or someone you love, you just didn't believe enough or love enough. This is the opposite of that.

In those moments when you feel the world crashing down around you when hope is like an extinguished flame and despair a constant companion, this thread of wisdom is for you. This is for the person so deep in grief or mourning that just to draw a breath feels too difficult.

It is a flicker of light to say even if you are not okay right now, someday life could be more beautiful than you can possibly imag-ine. You are doing what you can right now, breathing, being, and surviving. And that is enough. Because anything is possible, misery one day may be transformed into ecstatic happiness.

In my own life, I have seen this many times in different circumstances. Life can change in an instant. Maharishi taught me this lesson when he gave me opportunities that others would have said I was unqualified for that transformed my destiny in ways I may never fully understand. And I've seen it with situations big and small. It might not happen right away. It might take years. But with a desire and conviction something beautiful will come out.

I have also seen this in times of sadness. There were times in my life when I was so hurt by circumstances or feelings of failure that I didn't want to get out of bed in the morning. Everything seemed too difficult or too pointless.

Those days are now a distant memory. While some of the outer circumstances that ignited those feelings remain the same, my inner reality changed. I was once again reminded not to look outside but within. I found inner strength and conviction, not in some great glorious flash, but gradually, day by day. I also remembered Maharishi's words and the feeling he created: what we see outside is our own reflection. We can create from within. We are not dependent on anyone else's action or inaction.

I also found people who inspire me and who are striving with their whole hearts for Maharishi's vision. Some are long-time leaders, while others are younger and newer. If you had told me in those days that I would feel at peace and with a new direction, I would have had difficulty believing it.

A new life, within a life, is also its own kind of miracle. This book is one such new life. It is my call to those seeking more or searching for truth that we may all find each other and join to make something beautiful. Because anything is possible; the dream of a world of peace and happiness is possible.

Live Each Day

When you want to see the miracles of life—that anything is possible—the best advice I have is to live each day. It sounds so simple, but there is more.

To live each day is advice given in various ways throughout time and from numerous self-help teachers. But like most things, it is easier said than done. We get caught documenting for the future and worrying about the past; or looking to the past while worrying about the future. The combination of ways that we can manage to be anywhere but right in the moment is astonishing. We are practically superheroes of avoiding the moment.

But the moment is when the miracles happen. It is in the tender moments of life when we can touch infinity. This is not mood-making, and I am not asking you to try to find those beautiful moments. To live in the moment means to give the real essence and nature of life a chance to seep through your rushing mind or burdened heart and touch you.

It is in the moments, even the moments when we feel the most insecure or in doubt when we can reach beyond, to our own higher power, to the nature of our own lives.

Life is big, important, and significant. Every day is the most important day of your life. Every moment is the most important moment of your life. That is not said to create pressure but to create opportunities.

We do not live in the past or live for the future. We are not judged or accepted for what we have done but for who we are. In the end, when we leave this life, we carry with us only who we are in heart, mind, and consciousness. The more intelligence, creativity, purity, and bliss is available to us through the experience of our own inner consciousness, the more life will open new possibilities.

We can each be big or small, great or grand. We are already full of the light of God and expressing Divinity; but we have forgotten. In our limitations, we believe that we cannot be the expression of Divinity while doing laundry, walking the dog, making lunch, or any other of the millions of mundane activities that seem to crowd out the memory of our essential nature.

With such an enormous scope and possibility, the small steps and desires of life become, in a way, insignificant. And yet, to live the unbounded in the mundane existence is to step beyond the field of all possibilities and into the role of creator of all possibilities. It is at this level where one never has to say, "Is this it?"

In the words of Khalil Gibran, *"The timeless in you is aware of life's timelessness. And knows that yesterday is but today's memory and tomorrow is today's dream."*

We are all timeless beings, appearing to live within the boundaries of time and space. And yet, we only ever have today. It is today, in this instant, that we can make the greatest moment of life and change destiny forever. All possibilities are available in every moment. In the end, yesterday is already a memory, and tomorrow is but a dream. But today, at this moment, we are the architects of destiny and creators of all possibilities.

Seeing is Believing

How many of us have heard that seeing is believing? But have you ever seen without your eyes? Have you ever looked with your heart? Some people prefer only to see with their eyes. Others always look with the heart. Maybe the eyes can see, but perhaps the skin can see, as well.

You can see with your eyes, but there is a different type of seeing that comes with feeling. It is just as clear but less concrete. The only thing required to see with feeling is to trust the feeling. For me, that feeling started early.

When I was about seven years old, I was in the yellow bedroom of my childhood home with my parents. We were preparing to perform a simple ceremony of gratitude to the Tradition of Masters that had given knowledge of the fullness of life to Guru Dev and Maharishi. My father would perform the ceremony, which takes about five minutes and involves a few flowers and fruits respectfully offered. I stood a little away, a rose in my pressed hands, and listened as my parents began to sing. As they sang the names of the Masters of the Vedic Tradition, I felt a light, a presence in the room and inside of me. It was not like beings or ghosts appearing, but more like a flood of light. It was like the consciousness in the room got bigger.

You can imagine it like one moment standing in a bedroom, and suddenly you find yourself in a football stadium or large venue. What you thought was limited became big in a moment.

I looked at the far corner of the room, away from the table we were all facing. There appeared a radiance of light and wisdom. It was a feeling of stepping into eternity with my senses. As the words continued, I observed different forms, as if projected on a 3D movie screen, but transparent.

I seemed to feel them as much as I saw them, perhaps more. It was as if I was actually feeling the physical essence of the room, especially this new dimension, with my whole body. In this case, it was like feeling gradually led to seeing; but instead of seeing through my eyes, the vision went directly to my brain.

I felt reverence, and I felt love. It seemed like the most natural thing in the world. As my parents sang, I stood with my back to them, looking, feeling, as the Masters appeared one by one.

After hearing many other people's experiences and having others myself, I realize this was not an appearance of spirits, angels, or some other celestial field. It was not calling the Masters but simply glimpsing a field of eternal wisdom in a way I could understand and feel.

The whole experience lasted only a few minutes, but it deeply changed my perception of life. I realized that the Masters were not ancient people who lived some time ago but were available at this moment. It built a connection to the Tradition of Masters not through thinking but through experience.

It also made me see that what we think of as real and concrete is just a tiny portion of all that exists in the universe. What seems so important is so small. If these ancient Masters of the highest wisdom and enlightenment can bless a little girl standing in a bedroom with her parents, they must be all-time available everywhere. That understanding aligns with what I would later learn.

Over thirty years later, it is still difficult to articulate the significance of that experience because it was a knowing. There was no specific message. No guidance. But even to see, changed everything.

In the Vedic Tradition, there is a concept called "darshan." Darshan means sight. It usually refers to the blessings given by the Master or the transformation that occurs by seeing something holy or sacred. I received darshan that day.

The power of darshan is in transformation through sight. Just by looking or seeing, everything changes—the character, beliefs, values, and goals of a person. I didn't see any immediate outward change in myself, but to this day I can still feel that vision in my body.

I saw not with my eyes, where a memory image could later be recalled, but with my feeling. It was like the boundaries of my body became softer. Almost as if my awareness was reaching out like tentacles into the environment.

If seeing is believing, then seeing beyond the eyes is believing beyond the eyes. It means there is so much more to experience in this universe. There are so many more levels of creation. Like being stuck on the first level of a video game, we don't even realize how many more worlds there are to explore.

That was the day I started believing that anything is possible. Repeatedly, I am reminded of its truth. In the last few years, I saw that play out in India.

Tirupati

Tirumala Tirupati in Andhra Pradesh is one of the most famous points of pilgrimage in the world. Tirumala is the hilltop temple complex also called Vaikunta, while Tirupati is the town at its base. I first went there in 2017 to start a Maharishi Vedic Science teaching program at a university.

While there we had the opportunity to visit Lord Balaji—the form of Vishnu seated in the temple in Tirumala. With 50,000 to 100,000 people visiting the hilltop complex each day, Tirumala is alive with an unforgettable quality of vibrancy, reverence, spiritual zeal, and sheer humanity searching for something more.

As we entered the temple, we were pressed into a crush of pushing humanity. Spiritual zeal and fervor mixed together so that we were in a mass of bodies pressed together. It was also over 100 degrees. The combination of sweltering temperature and pressing humanity made me think I wouldn't feel anything. But I did. I looked into the eyes of Balaji and found a place within the temple to sit and meditate. It was powerful silence and familiarity.

That was the first of more than 15 visits to Lord Balaji. It created unexpected ripples in my awareness and memories of words, moments, and people in my life connecting to that moment. Perhaps there is far more than we realize in why we find ourselves in a specific spot at a certain time. I received a personal gift in that experience, but I was there for something beyond myself.

The project took a different form but did, eventually, move. Five years later, and with the focused dedication of many great teachers, there are several projects with students practicing TM in Tirupati and surrounding areas. It started small and slow, but the program for full self-development found a home in the holiest of holy cities, the most visited of all temple towns.

This project was a reminder that anything is possible. We appeared with the message of Maharishi in the most powerful city of spirituality in India. If we had tried to think out all the steps, it would have seemed impossible. The organization was too vast, and the number of teachers and Gurus was too enormous. But step by step, the impossible can become possible.

You are the Universe

What is the basis of this principle that anything is possible? It is the reality that we are all-powerful; our unlimited consciousness can know, do, and achieve anything. The expression of this reality from Taittiriya Upanishad 3.10.6 says:

अहं विश्वम्
"I am the Universe."

If anything is possible and all can be accessed from the power of consciousness, then, of course, having the same consciousness as the basis of the universe, I can be the universe, and you also are the universe. We think of ourselves as small, but we have the power of all possibilities within us.

Another similar expression is:

यथा पिण्डे तथा ब्रह्माण्डे
"As is the atom, so is the universe; as is the body, so is the cosmic body."

These expressions are two sides of the same coin. They encapsulate ideas of a drop affecting the ocean. The microcosm reflects the macrocosm. It also explains the concept of the butterfly effect, where a seemingly small action, like a butterfly beating its wings, can have a huge impact on world events, such as weather patterns.

But for the seekers of truth looking for practical application, these verses present a new view of reality. We tend to either look out into the universe or look at our relationship to the world as the universe is too large for most to even consider.

What if, instead, we look inside to the universe? What if our relationship with the world is our relationship with ourselves? And further, what if the ability to move the universe is no more difficult than moving our finger?

This is the final secret of this thread. In the Vedic tradition, it says that the universe is three-quarters unmanifest. That unmanifest is our own inner reality. Whether we realize it or not, we all experience it day in and day out.

What happens outside is the bombardment of thought, emotions, and physical processes on the most surface level of life. Beyond that, what happens quietly in the body is still small compared to what happens in the quiet of "Being" or consciousness. Being alone is. The power of all that you are is the power of all that the universe is. They are one and the same.

There is the famous idiom, "reach for the stars." Now is the time to look inside and find the most brilliant stars of the universe already shining within you. They are available within consciousness in your own inner self.

Action Steps

Here are some reflections, ideas, and actions to absorb and experience this thread of wisdom:

1. **Build Belief.** Don't limit yourself. The mind is powerful. Words are powerful. Don't waste your thought power on what you can't do. Plan what you can do now and build on that.

2. **Transcend.** Use your power to go beyond and feel the unlimited power within. Transcendental Meditation is the easiest way.

3. **Find Nature.** Go out into nature and take a technology break. Take a walk in the forest or look at the stars on a clear night. Feel the power of nature and see how it changes you.

4. **Write and Reflect.** When have you felt the most powerful? Reflect on the circumstances that made you see that you could accomplish more. Who were you with? What were you feeling?

5. **Look to Others.** Who is your favorite person or hero? How can you see them accomplishing something that seemed impossible? What does that mean for your life?

6. **Imagine** that you can use 100% of your mind and accomplish every desire. Which one would you want to accomplish first?

Happiness, laughter, and expansive experiences manifest in our lives because anything is possible.

Thread 3: Happiness is the Basis of Success

आनन्दाध्येव खल्विमानि भूतानि जायन्ते
आनन्देन जातानि जीवन्ति
आनन्दं प्रयन्त्यभिसंविशन्ति
"From bliss, indeed, all these beings originate;
Having been born, they are sustained by bliss;
They move towards and merge into bliss again."
~ Taittiriya Upanishad 3.6.1

Can you imagine being nothing other than bliss? What if the whole purpose of life is to move toward bliss? What if, even when we don't feel it, we are sustained by bliss? That is what this verse implies. Bliss is not only the goal. It is also our origin and our path. How does that relate to happiness?

Bliss is a concentration of happiness. If you see the sun reflecting on the water, happiness is the reflection on the water while bliss is the sun itself. The sun has greater intensity and greater heat and exists independently of anything else. The reflection on the water might be obscured by waves, fog, or darkness. The reflection can disappear. The sun itself, even if we do not see it, is always there.

In the same way, happiness reflects inner bliss. It might be affected or overshadowed by circumstances. The reality of bliss, the essential nature of us all, is like the sun, present regardless of outer circumstances.

In this sense, bliss is described as the nature of consciousness. It is the essential constituent from which everything we think of as the world and our lives arises. If all beings (including humans, plants, animals, and even inanimate objects) arise from bliss, are sustained by bliss, and merge again with bliss, bliss is described as the essential constituent, beyond any sense of you or me.

It is from this perspective that Maharishi said over and over, *"Life is bliss"* and *"Expansion of happiness is the purpose of creation."*

Even though we are made of bliss and sustained by bliss, stress or strain will obstruct this experience. Stress can be what we think of as daily life stress, or it can be the deeper stress in the nervous system, genetics, or DNA. Stress, abnormalities, and obstructions are not the normal state of the nervous system.

It doesn't have to be that way. Perfect health, and with it, perfect functioning of the nervous system can be achieved. Anything can be rectified, corrected, or removed. Stress and strain can be removed, allowing the blissful nature of life to shine through once more.

This is not just a theory but can be a practical reality. It has already been experienced by millions of people around the world throughout the ages. If we can be bliss and live in bliss, why waste time struggling and suffering?

If bliss is the nature of life and happiness its reflection in our thoughts, actions, behavior, and daily reality, then happiness can be an all-time reality.

The Purpose of Life

"Expansion of happiness is the purpose of life, and evolution is the process through which it is fulfilled. Life begins in a natural way, it evolves, and happiness expands. The expansion of happiness carries with it the expansion of intelligence, power, creativity, and everything that may be said to be of significance in life." ~ Maharishi Mahesh Yogi

If things make you happy, how can happiness be the basis of success? The simple answer is that happiness comes from the inside. Happiness can be found in a beautiful sunrise or in a rainbow, in the laughter of a child, or in a warm bath. But none of those things create happiness.

Happiness is the natural fragrance of a contented heart. Happiness does not take, it only gives. Happiness is at once the essence of love, peace, and humility and flows as the expression of inner bliss.

Happiness is without expectation of results or projection to the future. Happiness just is. There are many different things that make people happy: a hug from a loved one, a day at the beach, a vacation, a delicious meal, a good book, success in school or at work. All of these are things that people say make them happy. But do they really?

Let's take the day at the beach. Suppose that the weather is perfect, and you have a great group of friends joining you, but you wake up feeling off. You are tired, achy, and not in the mood to socialize. Then even if your friends are loving and kind, the weather perfect, and the food great, your day at the beach will feel dull. What changed was not the beach or the friends—it was the inner feeling.

It is obvious by now that how we feel inside affects how we perceive the outside world. But how does happiness create success? Happiness draws more happiness to it. It is the principle that like attracts like. Maharishi has said that *"Happiness radiates like the fragrance of a flower and draws all good things towards it."*

Imagine your happiness like that flower—perhaps sweet night jasmine or a summer rose, wafting on the breeze. Everyone who walks by you feels it. Everyone who talks to you smells it through your voice. Happiness is just like a subtle fragrance: it is in the air all around us.

Happiness is the best perfume, the most elegant accessory, and an incredible tool to create more success. Happiness begets happiness. Success begets success. It is a principle so embedded in the fabric of nature that we seem to have forgotten it.

It is so simple and so obvious that it seems like a joke. Really? That's it? All I have to do is be happy? And the simple answer is yes.

Does that mean someone should make a mood of being happy or try to force happiness? The answer is no—and yes. Here's what I mean: it is never helpful to force something beyond what is comfortable or natural. So of course, one should not fake a mood of feeling happy while feeling sad or any other range of emotions. In that case, the inner feeling still predominates—and it is the inside that counts.

But, when you have a choice, choose to be happy. Once you look for the opportunities, you'll start to find them. We all have a choice every day, many times a day, of how we react to situations. We can react with gratitude or happiness or we can react with upset, frustration, anger, or any other spectrum of emotion. All these emotions come naturally. But when we have a choice: do you choose happiness and gratitude or choose anger or frustration?

Gratitude Creates More Happiness

Countless experiences have taught me that it is always better to choose gratitude, and with gratitude comes happiness. It is so easy to fall into a trap of frustration or anger, but that, in the end, always comes with a price. You feel weaker, you lose opportunities, or you hurt someone you care about. Anger is never free, even if it seems to be.

In the Vedic tradition, they say that anger makes you weak. You lose your power and reasoning. You lose the strength of your purity in love and happiness to the weakness of anger. In moments of anger, you cannot accomplish all that you desire.

Happiness and gratitude, on the other hand, make you strong. They give you the power of righteousness and guide you toward your higher purpose. I chose gratitude specifically because on the surface, situations may seem unreasonable and unfair. In those moments, look to nature and ask, "What are you trying to teach me?" This moment of reflection usually reveals some weakness. Nature is the best teacher.

To give a simple example: I saw this once with a particularly aggressive Airbnb host. He pointed out everything he did and followed it up with the statements along the lines of, "You should be grateful to me" or "See how caring I am?" These statements were exaggerated to the point of ridiculousness. "The room was clean when you arrived, see how caring I am. I gave you toilet paper, you should be grateful."

Throughout my stay, he kept stating that he was the best host. I realized he was hoping for a positive review, but because of his pushy and domineering manner over little issues and unfair assumptions, it didn't create a good feeling.

After checking out, I walked down to the beach, sat on the dunes, and looked up at the wide blue sky. In a moment of quiet, it dawned on me: I've done the exact same thing at times to other people, although not to the same level.

But if this man's level of needing appreciation and casting blame wasn't so high, I wouldn't have understood the lesson: a good deed done in silence is filled with power and brings happiness. A good deed shouted from the rooftops for credit or gain loses its strength.

This reminded me of a beautiful scene from the end of a movie, of a chance encounter at a rural gas station between a woman healer and a boy dying of cancer. The boy sees her dog and wants to pet it or take it with him. She sees his illness and knows she can heal him. She says she will give him the dog if he gives her a hug.

In that hug, she heals the boy. The family drives away with the dog, thinking they received a generous gift from a stranger. They don't realize that the stranger saved the boy's life and changed his destiny forever. That quiet joy belongs to the healer.

This is the power of happiness and inner peace—the ability to do good for the sake of doing good. Like attracts like. Creating good attracts more good. That is the principle of nature. What we are, we draw toward us.

Karma

In Sanskrit, this principle is called karma. Karma means action. Action can be good, bad, or neutral. You can think of karma as throwing a basketball at a wall: the ball will bounce back to you. How hard you throw it, the angle you throw it at, and even the texture and strength of the wall will affect how the ball bounces back.

Now think that the action you are throwing is not just going to hit a wall. It is going somewhere far in the universe before bouncing back. In this case, if you threw a ball, it would probably take longer, it may encounter obstacles, or can even take on a different form altogether. Perhaps the ball becomes a Frisbee or a boomerang. That is karma.

With karma, it is not just the path of one ball you are following, but every action you perform every day. Sometimes the results of actions will come back very quickly. Have you heard the term instant karma? Instant karma is just that—instant results of your action. Perhaps you make an unkind statement about someone, and a few seconds later you stub your toe. Some people would say that is instant karma.

Other times karma can take weeks, months, years, or lifetimes. The results of actions received today could have been generated last week, ten years ago, or in another lifetime. To track karma is an unfathomable and pointless task. And yet, the principle of karma remains the same: what you put out into the universe comes back to you.

The best way to control karma is to control what you put out. Happiness, peace, harmony, and kindness sent into the environment and out to the universe bring the same back in kind. Be alert and aware of what you are putting out and how it comes back to you. Nature is always ready to teach a lesson or be a guide. Listen and learn.

One shocking example for me happened when I was hurt by a colleague's behavior. I said to someone else that I'd like to hit him for that. I didn't mean it literally; it was a way to express the hurt I felt. But nature had a lesson in store.

About half an hour later, I was walking from one room to an adjoining room that I thought was empty. In the process of quickly opening the door, it hit the colleague I'd been talking about in the face—hard. I didn't know he had come back to that room for something and was right behind the door.

I felt so guilty that what I'd said just before happened. That was a lesson to watch what you wish for and be alert about the intentions you put into the universe.

Instant karma can also be good. Perhaps you help someone with their groceries, and five minutes later you find out you won a prize —when you never normally win prizes. Nature works in both mysterious and predictable ways. The mysterious is the constant surprise of life. The predictable is this thread of wisdom: happiness is the basis of success. Happiness brings more happiness; good brings more good.

It is so simple and yet so profound. By putting happiness into the universe, happiness comes back to you. Happiness means outer success and inner fulfillment.

While it is certainly possible to be completely fulfilled on the inside without success on the outside, the ability to fulfill desires multiplies happiness. Happiness is not austerity. Happiness is 200% of life: 100% inner fulfillment and 100% outer fulfillment.

The principle that happiness is the basis of success is a more reliable strategy than the belief that the fulfillment of any specific desire will bring lasting happiness. The idea that we know what will bring us happiness is one of the great illusions we sell ourselves on repeatedly. The idea that we have the omniscient vision to see the source of true happiness and our true-life purpose is often a trap. We are our own worst enemies.

Think of the time you thought you only wanted money to be happy—and then found you still felt empty. Or how much someone you knew wanted to marry someone—and then had it end in bitter divorce years later. Without growth, evolution, and expansion toward the infinite, any finite boundary will start to feel like a limitation instead of a fulfillment.

It says in the Vedic literature that the laws of karma—meaning the process of action and reaction—are unfathomable. It is impossible to calculate if you do a specific action what the result will be for you, your family, or your friends. There is no way of knowing what ripples will be created now or in the future from any action.

There are countless novels exploring this concept: someone is given the opportunity to go back in time and right a wrong or save a life. Often, one little action changes everything. The protagonist comes away frantically trying to put it all back the way it was before. These stories illustrate one simple point: while we think we can control life, we are actually small parts of a much bigger whole.

The fact that we cannot control life is a relief. Can you imagine the pressure and burden of sitting and calculating, and double-checking the calculations, before taking any action? And then we'd want to cross-check that there isn't a better possible action that creates better results. We would become paralyzed in our own calculations and fail to fulfill anything.

Fortunately, this is not necessary. The formula is far simpler. Happiness, kindness, joy, compassion, and selfless giving all give back more than we could ever imagine. Happiness is a path and a goal. It is a means and an end.

Happiness is the beginning that opens the door for all good things to come. Happiness is one key, hidden in plain sight, to achieve eternal happiness. The path and the goal, in this case, are one.

Speaking with God

If you had a chance to ask God one question, what would you ask? That was a question I was confronted with as an 11-year-old in my family's living room at about 8:00 p.m. one summer evening. Let me explain: Another unique feature of growing up in Fairfield, Iowa, was the vast array of healers and spiritual teachers who came through town. My family did not usually visit with them, but some people we knew visited many of them.

I saw only later in life how Maharishi treated these spiritual people with great respect for what they could bring to the world. It was a unifying vision to see all people on all spiritual paths as part of one family, as we are all part of one world family.

There was one moment in my childhood that was the exception to the no-healers norm, and it happened when I was 11 years old. I still don't know the background of how it happened. Perhaps my aunt and uncle invited this neighbor over. In any case, she brought me a powerful lesson.

On that summer evening, I was on my way to bed when I saw one of our neighbors sitting like a regal presence in the center of the living room, facing my parents. They said she was going to speak to God, and I could ask a question. What?

I was not completely taken aback because I'd heard that something happened to this neighbor. In addition to being the mother of my favorite camp counselor and a beloved fifth-grade teacher, she had accidentally overdosed on allergy medication and was clinically dead before being revived. First, the rumor went around town that she had died; then another rumor spread that she had recovered, but was different.

When she was revived, she said she was an archangel who came to Earth to be a channel to God. She explained that the person we knew as our neighbor was gone, and she was there now. My reaction to that was something between disbelief, fear, and curiosity. Could it be? Over a period of six months to a year, many people in our small town went to see her and see what she did.

And now here she was, sitting in our living room. The moment I entered the room, she asked me what I wanted to ask God.

Talk about pressure. I had one chance, on the spur of the moment, to ask any question to God directly. If that happened to you, what would you ask? In retrospect, I see how many incredible friends I had growing up. But as an insecure 11-year-old, I asked the first thing that came to my mind.

"Will I ever have any friends?"

She sat quietly for a moment, and her eyes rolled back in her head. And then she replied. She looked me right in the eyes and said, "Just continue being yourself. Your great friends will find you. Just be yourself."

I don't know what happened to that neighbor, but I know that her prophecy of that day came true. It took a couple of more awkward years, but I finally started to find friends who were more than family. I found my people and continue to find people who I feel like I've known forever.

To my 11-year-old self, to ever find real friends seemed impossible. But I continued to pursue my passions, laugh, and play. And along the way, I found people who inspired me to be better in every way. I found friends who take my breath away with their brilliant minds, compassionate hearts, and all that they are. My friends found me, just as she predicted, and some had been there all along.

Now we can reverse the question: if you could pretend to be all-powerful and tell an insecure 11-year-old anything, what would you tell her? Probably to just be herself, that her friends would find her. It was perfect advice.

Was it God speaking, or just a well-meaning adult? I choose to believe it was God. Not because she could necessarily "speak" to God but because God speaks to all of us through whatever voices are available—birds and trees, flowers and bushes, friends and foes.

If God could speak to each of us, that would probably be the message, as it is stated in the many great world religions: Be yourself. Be happy. Love one another. Give. Be kind. Let the best of your heart shine in happiness, and your friends will always find you. Be yourself and be happy. If you could ask God anything, isn't that what you would want to hear back?

Action Steps

Here are some reflections, ideas, and actions to absorb and experience this thread of wisdom:

1. **Laugh.** I mean, really laugh. Find someone with whom you can laugh until you are crying or falling on the floor. Laugh hard and laugh often. Don't force it, but the process of laughing revitalizes physiology and psychology. You can even start just by smiling. Even laughing every once in a while will start to put greater happiness into your body and life.

2. **Do something that you love** or that makes you feel renewed every day. For me, that is often a walk or swim in nature, but it can be anything that makes you feel grateful for the opportunity to be alive and experience life.

3. **Indulge** in something that makes you feel joyful, guilt-free. You deserve joy and happiness in your life.

4. **Transcend.** Bliss is an inner reality. Without a path to experience it, reaching it is like a game of chance. It is also physical. The more the nervous system is trained to maintain the experience of bliss, the more bliss can be experienced. Transcendental Meditation is the most simple and effective path to cultivate the nervous system to experience and maintain bliss.

5. **Rate Your Happiness.** "The purpose of evolution is the expansion of happiness." ~ Maharishi.

Rate your happiness in different areas of your life on a scale of 1 to 10. You can do this in as many areas as you'd like. I suggest starting with physical, mental, emotional, and spiritual. Save the scores you give yourself and come back to them when you finish the book or in a month.

6. Recount a few moments, in various areas of your life, when your happiness and good mood brought you success. Conversely, remember the times you were very unhappy and how that blocked your progress.

Self-referral happiness, kindness, and love reverberate in expanded experiences,
manifesting healthy accomplishments miraculously.

Thread 4: Never Judge— Everything Can be Right or Wrong

"Now then we will explain Dharma"
~ Vaisheshik Verse 1
"Now begins the inquiry of duty (Dharma)"
~ Karma Mimamsa Verse 1

What is dharma? Dharma rhymes with karma. Karma and dharma are, in many ways, two sides of the same coin. The simplest definition of dharma is "action in accordance with natural law." But what does that mean? Isn't natural law, anyway, governing all our lives?

Dharma is that which upholds evolution. Dharma is action which brings good to each of us individually - and the environment. In that sense, dharma is action that is in alignment with the law of nature governing the universe. It is the action that is right for you —and which brings maximum good to everyone around you. Dharma is the power of action that allows for the fastest evolution with the greatest comfort.

The still simpler and more direct answer is that dharma is what you were born to do. It is what, in a perfect world where all the forces are conspiring in your favor, you will find yourself doing.

Your dharma is the activity you can do that brings the greatest happiness and fulfillment to you and allows you to contribute maximum to society.

Your dharma, in a sense, is your dream job. But dharma isn't necessarily glamorous or glorious, it can also be simple. Dharma is the activity that allows you to evolve the most quickly. For some, that might be as a celebrity. For others, that is working in a small shop, working as a doctor or a researcher, teaching, or staying at home with their children. While there is some overlap, there are as many dharmas as there are people in the world. We are each born for our own unique dharma.

We are all unique in our physical appearance and personalities, and in the same way, our dharmas are all unique. There can be congruences, especially in families. On the physical side, you share characteristics of eye and hair color, build, and food preferences. On the side of dharma, you share predilections and other preferences, like an aptitude for math, a love of the water, or infectious laughter.

These basic characteristics that can be shared by many converge to create your own special dharma. Your dharma is your destiny. It is who you are and what you are meant to do in the deepest core of your soul. If you could speak directly to your soul, what would it tell you to do? That is your dharma.

Dharma is as elusive as it is incredible. Some people are sure they know their dharma, while others still wonder in their 40s, 50s, or 80s. It is never too late to find your dharma—or for your dharma to find you. Sometimes, dharma becomes clear later in life. That is how dharma and karma tie in together.

Karma is action and reaction, which we've discussed. What is happening to you at this moment, how you feel about it, and even how you react to it, is on the basis of your past actions. That means that if your dharma is not yet clear, it can be because of karma.

In a way, it sounds like a trap. But it is actually a trap door to all possibilities. Because to understand dharma and karma is to understand that, at every moment, we can create our own destiny, regenerate our karma, and no longer be caught in a cycle of wondering what we are here for. Everyone's dharma is first a duty to themselves to be in harmony with natural law.

The shortcut to that is, first and foremost, consciousness. Pure consciousness is the universal dharma. Pure consciousness is the connection between the individual and the universal life. That is the first duty of everyone.

It is everyone's destiny to unfold their highest potential and gain more in life. Without this fundamental basis, all other efforts will be as difficult to control as a small boat at sea in a hurricane. Many people are naturally drawn to what they are good at, but regardless of outer dharma, inner dharma is to gain fulfillment.

The Vedic expression for this is *'Vedo akhilo dharma mulam'* *(Manu Smriti 2.6)*, which translates literally as Ved is the root of all the laws, but it can also mean Ved is the root of all dharma. What is Ved in this case? Ved is total knowledge available in the consciousness of everyone. That is to say, the root of all dharma and the wisdom to achieve it is already within each of us. Total knowledge, the ability to accomplish the highest in life, is already within each of us.

———

To be in the moment, without looking either to the past or the future, opens the door for the best opportunities, the highest display of dharma, to be available. When we look peacefully and accept, the enormous time, energy, and mental turmoil that goes into worrying about either the past or the future are saved for the present.

We underestimate how much mental energy we spend on either judging others or judging ourselves. The answer to questioning someone else's motives is never to judge. This is a challenging one, as it is an unconscious and automatic response. From simple things like someone's shoes, hair, or what they posted on Instagram, to bigger things like someone's beliefs, ideals, or priorities.

To judge is to measure ourselves against others. It is an unconscious evolutionary behavior that is so ingrained that spiritual teachers throughout the ages have warned against it or advised cultivating indifference.

It is worth warning against. It is also not an easy habit to change. Trying to cultivate anything—indifference, happiness, or anything else, will probably result in a lack of that quality. By trying, we put our attention on the lack. And, as before, what you put your attention on grows stronger in your life.

The deeper lesson here is that by judging, we are judging ourselves —better or worse, wise or stupid, richer or poorer. By judging ourselves, we are eroding the fine fibers of our hearts and putting our infinite potential into a small box.

Instead of our unlimited brilliance of creativity, love, and light, we are defining ourselves simply as more or less than, better or worse. We have taken the infinite potential of our hearts, souls, and consciousness and confined it in small boundaries.

This means that by judging others we are limiting ourselves. We then define good or bad in absolutes and forget our infinite, unbounded potential. Good or bad is never absolute. Only the absolute level of consciousness, which is unlimited, unbounded and both ever-changing and never-changing, can actually be called an absolute.

We've said not to judge but also not to TRY not to judge. What is the essence of this thread of wisdom?

The answer, again, is in knowledge. Knowledge has the power to transform a person. The greater the knowledge, the greater the power to transform. This thread is a reminder of the power of knowledge.

Right and Wrong are Relative

What is right for one person in one situation might be wrong for another. This is simple and obvious. But even something that is completely good for one person might be wrong for another. This knowledge of right and wrong is enough to transform how we view others and their actions.

This goes for every area of life—from what we eat and how we exercise, to how we define love, how we raise our children, and how we do (or don't) believe in God. What is right for one person might not be right for another. And that still doesn't make it wrong.

A society can become so divided along political lines, religious lines, or even between favorite sports teams. It is natural to become tribalistic and judge those deemed "other." While it is wonderful to feel close to a group of like-minded people, judging others takes away limited time and energy from developing ourselves.

In addition, while what others are doing may be wrong for you, it could be perfectly right for them. Having traveled to more than 50 countries and having visited many traditional cultures, I've learned that pretty much everything in life can be different, and yet for those cultures, it is right.

It is not food, clothing, customs, beliefs, etiquette, age of adult-hood, religion, global contributions, the definition of success, standards of beauty, or any other measure of society that is ever right or wrong. It is the intention of the hearts and the alignment with the local laws of nature that makes something right or wrong for a specific person, area, or situation.

The laws of nature are different in different parts of the world. How a home is designed in the Amazon will be vastly different from how it is designed in the Arctic. How people eat, dress, interact with each other, and even what they believe will also differ. They could practice the same religion—but come to a different interpretation of how it should be practiced or what it means.

This is because different geographic and climatic conditions give rise to the laws of nature governing the lives of the people in different parts of the world.

But what about clear right and wrong? How can something so definitely wrong be right in a certain instance? How can something so right ever be wrong? That is one of the many interesting features of life. The only thing Absolute—is the Absolute—the level of pure undivided consciousness where we are all one. Everything else is changing.

What is the Absolute? The Absolute is a level of non-changing consciousness. Physicists have toyed with ideas, models, and theories around it for decades, although none have yet been entirely successful. Ancient Rishi have described it for millennia since time immemorial. The simplest definition of the Absolute is a level of life where everything that appears different is unified—from the different force and matter fields that govern the universe and the different laws of nature, like gravity, to everything we have, experience, and are.

The Absolute is not a level most people are familiar with, or particularly comfortable acknowledging. The Absolute is consciousness in its most pure, unmanifest form. For now, it is enough to know that it exists. And in existence, it remains the only level of life that is not changing. Everything else is constantly changing.

From the weather to the growth of children, to the structure of governments, to the currents in the ocean, and the growth of plants, change happens on both big and small scales in ways that are both obvious and imperceptible. All these changes, big and small, we see either in the moment or in retrospect.

In a short 18 years, a child grows from a newborn to an adult. In a year, the hair on your head grows an average of four inches. Every tree, plant, and living being is changing, evolving, and growing. Even rock, which seems so stable and immovable, is eroded by water, salt, wind, or rain over decades or millennia. The idea that anything is completely set is an illusion.

If everything is always changing, and each of us is our own unique universe of past experiences, cultural values, worldviews, individual talents, and destiny, it makes sense that no two people would have the exact same path or definition of right and wrong.

What is good for one person may be bad for another. The best way to raise one child may only be mediocre for another child. We all already know this. What makes you happy at one time may not make you happy at another. Someone you love very much can at times make you very happy and at other times upset.

From this perspective and our vast experience, it's clear that life is ever-changing. In addition to internal changes, different geographic and climatic conditions give rise to different cultures and laws of nature in different parts of the world. And even within each of us, what is good at one time might not be good at another.

It is baffling then that being the wise, intelligent, aware human beings that we are, we still fall into the trap of comparison or judgment. This is exacerbated by social media and smartphones that create more opportunities to compare and judge than ever before.

True and lasting peace does not come from being better or worse than anyone else. Wealth, beauty, strength, generosity, power, flexibility, and fortunate circumstances are all relative measures that do not bring lasting happiness. However, by passing judgment, whether good or bad, on others, we are linking our desires to them and sowing seeds in our hearts that can lead either to more desires or unhappiness.

What is the formula then not to judge? It is simple innocence. It is being present and grateful for what is happening, and it is being patient with yourself. Because, usually, we are our own harshest critics.

The first step to stop judging others is to stop judging yourself. That doesn't mean to stop having goals or working to improve areas of your life. It means giving yourself the grace to be as you are in the moment. When you can do that, dharma becomes almost automatic.

Changing Perception

Not only are outer situations ever-changing, the inner reality of our thinking, perception, and feeling is also ever-changing. It is one thing to acknowledge the outer change, but deeper understanding and peace come from recognizing the inner change of perception.

Think of a mountain with a view of the valley on the other side. While walking up the side of the mountain, you will have changing views of the trees, rocks, path, and some of what was behind you. But from the top of the mountain, the view looks completely different than from the start of the path.

If you ask someone starting the path what it is like, he or she will give one answer. They might say the path is hard or easy, rocky, muddy, or other qualities. By the end of the path, that beginning portion will be a small section of the whole, and its qualities will be diluted by everything that came after.

The same is true of life. From any point on the path of life, the view will look different. The interesting point about this is that not only do we all view the world from different perspectives depending on where we are on the path, but we also view the world from a different perspective depending on our own inner perception or consciousness.

What do I mean by inner perception? Think of days when you were tired, upset, or angry and how the whole world seemed to be colored by those feelings and everything seemed more difficult. And think of a day when you were happy or content. On happy days, even usual annoyances could seem pleasing or cute. This is the power of our own inner perception.

Two people standing on the same path and looking at the same view can have different views depending on their inner perception. Does that mean that everyone's view is just opinion and mood? How do we find lasting truth? Does lasting truth accompany lasting happiness? And does that mean we are at the mercy of our emotions and moods?

If indeed opinions and moods are the essence of life, I am in trouble, and you probably are, too. Fortunately, that is not the ultimate reality of life. What is the ultimate reality?

By now you know the Absolute non-changing level of life. Every level of perception is always changing except for this finest level—absolute pure consciousness. The Absolute, being absolute, is ever the same, non-changing, unbounded, and eternal.

We are all part of the Absolute—and the whole of the Absolute. We have only forgotten our unshakeable, eternal basis. When we stop judging, bit by bit, the part of us that is unshakeable, infinite, and absolute starts to creep in and give us the strength and clarity to find our dharma and live our most fulfilling, most beautiful life.

Freedom from Self-judgment

If we are going to stop judging, the first person we need to stop judging is ourselves. When we stop judging ourselves, we give ourselves permission to be all that we are.

The secondary effect of this is that whatever bad habits or vices we are holding onto—everything from a sugar obsession to binging on Netflix to more serious concerns such as an addiction—start to lose appeal. All these mechanisms are an escape from feeling or being what we are.

In accepting ourselves fully, as we are in the moment, we set ourselves free. With freedom from judgment and time, whatever we were using to hide from ourselves and our feelings loses its power over us. We simply are.

This thread of wisdom has been a key to opening doors I never thought I could in my life. It was the key to overcoming what was the verge of life-long anorexia. Later, it was the key to overcoming a binge-eating disorder.

In those cases, it was only when I gave myself complete permission to eat what I wanted, when I wanted, and accept the body that came with that without judgment that the urge to either restrict or binge completely vanished.

When I stopped trying to control how I thought my body should be and instead listened to what it was telling me, I was freed. It was only by bringing a second element—an element of love and openness without judgment—that I was able to stop wasting precious time and mental energy on food, weight, and planning the next meal.

For me, this deep listening was something that carried over into other areas of life. Freedom from judgment is accepting the body's own inner intelligence.

Even more important for my seeker's soul—to stop judging myself—became the key for me to reach Maharishi and learn directly from him. And it became the key to inner happiness.

This is an important point in the judgment-free zone: giving up judgment does not mean giving up on goals, desires, and aspirations. It is the opposite: by giving up judgment, you give your incredible, powerful inner self the freedom to help you accomplish all your goals, desires, and aspirations. To avoid judging is to set yourself free.

When I stopped judging myself based on the criteria of those around me, I was able to be myself around Maharishi without worrying about the judgment of others. To be like them, for me, was not natural. To talk like them, defer like them, or even describe like them was not natural to me. I was too loud, too descriptive and also too vague, and not worried about being corrected. I just wanted to talk to Maharishi!

While sharing my experiences with Maharishi I felt seen and understood for the first time. It was like he could see into the depth of who I was, the moments of my greatest heights, and pull that out with me. It made me feel unimaginably happy, and I could see that by being me I was becoming more of what Maharishi saw.

That was when I saw for the first time that there is no one spiritual path. There is no checklist to mark, no landmarks at which to take selfies. It is guided by the inner wisdom and destiny of each of us and takes us past the points and vistas more important for us.

To stop judging is to relinquish control and the idea that you know what should be—and experience what you are. In that, joy, happiness, and peace can be unlimited and the possibilities unbounded. What if the greatest you can imagine is only 5% of all you are? When you stop judging, you set yourself free and open new doors that otherwise could stay closed for a lifetime.

To stop judging is to recognize that the plan of nature or God is greater than what you think it should be. The plan of your own inner wisdom is more than you could ever imagine. To stop judging is to set yourself free and, in that, the dharma latent inside will guide you on the path to your highest purpose.

How to Find Your Dharma

Your unique dharma is a confluence of what you are good at, what you love to do, what you are uniquely equipped to put out into the world, how you can help others, and the environment you live in. There's more on this at the end of the chapter.

The highest dharma of everyone is enlightenment, liberation, and unity consciousness. But the path to reaching that dharma is different for everyone.

The dharma for one individual supports the dharma of the whole society. True dharma is in alignment and harmony with the individual and the collective—they are not mutually exclusive. The secret to be shared here is that dharma is more than what to do. Dharma encompasses an essential nature of each person—the soul's longing to realize itself.

Dharma is to keep in constant alliance with cosmic intelligence as life goes on. As the seconds move on in life, the key is to see that you are not disconnected from natural law. Discussing dharma when talking about judging is natural. We don't judge the outside, but we do justice to life on the inside.

Dharma is an inner duty. It is a personal discretion. The first dharma of each person is with the self. As the seconds of life are passing, you cannot lose the connection with that intelligence, that inner wisdom which is called dharma.

How can this be done in day-to-day life? There is a simple formula I learned from Maharishi:

- If you know something is right, do it.
- If you know you don't have to do it or that it is wrong, postpone it or don't do it.
- If you have a doubt that something is good, wait. This allows you to see if it falls into one of the first two categories.

This can be summarized in a phrase: do what you know to be right; don't do what you know to be wrong; if in doubt, wait.

The Story of Milarepa

The story of Milarepa is the story of survival and persistence. It is of a man, like any of us, choosing to do what is necessary under pressures of environment and obligations of family. But Milarepa's story takes a unique turn in that after a time, Milarepa had his own version of "is this it?" and began to search for spiritual truth or enlightenment. In the search, through a long process, he did realize enlightenment.

Throughout the story of Milarepa, there are moments to judge, from the way he chooses to protect his family to the path his master gives him for enlightenment. But this path, for Milarepa, led to liberation. The story of Milarepa is the essence of never judging. Here, he tells his own story:

> *I am Milarepa. You might know me by other names or might have only heard me as a whisper in the wind. For I am there, too: in the blades of grass as they dance in the sunshine and the dew; in the song of the birds; in the rainbow; and in the storm. You might not know me, but at this very moment, you are living my path and my story.*

> *For I am the one. All that was and all that will be is within me. I see without seeing and yet live a million lives in a billion bodies in ten million universes and a multitude of galaxies. I am everywhere, and yet, you have probably never seen me.*

Those who think I have a name and a place will call me Milarepa and put me in the holy Mount Kailash on the Tibetan plateau. There is my cave of Tapasya (spiritual practices and renunciation). But I can be found not only in the caves or hills of high plateaus. I am in your child and in you. I am in your enemies and in your friends. I am in your weakness and in your strength.

While there was never a time when I was not, like you, I was born to a mother and grew as a child. Like you, I wanted to please my mother. And also, perhaps like you, I could never do enough, but I tried with all my might.

When I was a boy, we were surrounded by riches. Luscious silks covered the walls, and ornate palanquins transported my mother from serene jasmine gardens to mango groves to private floral baths and back to the main house. For all extents and purposes, she lived like a queen. Trays laden with dates, figs, grapes, almonds, mangos, pots of honey, and fresh coconut cream filled our days.

I ran wild with the other children, tearing our silk pants and returning home, delightedly caked with mud, the jeweled belts around our waists painted a soft reddish brown from the dirt.

One day, when I returned from playing, I found my mother with tear-streaked cheeks, looking off into the distance, as though she was no longer there. She didn't scold me for returning muddy or offer the sweet pistachio honey cakes I was so fond of. I nestled into her lap, and she stroked my head.

It felt like being touched by a ghost. At that moment, I vowed to do everything to bring my mother back and protect her from this mysterious illness.

Later, she told me that my father had passed away; and because of some antiquated laws, all our wealth would go to my father's wicked brother, and we would be his charges.

Overnight, the house transformed from one of joy and abundance into one of sober scarcity. The fruits I loved to snack on vanished, as did the silk from the walls and the beautiful gems. Everything of value was stripped from the house. Even the fruit trees in the orchard were systematically harvested and taken to the market.

As I grew from a boy to a man, I watched my mother transform from a woman of beauty and grace to one of hatred and revenge. Bitterness filled her heart. She pleaded with me to learn the dark arts of magic to take revenge on my uncle.

Like a dutiful son, I learned, and soon mastered the dark arts. People from far and wide would seek me out to help them extract what they felt was justice. I crippled evil stepmothers and killed enemies. I won battles for the unrighteous and deprived farmers of rain. Whatever they asked, I could exact the revenge. But you see, these arts are not without a price; and one day, the price was my beloved mother herself.

Left with nothing in this world and no desire to live, I began wandering in search of a master to absolve me of the destruction I had caused to others and to show me the path of light.

In the high Tibetan plateau, I found such a master. He embraced me in his Ashram (hermitage) as his son and took me to the path of light. "First, my son," he said, "you must do all that I say."

For one thousand days, my master had me dig holes and foundations for homes from dawn until dusk. In the nights, he would have me dig the wells. He was a strict taskmaster and would not let me stop. Whenever I complained that I was gaining no knowledge or progress on the path to liberation, he would reply simply with, "Continue."

After a thousand days, my master brought me into his room. 'Now, my son, you are ready for initiation. I have made you do hard physical labor because it was the fastest way to clear your sins. You dug out the black from the dark arts with the holes in the earth. Mother Earth has protected you and brought you home. You were born of this earth and will return to this earth, as your parents have before you. But Mother Earth has given you the unique opportunity to carry beyond this physical body. Now, come with me."

The path of my master from that moment on was a path of light. I cannot tell you whether it was a day or an eon, for time no longer matters. Night and day have become a continuum of bliss.

I, who was the deepest of sinners and destroyed lives, was given a path of liberation. I am revered the world over for my enlightenment and wisdom. And yet it is not "I" or "mine." I simply speak what is.

There is no path, and yet you are on the path. There is no goal, and you are the goal. There is no place for judgment, only for reflection, and reverence for the opportunity of life.

Think not of what you have been, or you will never become what you are meant to be. I was a prince, I was a dark wizard, and now I am all. Do not stay as one. Become all. Be all, for you already are.

This is the conclusion also of the lesson on dharma. No matter how far from the path you feel you've strayed or how impossible the goal, dharma is the means to take you to who you are meant to be. It is built into each of us. It is the greatest destiny we could imagine, and it is the highest fulfillment.

There is an expression from the Upanishads that summarizes this thread. It says:

आत्मा वा अरे द्रष्टव्यः श्रोतव्यः मन्तव्यः निदिध्यासितव्य
*"That Atma alone, that simplest state of awareness alone, is worthy
of seeing, hearing, contemplating, and realizing."*
~ Yāgyavalkya, Bṛihadāraṇyaka Upanishad 2.4.5

What does that mean? Atma is the Sanskrit word for pure consciousness, or "the self of every individual." It is the higher self we all have, latent at the source of thought. It is called "that simplest state of awareness alone" to refer to its existence at the source of thought. When the mind settles down in its most quiet state, Atma, or pure consciousness, is available.

The brilliance of this verse is that it is not pushing you to look outside—it is guiding you to look inside. To see, hear, contemplate, and realize Atma is to open a door inside yourself. It is to acknowledge that productivity is not only on the outside. There is a world of productivity available on the inside.

The world of inner realization is rarely seen or heard, except by the ones seeking to unfold their higher consciousness and inner vision. But to contemplate, to learn about, to understand the power of that inner Atma is the purpose of this book. It is a process to reach beyond, understand, and unfold this inner reality.

This expression is another way to say, "Never judge others." You do not know their inner world. You rarely even know their full outer circumstances. To never judge frees time, space, and energy to see, hear, contemplate, and realize your own higher power, to fulfill your own dreams.

The more time we spend judging others—or ourselves—the less time we have to devote to the development of our own consciousness. Think of the number of hours you spend in a day or a week worrying about what you will eat, your weight, what others think of you, or what you are going to do next week or in five years.

All these worries, considerations, and judgments take away from the essential reality that we are, in our deepest beings, all-powerful Atma. We are worthy of being seen and heard. Our inner power is worthy of being contemplated. And beyond all else, it is worth realizing!

To never judge others is also a guide to never judge ourselves. Take that energy, creativity, and analytic ability and put it into spending time with your own deepest self. Practice Transcendental Meditation. Learn about Atma. Learn about the experiences of Atma.

Listen to your intuition and give yourself the grace to just be, as you are, at this moment. When we are without judgment, we allow the highest dharma, destiny, to find us and bring better opportunities than we could imagine.

Action Steps

Here are some reflections, ideas, and actions to absorb and experience this thread of wisdom:

1. Be Patient. Remember that we've all been there. Life tends to bring back to us what we give out. This is the law of karma. If you are faced with someone who is selfish, unreliable, pushy, too timid, greedy, angry, aggressive, or any other quality you find too much, reflect on that quality in yourself. Do you see a reflection? What is nature trying to tell you? Most often, finding some resonance creates both compassion and peace. Like a Chinese finger trap, locating your reflection in the situation sets you free.

2. Appreciate. Appreciation builds gratitude and peace.

- Appreciate something about your body, mind, and soul.
- Appreciate something about those around you.
- Find something genuinely joyful and point it out.

- When you focus on the good, more good grows around you.

3. Write. Write a story from another perspective. If you find yourself judging a situation, sit quietly and then write the same situation from the other person's perspective. What were they thinking? What were they trying to achieve? How can you help them?

4. Find Compassion. Write the 10 most important judgments you do in life, and write something that doesn't imply judgment, but compassion. How do you feel doing that? For example, if you say, "I dislike when so-and-so does X," it could become "I find (something that is good) when so-and-so does X." How does your judgment limit your opportunities?

5. Find Your Dharma. Make a list of:

- What do you love to do?
- What are you good at?
- What do people need that you can offer?
- What is needed in your environment?
- What are you uniquely qualified to give or help people with?

From this list, start to note the overlap or where they combine. When you find what you love to do, what you're good at, and what you can offer to others in your environment, you will start to feel yourself in your dharma.

Happiness, laughter, and expansive experiences manifest in our lives when we stop judging ourselves or others.

Thread 5: Woman is Divine

Within each person, there is an infinite power of consciousness. It is a power of happiness, a power of truth, and a power of love. Women are uniquely skilled and capable of bringing this power from within out to those we love. It is not a superficial thing. It is a power that can move oceans and change destinies.

When we think then of women's rights and women's power, or lack thereof throughout recent history, we miss one simple truth: that we are all already more powerful, more Divine, and more ready to transform the world than we have ever given ourselves credit for.

So many wise, brave, determined women have done incredible work over decades and centuries for our essential voices to be heard. And there is so much more to do. This needs to continue on every level, as the momentum is building.

But there is an element not yet considered. Beyond the some-times-gradual outward shifts, we have the power to transform the world into the world we desire from within. This is the power of consciousness. It is our time to transform the world, not through force or complaining about a system as it was, but by first bringing a new paradigm within ourselves.

In the world in which we live, it is so easy to focus on the problems and everything that can and should change to create a more equitable and evolutionary society. There is so much that needs to change. And we need to find a balance. But perhaps not only for the reasons you'd think.

Yes, recognizing women's power is good for women. But it is also good for men. And it is good for families. It is one essential part of the whole that enriches every other part. Here is what I mean:

In the previous chapter, we spoke about dharma. The first dharma of every person is with the self. As the seconds of life pass, we cannot lose this connection with the highest inner intelligence. This value, which could be called cosmic or divine, is the birthright and essential nature of every human being.

Within the human nervous system, there are two basic functions: analysis and synthesis. We can create a whole, see the big picture, and plan. And we can also analyze, dissect, and understand the pieces of that whole. These two qualities, in the simplest sense, are the masculine and feminine principles within each person. We all have both.

The feminine principle is receptive—it unifies, creates wholeness, and pulls together opposites. The masculine principle analyzes and divides. It is not that women have one quality and men another, but for the sake of defining principles, these are the qualities traditionally given to masculine and feminine within each of us.

Then why would we say women are divine specifically if, of course, everyone is divine? In Sanskrit and in Latin, Gaya is the name for Mother Earth. In nearly every culture of the world, the planet we live on is called Mother Earth. The feminine principle is the home that nourishes us. It is the name we give to the unique combination of natural laws that make up our planet.

Gaya is she who protects Mother Earth. In the Vedic tradition, the mother of all the Devatas, a supreme form of divine intelligence, is called Gayatri. *Gaya*—earth and *tri*—mother. The mother of all is earth herself.

In many great cultures of the world—the Pachamama, the Mayas and Incas of Latin America, the Vedic culture, the Egyptian culture, the Balinese—the principle of Gaya, the receptive power of Mother Earth, is embodied in the heart of women.

As women, we are not only givers of life but protectors of life. Honoring and protecting the protectors of life will make everyone better—all men, families, and communities of the world. Enhancing the specific power of women enhances what is good for everyone.

Every woman has within her divine power. We can call this shakti. Shakti is a word for the power of purity and love. It is not power through taking but the inner power of strength and also of softness.

Women have this nourishing power of shakti. We are born with it. That's not to say that men cannot also develop it. Just as we are all born with specific skills or aptitudes, an inborn talent of every woman is to protect and nourish life.

It says in the Smritis that women should be honored and adored for all good to come on earth. It goes on to say that wherever women are honored, all of nature rejoices. But where women are dishonored, even sacred spiritual ceremonies will not yield results.

In certain glib ways, even in western cultures, we have a similar principle. I've heard people say, "When mom's happy, everyone is happy." While it is more superficial, the basis is the same. Protect and nourish the protector and nourisher of the family, and everyone will flourish.

There is a special quality and property of women and that is to be protected and enhanced.

Living the Divine

We come into this world with only what we are: a body, a heart to feel, a brain to think, and a soul or consciousness that is beyond everything. It is nothing—and yet it is everything. That physiology and nervous system are more than flesh and bones—more than purity or impurity—more than sickness or health. It is also more than the ability to think, feel, perceive, and even love.

The human nervous system can project, live, and breathe the divine. If you think of the most beautiful, magical, and fulfilling moment of your life—when everything seemed to click or when you were happier than you could ever imagine—that is the beginning. That is the first step on the path.

To say that women and men are divine is not an exaggeration. It is a reality. It is the fullness of life flowing within itself. Where does life go? What path does it take? Is it pre-determination or free will? All these questions are asked on the path. It's natural to want answers.

People look for answers in books, from teachers, or in what other people think or how the world has done it. People always want answers outside of themselves. But as the answers can be found inside and the solutions conceived inside, the ability to implement wisdom also comes from inside.

The first time I realized that we are so much bigger than we think we are, I was nine years old. I had just learned pranayam, a simple breathing exercise, in preparation for learning the Transcendental Meditation technique a few weeks later.

It was my first day practicing. I closed my eyes and it was like I was in another world. My body felt like it was made of a cushion of light. There was ecstatic happiness and a feeling that I was home. There was also this predominant feeling of so much comfort, like the most comfortable place I'd ever been. I wanted to stay there forever.

In that experience, the social angst of a nine-year-old, from family worries to friend worries, dissolved. But more than that, everything seemed very small. My fourth-grade classroom seemed very small. My school seemed very small. Even the USA, which had seemed inconceivably large to me before, seemed very small.

That was one of the first seeds of seeking in me. Once you can see, feel, and experience how truly small everything that appears important is—life changes.

I remember after that experience, looking and hoping to get back to it. Not every day doing my breathing exercises brought that, but the memory spurred me to hope for it. It was like a memory of the best moment of my life. I kept thinking, "Did that actually happen to me?"

Signposts on the Path of the Divine

While that experience with pranayam was the first, it wasn't the last. A few years later, while I was at a three-week summer camp before starting the not-so-subtly-named Ideal Girls' School, the same sense of peace started to settle in. This time it lasted much longer than five or ten minutes.

It stretched on for days, with each day feeling like I had sunk more deeply into the ultra-comfortable light-pillow-pudding of happiness. I couldn't believe it kept going. Was this me? Things that would make me upset rolled off. Things that would make me happy made me bounce with glee. And there was this predominant peace so thick I could cut it with a knife. It was in the air, it was in my skin, and somehow, especially, it was in the sky.

In looking back with a new perspective, those experiences were part of destiny and a higher purpose. Nature opens windows, doors, or even small cracks that can reveal new opportunities and levels of experience. Maybe they are whispers or guidance that change the direction of our path even a little.

Even a slight change in direction, over time, can have a big impact. Sometimes an orchestrated plan for a higher purpose is not a grand flash or life-changing moment, but even a split second to remember your divine nature. Even a second remembering that we are, in fact, divine can be enough to change the course of a life.

In my case, if I hadn't had that experience when I was nine, I wouldn't have decided never to miss a meditation, no matter how boring it became. That was the moment when I first saw Maharishi not as a person, a personality, or a guide, but as a master imparting higher blessings than I could previously comprehend.

My experience of meditation for that first year was often not particularly profound, but that first experience of pranayam was so strong in my memory and feeling that I would keep at it for anything. It became a point of pride: I never missed a meditation.

Likewise, that overpowering peace that settled in like a blanket around me at 14 changed my life. Without that experience, I would not have decided to leave my horse, my family, and my life in Iowa to attend the Ideal Girls' School (IGS).

Without going to IGS, I never would have become frustrated and started to search for a Vedic education, written Maharishi a letter, or become a passionate seeker of truth. Some might conclude that because of the experiences, I changed my life. While that is true, I believe I was always destined for the life I have had, and the experiences were well-timed signposts to make sure I made the right turn and took the direction I was always moving toward.

An outside observer could say I took a sharp pivot. For me, it was a natural response to an inner calling. These inner callings come to all of us if we are fortunate enough to hear them.

Sometimes they hit us so hard that we have no choice but to listen. Other times, they are subtle, almost like a test to see if we are ready. However they come, they are both our destiny and our choice, pushing us toward something greater.

Khalil Gibran said, "*We choose our joys and sorrows long before we experience them.*" This choice of destiny is something we do not do only with joys and sorrows, but also with friends, family, work, accomplishments—and spiritual longings.

We put ourselves on the path, and like spiritual post-it notes, we remind ourselves along the way of where we are going. We also choose to forget our essential nature. We forget that we are divine and all-powerful and start believing that we must live in limitations of how it was or has been, instead of how it should or can be.

The memory that we are divine is already within each of us. This is the memory that we are more than the most we could ever imagine. More than the best experience of our lives. More than the most beautiful image of an ideal life of any person. We are, man or woman, old or young, searching and longing, or lost and confused, divine. The memory is all that is missing. And even the memory we already have.

This grand and lofty ideal is uplifting and inspiring but can seem very far away when caught in the mundane pressure of daily life—work, family, home, kids, cleaning, laundry, meals, traffic, etc. The tiny points of daily reality appear as the overpowering theme. How is it possible to shift, in an instant, from minutiae to divinity?

It can happen in an instant, at any instant, at any time. The flash of memory of divine reality can happen in the shower, on a bus, or while stuck in traffic. It can happen while walking in nature or rushing to work. The spark of the divine is waiting for its moment to shine. It is waiting to shift all that we thought of, to all we can be.

The Story of Nefertiti

Nefertiti was born around 1370 BC. As one of the great queens of ancient Egypt, her legacy is in her unwritten history. Nefertiti had a deep-seated belief that women were all-powerful divine goddesses. Her ideas became the seeds of many female-centric religions and spiritual traditions, as well as the worship of the sun as a form of the divine. Nefertiti gave birth to six daughters, called the six daughters of the sun god. This is her story:

The ancient time has passed. As the sun shines everywhere, so do the divine blessings shine on all. The power is with the sun, which gives all life. Each ray of the sun, like a ray of grace, brings health, vitality, and nourishment to all. To live with the sun is to live a nourished life. All should worship the sun and worship the divine mother who gave birth to us all.

Every day I pass through the temple gates, covering my head and my kohl-lined eyes, catching the scent of my own jasmine fragrance as I go to make offerings to Aten. "A" is the wholeness of life, and "ten" is the wholeness of life circling on itself. Aten represents realization—enlightenment—for the people of Mother Earth.

It is the mothers who can carry us there—and the mothers who can carry us away. It is we, the women, who can bring the revival. We let them appear strong, but we worship, we light the flame, we give birth to the new generation, and instill belief in their hearts.

My daughters already know their role. Beautiful and elegant, they are also strong in character, sharp in intellect, and wise enough to know when to surrender to the divine. There is no place and time that is not for surrender. We are divine. Be one and all. See the scope and the grandeur within each of us through surrender to that higher power.

I walk with two of my daughters, Meriaten and Meketanten, into the desert, the cool of the night whipping our robes and the fragrance of flowers mixing with the sand in the wind. The stars are high above, guiding us. They speak of a new time. They speak of revival and loss. They also speak of the fight for power and ultimate betrayal. And so, we come to pray.

We sit in the silence of the night when no birds sing and vastness stretches out around us. It is always darkest before dawn, and in the darkness, we begin our prayer. Our voices rise like a thousand choruses, each one moving and holding as one.

Our prayer to the sun god begins before he is seen. Although we pray to the sun, we also pray to the divine mother in each of us. Young and old, joining together with the power of the night to greet the sun.

With the rising dawn, each ray comes from the sun—I—a thousand and eight rays—worship with the names of the great sun god who is in fact the mother of all. She, He, They give life to all on earth.

And I see in the sun the power of my love. I, Nefertiti, the one and all, the goddess of power, of the divine mother who shines like a thousand suns from her forehead.

Whether the stars tell the story of the destiny to come, or the divine power within will change reality, the story will be told. But in every story, we are mothers and daughters joining hands, from thousands of generations before and thousands of generations to come, in this moment with the rays of the sun to bring forth into the earth a new life, a new divine light.

You may think my story is long gone, written in the history books with stones in museums, but I exist everywhere. Perhaps that story did come to pass as a power struggle and betrayal, but I was not just a queen who lived in some ancient kingdom.

I live in the hearts and souls of women around the world. From the rays of my hair, from the rays of the sun, I live on. It might be, as the stars spoke to me, that I became one with the sun. I am the one. My power lies in my daughters, and their daughters, and their daughters, and so on for millions of years and all millennia.

You believe the ancient Egyptians are long gone. But the ancient Egyptians walk amongst you. My power and the power of the sun together breathe in you, in your heart and soul as the mother of all.

The World is as You Are

The story of Nefertiti and the Gaya of the great traditions reminds us of who we are. By focusing on the problem, we forget that our essential power is in attention. What you put your attention on grows stronger in your life.

"The world is as you are" was one of Maharishi's simple teachings for children. And yet that simple sentence has profound implications for every person's life. If the world is as you are, then by changing yourself, you can change the world. It can start small, with a smile or a small choice, but it will grow and flourish as one change leads to another. To change the world, first, you must change yourself.

When you focus on the problem, the failure, or the lack, you see more of that. Changing circumstances, situations, and environment means changing the inner reality that is drawing that to you. This is not to say that those who are victims of terrible circumstances are at fault, but that in even the most difficult and impossible situations, there is the possibility of light. It starts with thought and recognition.

I have also felt hopeless in situations that seem to have no resolution. The pandemic has left many people with a feeling of "will this ever end?" Like a global pandemic, there are situations out of our individual control. What we can and do control is our response to them and the opportunities we create.

We have the opportunity each day to connect to our own divine nature and to honor the women in our lives. That includes honoring ourselves and other women around us. When together we rise up, the shakti within—the divine waiting to be expressed —will seek and find channels to protect and nourish our families, communities, and the world.

Where women are honored, all good comes. When we as women find that essential nature and honor it in ourselves and others, we can enhance the differences in our beautiful world while raising up others, as well as ourselves.

Action Steps

Here are some reflections, ideas, and actions to absorb and experience this thread of wisdom:

1. Use Attention. Use your inner power to change a situation. Instead of fighting, protesting, or objecting to something you see as wrong or unjust, see it, quietly set the intention of your desire, and leave it. Watch how your quiet attention starts to shift the situation.

Start with small situations that don't involve many other people. With practice, you can reach bigger situations through the power of your attention. Please learn the TM-Sidhi (advanced TM program) to do this even better.

2. Admire. "Wherever women are honored there is happiness and joyfulness." ~ Smritis

Collect photos on your phone or Instagram of various expressions of women in your life that you appreciate. Why are these photos important to you? What about their expressions reach you? How does this connect to the expression "woman is divine"?

All human and material boundaries reconnect as holistic, making Absolute Self manifest Intelligence.

Thread 6: The Answer to Love is to Love More

"Love is the force of life. The flower of life blooms, and when it blooms, it radiates love all around."
~ Maharishi Mahesh Yogi

The flower of life blooms, and when it blooms, it radiates love all around. Love is the force of life. What an incredible power is love! Love is both a path and a goal. Whenever you are loving, you bring justice to life.

Love is not just an emotion. Love is honored when it makes something right. With loving, life is honored; and the lives of those being loved improve.

The single ability I am most grateful for is the ability to love. Love makes hard moments beautiful and tender moments divine. Love bridges gaps and gulfs too wide to span and creates unity. Every expression of love at every moment of life expresses the most significant, valuable essence of the life of a human being.

While it can come naturally, love can also be cultivated and will grow. I'm not talking only about romantic love, although love certainly encompasses romance. But the paths and channels of love are as diverse as our relationships: love of family, of friends, of the world, of the divine, and of life.

I first noticed the ability to keep loving when I was young. I cared so much about what happened to others in my small town. Of course, small towns are ripe with gossip, and ours was no exception, but I was not just joining the gossip mill. I felt like a silent cheerleader wishing for the success of my classmates, my teachers, my friends, and even other students in school that I didn't know.

I wanted them to achieve all they dreamed to be and more. I am so happy when I hear of their successes, their happiness, and their progress. Perhaps some will say this is strange. But I realized long ago that I will always care about the people I hold dear, no matter how our paths diverge.

From a distance, I'm celebrating the middle-school best friend who is now happily married and a well-known sommelier at a Michelin-starred restaurant. I'm rooting for the now tri-lingual, high-powered NYC lawyer who used to be in my gymnastics class and was one of the kindest people I knew. There are many others with so many accolades that it would be difficult to list here. But even as decades pass, the care doesn't fade. I am wishing and rooting for the success of people whose paths I crossed on the journey of life. But most of all, I am wishing for their happiness and peace.

In the age of social media, we can usually discover what the people who are no longer directly a part of our lives are doing, or at least see a snapshot of their highlight reels. Many see that as a rabbit hole of comparison or jealousy, giving rise to feelings of inadequacy. I choose to love the people I am connected with and wish them well. That simple, daily act of loving frees the soul to love more.

Different Currents of Love

We can talk about different types of love based on connection, from acquaintances to friends, romantic partners, and even to love of the divine directly. The answer to all types of love is the same: love more.

What is described above is the first kind of love: the choice to love everyone in your life, however distantly they are still connected, regardless of their behavior toward you. Just that simple act is liberating. It frees you from the trap of comparison and brings simple joy with each new accomplishment. It might not appear like a life-altering choice, but it starts to change your perspective on others and on life.

There is a second kind of love that is more challenging: it is the choice to love those who have consciously hurt you. It is more difficult to genuinely rise to love after being hurt. This is real power and takes a pure heart. We've all been hurt, and unfortunately, in most cases, we've all also hurt someone, either intentionally or unintentionally. The act of loving those who've hurt you is in this way also an act of love to yourself.

It feels good to be kind to someone, even when it is unfair. This act of love takes constant cultivation. There is an ancient Tibetan saying that to hold onto a grudge is like swallowing poison and expecting it to hurt the other person. The only person who is hurt by being angry, upset, or holding a grudge is you. By choosing to love, you set yourself free.

Let go and love. Live life with love. Stop presuming you are the judge or the jury and just be in love. It costs nothing—and yet it means everything. The door is open; let your heart be open to the gift of life and love.

While everyone can enjoy the first kind of love—spreading love to everyone—when and how we have opportunities to love, even in the face of hurt, varies. We all experience different challenges, situations, tests, and opportunities for growth in all phases of life and all types of love.

Loving is an act of patience with yourself. It is a constant process of forgiving, going beyond, and seeing the good in whatever little glimmer exists. To be able to love is first to be able to love yourself and to allow yourself to open up.

The process of loving, like a snowball rolling down a hill, builds its own momentum. You start with what you have and push it along gently until eventually, it moves on its own. And once it starts to move, there is no stopping love.

It is a flow of freedom and liberation. Love opens the heart and mind to a sort of unboundedness and peace. Love, in many ways, is both its own path and that which clears the path to make it sweeter.

Another kind of love is romantic love. While romantic love is often portrayed as the pinnacle of "happily ever after" (and it can certainly be this), for many, the ideal of romantic love and the reality of day-to-day, year-to-year existence are very different. In many cases, romance becomes comfort and familiarity. Many will be happy with a comfortable friendship or companionship. Others wish to have the romantic passion and overflowing love more commonly seen early in a relationship.

Is it possible for romantic love to continue and grow indefinitely? Yes. Unbounded love does not happen based on desire or will, date nights, or other superficial approaches to create a feeling of newness. Romantic love between two people will only continue to grow if both continue to grow in themselves.

When two people can grow together, love will grow with them. Love is an unbounded reality. When the unbounded love of connection is squeezed into mundane routines of living, it becomes snuffed out like a flame without oxygen. The unboundedness of love becomes so cramped that the joy of loving cannot reach its full expression.

When, in contrast, two people open themselves to the unbounded and live it more and more in daily life, then love has an avenue to flow in the unbounded. Love is no longer boring or stagnant. It becomes another path to reach the unbounded and live the unbounded love in daily existence.

When this happens, love connects the divine to the individuals loving. When two people can grow in love together, their love will grow with them, enriching and unfolding all that they are. To love more together is a path to unboundedness. The start of love might be the foundation. But the house, country, and world of love is built day by day and year by year when two people connect to both the divine and their higher purpose while loving each other.

There is no end to the possibility of love. Romance and lasting relationships blossom when two individuals can grow together for the divine in themselves. Then they reach through their love to touch the divine. Love becomes more than attraction—it becomes transcendent.

About love reaching the unbounded Maharishi has said,

> *"Absolute love means love without any reason, without any cause, without any purpose. Love for the sake of love, and that is spontaneous, absolute flow of love.*
>
> *In the world [love] for this, for this, for this—love for something is due to its value. Love for a flower is 'it is so good, very good smell and good shape and this'. But when the flower fades, and is not so good to look at and doesn't give fragrance, then the love stops. We cast it off, throw it away. Wherever there is relative consideration there the love is relative. Where there is no consideration, it is*

spontaneous, and reason cannot be attributed to it, reason cannot analyze it, then it is absolute love.

When the mind gets to the absolute state of Being, it gets to that universal consciousness, unbounded state of Being, then only the mind becomes capable of expressing that absolute state of love. Some of it is expressed. One goes down and comes out and more, and more begins to be expressed. You heard of universal love— means love for everything without reason, the heart is full with love, it doesn't shrink on anything. Then it is the outflow or the expression of absolute love." (Bad Mergentheim, Germany, 1964)

Love of the Highest

"And when the heart and mind is capable of absolute love, then that is the fertile platform for God, for God's love." - Maharishi

Beyond even the love of another person is love to the divine directly. This can be experienced through devotion—to God, to a Master, or to a path. Maharishi explains that devotion is love mixed with respect. Respect for something higher and greater makes a person grow in love and in their ability to love. This is the power of devotion. By looking to something greater than ourselves, we start to become greater, and we surrender.

Maharishi says when love becomes supreme, one surrenders. This love becomes pure and makes the person devoted. The devotee surrenders and then becomes unified with the beloved.

Devotion carries us beyond ourselves, even momentarily, and fills us with something greater. The full extent of divine love is to be explored and lived through the channel of each person's perception. The knowledge that it exists and can be experienced is enough to desire this divine love and welcome it into your life.

How can knowledge of unbounded love be applied practically? There is a saying, "What you put your attention on grows" that makes the case for putting attention on the growth of love.

Science described this principle in measurement theory. It states that just by observing something, the observer changes the object of observation. By being aware of love and desiring to bring more of it into our lives, love and compassion grow. In social sciences, it has been repeatedly noted that even a few minutes of attention to moral teaching (such as the Bible or the constitution of a country) makes people act in a manner that is more honest and more compassionate.

The idea that divine love exists and can be experienced is enough of a reminder to start to bring the power of that love into your life. Divine means that which is beyond this earth or human realms—that which is omnipresent, omniscient, and omnipotent. However you see or define the divine, that which is greater than the greatest and described as divine, it can also be reached and experienced. And the path to the divine is love—and to continue to grow in love. The solution to love is to love more.

Dissolving Maya

Rumi summarized this concept of opening to love beautifully when he said, *"Your task is not to seek for love, but merely to seek and find all the barriers within yourself that you have built against it."*

We are all love in our essential nature. We are loving beings, made of love, flowing toward love, filled with love, and living for love. But most of us have forgotten that. Like Rumi says, we build barriers, walls, forts, and castles to convince ourselves that we are safe and secure. Because if we have these walls or boundaries, we must be safe. But those walls, barriers, and boundaries only serve to hide from us our own essential truth.

There is a concept in the Vedic tradition called Maya. Maya translates as "that which is not." Maya is said to be responsible for the whole illusion of creation. We could say that the walls and boundaries we put up within ourselves are Maya. They appear to protect us or keep us safe when they do not exist.

There is so much talk in the world about self-love. To truly express self-love is to allow ourselves to love fully and completely without abandon—not only ourselves but everything else for which we feel love. To love is to live and to blossom. When you watch a large white lotus or a soft red rose blossom, all that was tightly hidden in the bud unfurls as if by magic. What was once hard like a ball becomes soft, fragrant, and sensual.

That soft, fragrant, sensual quality is what attracts us to the flowers. We love to smell them, touch their soft petals, and admire the shades of colors and play of light. It is in blooming that the flower, in its most vulnerable state, becomes the most powerful and beautiful.

We are all like flowers, tight and hard like balls if we do not allow ourselves to love. We hold everything so tightly that there is no sap, no fragrance, no soft petal to be found. The softness does not make us weak but, instead, infinitely strong. To love fully and completely is one of the greatest superpowers in the universe.

Full love can never be hurt because it expects nothing, it requires nothing, and it asks for nothing. It is the joy of loving that makes love flow, and it is in the adoration of the beloved that the petals of love blossom.

When allowed to love, the human heart opens like a lotus flower. The soft petals become visible, each unique, soft, curved, elegant, and multifaceted. The fragrance of love is felt all around, and the beauty of love is seen in the skin, the face, the hair, and the manner of being.

To love is to allow life to blossom and kiss infinity. It is to allow the human heart to touch the divine and feel at home. To love is a daily reminder that the greatest beauty is inside, all around, and always available. To love fully is to become one.

> *"A tender spark of love lights the light in loneliness. It burns alive the pangs of the bygone past and spreads the light of hope and joy and fulfillment. And a tiny spark of love does it."*
> ~ Maharishi Mahesh Yogi, *Love and God*

Such is the power of love. So much is written about what love can do, how to love, or how to attract love, and yet love is so simple. Be love, love, and let your heart flow. Tear down the boundaries built against it and let the light of love in your heart burn away the pain of the past and light the future with hope and peace.

Experiencing Love

Experiences of love bloom for me like petals on a flower. Every time I feel like "this is it," when I am beyond the beyond filled with love, it grows bigger. That is the beauty of love. There is no limit. Sometimes that love is directed to God or to the divine, and sometimes it is more personal. In either case, they fuse together. Two become one. The act of loving is an act of unifying.

Upon viewing certain Devatas, forms of natural law that are often depicted as sculptures or images in the form of divine beings, I felt a similar quality of enormous divine love. These are most commonly seen in temples throughout Asia but are universal depictions of some essence of each person's own inner divine potential.

That feeling of love and connection when seeing these forms came spontaneously and was not at all expected. It was like some old memories awakened. It was surprising because I didn't really expect to experience or notice anything in the temples. I felt that they must do something good and was an innocent witness. The structure, the form, and the power of the divine awakened there in me were enormous, and yet there was also a specific, personal quality.

There was a temple in Japan, on a lake south of Tokyo, in which the goddess of the temple appeared as I sat there. She emanated so much love, so much compassion. It was like being embraced in the most complete essence of a mother. Love, acceptance, nourishment, a vision of the future, and a desire to help you accomplish, all rolled into a feeling of overwhelming love. Her love was so powerful that I, in turn, immediately felt tremendous love for her.

The goddess I saw was wearing red and black in color. She was huge, powerful. But her power was love—pure love. An ocean was too small to contain her magnitude of love. It was like she was there, century after century, pouring love from the essence of who she is.

This type of love tears down the ideas of certain types of relationships, attraction, or need for acceptance. It was pure love, without attachment, without even a concrete form. Who was she? Why did I know her? Why on seeing her did I immediately feel at home? Those are the answers for the infinite, but the answer to love remains: to love more.

The Story of Goddess Arundhati

You can see Arundhati sparkling in the night sky whenever you look at the big dipper (Ursa Major). Arundhati is there with Vaishishta, one of the greatest Rishi of all time. Arundhati was the wife of Vaishishta, legendary for her love and devotion.

Anyone who has heard of the Vedic Tradition has heard of Vaishishta, but many don't know that Arundhati is also a great Rishi. She is one with Vaishishta. They are not two, but they appear as two, as two Rishi, and as husband and wife.

The devotion of Arundhati and Vaishishta is so legendary that in parts of India newly married couples will look to the stars in the sky where Arundhati and Vaishishta reside. They look for her blessings for perfect devotion. The two separate stars—Mizar and Alcor—sparkle in such a way that they appear united.

Mizar and Alcor don't just appear to be one; they actually orbit around each other, without either one ever becoming dominant. In a rare phenomenon, instead of one circling the other, they rotate together, as if in a dance, in perfect balance. Their perfect balance is seen as an example of unification through love. This is the representation of Vaishishta and Arundhati's love.

Arundhati's story is eternal. While it may have taken place thousands of years ago, the essence of the story replays itself throughout time.

The story of Arundhati is one of unconditional love and devotion —of love so powerful that the reality is immediately clear. Her love is beyond fairytales or great romances. Her love made her unified with her husband, so one was the other.

She came from a family of wise Rishi (seers, or knowers of reality), and was a great Rishi in her own right. Arundhati and Vaishishta lived for many years in an ashram, a spiritual hermitage, with six other great Rishi and their wives. These seven Rishi, known as the *Saptarishi*, are said to have the knowledge to create the world.

In the story of the Saptarishi and Arundhati, a form of Shiva (a form of Natural Law or Devata) appears as a beautiful man whose charm was so overpowering that the wives of the Saptarishi were drawn away to him. The only one who remained was Arundhati.

Taken on the surface, this appears to be a parable of women's subservience and devotion to their husbands and duties. But looking more deeply, it is a story of the power of love to unify consciousness. When two are no longer two, but one, they are invincible. Then love transcends human needs and human concepts and slips into the field of the divine.

The devotion of Arundhati is an example of this thread: the answer to love is to love more. Arundhati was melted in her love for Vaishishta. She saw only and always Vaishishta, not only with her outer vision but in her heart. She accompanied him always whether she was with him physically or not. Whether eating, walking, meditating, or singing, she moved in love with Vaishishta.

Arundhati did this not by trying but by the quiet reality of her heart and soul flowing with love. The primary beneficiary of this overflowing heart was Arundhati herself. In her simple purity, she achieved immortality and unity.

This story is not meant to be taken literally. It is a gentle reminder that the path to unity, liberation, and eternity can be opened through an overflowing, simple heart. A heart full of love, flowing without restriction, creates unity and opens the one loving to the unbounded purity of totality itself.

Tonight you can look up and see Ursa Major, the Big Dipper, or Great Bear in the sky; and sparkling in the second star from the end of the handle, you will find Arundhati, the divine woman whose brilliance complements and equals the great Rishi with her love. She is there eternally reminding us all that the answer to love is to love more.

Action Steps

Here are some reflections, ideas, and actions to absorb and experience this thread of wisdom:

1. Cherish Love. Make a point to prioritize love of all kinds. We can get so caught up in goals, destinations, deadlines, and to-dos that it is easy to forget that the most important to-do is within ourselves. In the end, it is the only thing we take with us. Give time to the people you love and find ways to express and share love in the coming week. As Maharishi says in *Love and God*, *"No drop of precious love is ever wasted..."*

2. Reflect and Write. Notice moments where any experience of love happened to you last week and find out how this was significant for your life. How did that experience move your life?

3. Remember. Now, look at your life as a whole and find the five most important moments of love in your life. From those, see where you are now. How were those moments instrumental in your evolution and progress? Why?

4. Create. Relate one of the very best moments of love in your life to a poem, song, art, or another expression so you can connect back to that experience. Through a non-verbal expression, you connect back to that moment and see how precious love is.

5. How Much Have I Loved? Notice moments of life (in your own life or in the lives of your heroes) where love allowed a great injustice to be corrected. See how love is important to do justice to life. From the wise Father Gabriel Mejia of Colombia: *"At the end of our lives, we will be judged by our level of love."* Ask yourself, "How much have I done justice to life with love?"

Vedic experiences develop open hearts and miracles.

Thread 7: What You Put Your Attention on Grows Stronger

भद्रं कर्णेभिः शृणुयाम देवा
भद्रं पश्येमाक्षभिर्यजत्राः
"All good I should hear from the ears.
All good I should see through the eyes."
~ Rk Veda 1.89.8 (also the introduction to the Upanishads of
Atharva Veda)

This invocation is not a prayer that all should be perfect but a reminder that we can find the good or the beautiful in all that we see, hear, and perceive. This is the essence of what you put your attention on grows stronger.

Seeing, hearing, and perceiving "all good" reduces pinches and friction in the heart, unfolding a sense of freedom. Seeing only good, we free ourselves from the need to correct or do something. If we see a problem, there is a sense of responsibility to solve it. If we see good, we create happiness and freedom for ourselves.

But it is not just seeing good. This thread, in some cases, can also be "what you see, you become." Attention is a powerful tool not to be underestimated. Attention is the time we give to feed our minds, our hearts, and our souls. Attention brings everything to life around us.

Have you ever kissed a child's scraped knee, and they say it is all better? The scrape is still there, but the loving attention has made it better. In an innocent child's eyes, a kiss on a scraped knee made it all better. Why not for adults, too?

With attention alone, we can start transforming our lives. When we practice piano every day for years, the connections in the brain and the ability to play grows immensely. That is simple, focused attention that we can use to structure our lives. But much of our attention and the direction we give it is based on our environment or subconscious focus. This current of focus and attention builds who we are now into who we can become.

Put another way, wherever attention goes, that grows. A businesswoman will focus her attention on every aspect of her business—from accounting to customer service, marketing or production—her regular attention helps the business grow.

In physics, this is called the observer effect or measurement theory. It simply states that the act of observing does something to the object of observation. Even if you don't physically affect the object of observation—you don't have to touch it—the process of attention changes the previous state of the object.

We've all seen graphs showing an iceberg as an analogy for success. What you see above the water, the "success," is merely a tiny portion of the iceberg. What goes on behind the scenes, below the water, is the real iceberg. Success is comprised of hard work, connections, persistence, failure, and luck. But there is one missing ingredient: attention.

The ability to use attention is to free ourselves from expectations of what we have to be or when we have to achieve it, and simply, consistently show up for ourselves. Attention is a process of observing where you are at this moment and observing where you would like to be. Attention is like watering the flowers of your potential and bringing new life to blossom.

Attention can look different for each person. Some may prefer visualization, seeing what they want to achieve each day or each week. Others may prefer lists, selecting a few achievable goals. Still others may find vision boards, journaling, or some other strategy to be the most beneficial. Whatever strategy you choose, the key is in what we can control—what we can do from our side through attention.

You might have a goal to earn a million dollars this year. But without concrete steps to achieve it, it is just a wish. You can still see the million dollars in your mind, and you may even write it down and pin it up. But you should also visualize where you need to concentrate your attention on the goals that require focus and action today. Maybe that is a new business venture. Maybe that is a new connection. Or maybe it is making a list of possibilities to try and then testing them.

The process of attention is also one of letting go of expectations and preconceived ideas. Letting go of limiting beliefs, actions, and anything else that is holding you back from your goals allows the process of attention to transform you. Through attention, you are showing up for yourself in a process of continual re-birth.

Maharishi has said that the process of evolution is the process of giving up what we are for what we can become. What we can become is infinitely more beautiful, more powerful, and happier than we can ever imagine.

The Man in the Hut

In the Vedic texts, there is a story used to illustrate the reality that what we can become is greater than we could ever imagine. The story is of a man living in a small hut on the edge of a large forest. On the other side of the forest is a magnificent castle.

The lands of the castle are filled with mines of all the precious stones and metals: diamonds, rubies, emeralds, sapphires, gold, silver, and platinum. The castle has with it such an enormous wealth that it is almost unfathomable.

One day, the man living in the little hut was performing his usual daily activities of cooking, eating, and washing when he is told that the castle now belongs to him. Now, as the owner of the castle, all the riches of all the grounds also belong to him. He can take up residence in the castle immediately.

But the man in his simple hut near the forest doesn't want to move. He likes the view of the stream from his hut. He feels attached to the pots he cooks with and the comfort of his simple bed. The hut is familiar. Even though the castle offers far greater comfort and wealth, he cries at the idea of leaving his hut. The hut belongs to the lands of the castle, so he will not lose the hut, but the thought of moving causes him to mourn the loss of the hut.

This is the analogy of a human being, so accustomed to their limitations and limiting beliefs that they are attached and cannot move forward. Even when an incredible opportunity presents itself, the man in the hut is attached to the hut. Never mind the comfort, the beauty, the possibilities, and even the happiness of the castle. He cries for the hut.

In various ways, at various times, the man in the hut is all of us. We become so comfortable with our own attachments and boundaries that we forget we have unbounded potential. We put ourselves into boxes of what we think we are good at, or what we think we deserve, instead of remembering all that we can become.

When we go beyond ourselves, to our unbounded potential of consciousness, we find ourselves in a new way. We gain a bigger vision than the small boxes we thought were so important. The castle and grounds in the analogy above are our unlimited potential, which we reach not by forcing, trying, or breaking through, but simply by being more and more of who we are and developing inner consciousness. With a commitment to inner experience, outer attention also creates new opportunities.

This is the power of attention. This is why the saying, *"what you put your attention on grows stronger in your life"* is so important. Put your attention on the good, the wise, and the beautiful. Put your attention on that which you want to become. And like watering the flower of your possibilities, watch as the beauty of all that you can be grows and blossoms from the seed of who you are now.

What You See, You Become

Attention manifests itself in everything. Who we are inside is reflected outside in our presence. It is reflected in the way we carry ourselves, the way we speak, and the way we respond to the world. Our inner attention, which seems like an intimate secret, is projected into the world every day through our bodies, speech, and actions.

Have you ever met an older couple who look almost like twins? After decades of living together, their mannerisms are the same, they say things at the same time, and they even look the same. This idea that when we are around someone frequently, we begin to resemble them is well understood. Social psychologists say that our thinking reflects the combination of the five people with whom we spend the most time. They influence our thoughts, perceptions, and worldview.

But what about the one person we spend the most time with? How do we influence or improve ourselves? The principle is, "*What you see, you become.*" This can be both literally and figuratively. In the literal sense, what we put our attention on grows stronger in our lives.

When you watch the news, the perspective and presentation of the newscaster color your thinking. When you scroll through social media, other people's "perfect" lives make you want your life to look the same. When you read a book or magazine, it not only teaches you something new but presents new perspectives that you may integrate as your own. All of these perceptions may subtly alter your perspective in ways that may not be immediately obvious.

In the Vedic tradition, they say you not only consume food through your mouth but you digest experiences through all the senses. What you eat is broken down into nutrients that build health in your body. What you see is taken through your eyes and digested by your mind and influences your perception. Likewise, what you hear is taken through your ears, what you smell through the nose, and what you feel is consumed by the skin and processed into feelings.

We've all experienced a gentle, loving touch and the way it immediately calms and relaxes our bodies and brings warmth to our hearts. Our bodies digest and respond to touch, just as they digest and respond to the impulses and information we put in through every sense.

What we see, hear, touch, taste, and smell on a regular basis is the food through which we feed our bodies, minds, emotions, and deepest feelings about ourselves and life. We need to constantly nourish ourselves. Just as a constant diet of junk food will leave the body lacking key nutrients, a life devoid of nourishment through all the senses will leave a feeling of lack we cannot define.

What you see you become is the path of a million daily perceptions, not a single defining moment. That gives courage because there are a million second chances every day. It is what we do in the spaces between time, how we fill ourselves, and what we choose to dedicate our time to. Attention is both conscious and unconscious.

"What you see you become" is a reminder to feed your body, mind, and soul with what you want to become. This doesn't mean just vision boards or reminders on the bathroom mirror but also deeper nourishment of knowledge.

Knowledge for Transformation

In Maharishi's *New Translation and Commentary of the Bhagavad Gita*, it says, *"Truly there is in this world nothing so purifying as knowledge."* Knowledge transforms who we are and what we think is possible. Knowledge takes us from where we are to what we can become.

Think of when early travelers learned that the world is not flat. That single piece of knowledge opened a world of possibilities for travel and exploration—without the risk of falling off the end of the earth.

Higher knowledge and higher experience make an empty person into a full person. Knowledge inspires us in simple and profound ways. Knowledge purifies because it refines the intellect and the heart to open new possibilities. The best knowledge is not only for intellectual understanding but for experience, as well.

Complete knowledge is for complete experience. Powerful knowledge can reach us so deeply that it changes not only the way we think and feel but the way we perceive the world and our ability to fulfill our desires in the world.

The power of knowledge is for action. There are more books in the libraries of the world than any human can read and memorize. But one book with useful knowledge can change a person's life. If knowledge increases the ability to fulfill desires and gain greater fulfillment in life, what a door of possibilities that can be!

Knowledge of human consciousness and human potential opens a greater world of possibilities than what is traditionally defined as possible in life. It makes the impossible within reach. Knowledge of the full development of human consciousness means that anything we thought was possible can, indeed, be possible.

Suddenly, the arbitrary limitations and rules we put on our lives dissolve. In the words of Rumi, *"You were born with wings, why prefer to crawl through life?"* You were born with more possibilities than you could ever imagine. You were born to fly. We were all born to fly.

This thread of wisdom is dedicated to every child, no matter how old and hardened by life, who wished they could fly. What you put your attention on grows. What you see, you become. There is no goal, no possibility, and no desire too great to achieve with the full power of your mind and consciousness. By sacrificing who you are for who you can become, you can achieve anything.

If you don't know where to start, start where you are now. And Dream.

> *"There is a candle in your heart, ready to be kindled.*
> *There is a void in your soul, ready to be filled.*
> *You feel it, don't you?"*
> ~ Rumi

You feel it, don't you?

Hearing

My first year at the Ideal Girls' School was when I was 14, in ninth grade. During that year, I learned the advanced programs of the TM Technique called the TM-Sidhi program. I made lifelong friends and gained confidence and self-assurance. And the fire of desire for enlightenment lit itself in me as never before.

It was during the time I was learning the advanced Transcendental Meditation programs that my experience changed. One day I was speaking to a teacher, and I noticed she was repeating everything. She would say a few sentences and then say them again. Granted, it is not unusual for teachers to repeat themselves. But she was repeating everything—verbatim. *That's strange*, I thought.

"Why is she repeating everything?" I asked the other students. "She's not," one of my friends replied and looked quizzically at me, wondering what I was talking about.

Later in the day, I was talking to my friend Robin when some words popped into my head—so I said them. "Hey!" she exclaimed, "I was just thinking that!" Again, it's not uncommon for good friends to think the same thing at the same time. As the old expression goes, "Great minds think alike."

But it kept happening, day after day, with everyone I encountered. I knew what they were going to say before they said it. I realized after some time that the teacher who was diligently repeating everything twice was actually thinking out what she would say—and then saying it.

After a few days, I confessed what I thought was happening to Robin. "I know! Me, too!" she exclaimed. "Here, let's test it with each other." With that, Robin and I began months of testing each other, first on "hearing" each other's thoughts and then on "seeing" colors around us like colorful, transparent clouds around people and objects. It was thrilling.

The interesting thing about both the seeing and the hearing was that there was never any judgment. It just was. No good or bad, rarely even a sense of who it was connected to. It was more like stepping into a river and watching things float by.

Robin and I would, metaphorically, point out branches, logs, boats, and innertubes as they floated down the river. "Hey! Did you see that?" we would exclaim to each other throughout the day. It was just as obvious and just as simple. I am sure that this developed as much as it did because we were so focused on it. What you put your attention on grows stronger. It was a time for us to discover that what we think is seeing or hearing is a small portion of reality.

Everyone has their own voice that they speak in, like the voice we hear in our heads. I remember being confused one day when I heard a voice inside that sounded just like mine as I was thinking about my mother's mother and missing her. There were also other thoughts and emotions that rolled in that I knew were not mine.

What was that? I thought. When I spoke to my mother later that day and shared those thoughts, she scowled, "Those were my thoughts! Stay out of my head." Apparently, just as our spoken voices sound almost identical, the voice my mother uses in her head is very similar to my own. Perhaps self-talk and the voices we use to address ourselves also run in families.

It was around that time that I lost interest in this ability. It had become too invasive. It was thrilling to know that such levels existed, then it became a fun party trick to impress my brother, and then I just lost interest. For a long time, it seemed to turn off or become much quieter.

In the Vedic tradition, there is a term "Vedic eyes" or "Vedic ears" to refer to not what is seen through the physical eyes or ears but through the subtle channels of perception. It is not seeing or hearing in the traditional sense but more of knowing, intuiting, or perceiving with inner vision.

Many times, this experience can be as clear as seeing with the physical eyes or ears, but the way it is perceived or felt is different. Other times, it is much more subtle, like a faint feeling. Most people have at least glimpsed this type of experience. It can come as intuition, understanding, or a glimpse deeper into a situation.

The senses in this way reach into the celestial fields of life, what some might call the world of the angels, or devatas, or subtle beings. We are all celestial beings, appearing in our outer shells through relative perception. And more subtle than that, we are all the radiant, diverse expressions of consciousness. These experiences were some of my first glimpses into higher states of consciousness and the realization that this knowledge is not for the intellect, but for direct experience.

What we put our attention on is a reminder that there are much bigger levels of life than the existence we think of as real. With the desire for knowledge, along with experience and patience, nature will find ways and means to reach us and show us greater experiences and greater realities.

The Story of Lopamudra

Lopamudra is one of the Rishi of the Rk Veda. A Rishi is a seer, but modern historians would call a Rishi an author. The term Rishi encompasses the unique ability of cognition to bring forth true knowledge.

Lopamudra is one great female Rishi. Lopamudra's name means "lost parts" as she is said to have been created from the most powerful and beautiful parts of plants and animals such as the eyes of a deer, the grace of a panther, the speed of a cheetah, etc. She was at once human and divine.

Lopamudra is the wife of Rishi Agastya, one of the most famous great seers of the Vedic Tradition. Like Arundhati, Lopamudra is a great Rishi equal to her husband in wisdom, vision, and love. With her love, Lopamudra helped Agastya rise to the highest unity. Together, they became more than either could be alone.

This tradition of unity is the story of Lopamudra. Her story is told in various ways, but the essence is simple. She came to this earth as separate from Agastya; together, they reached the highest unity. Here is Lopamudra's story, as told in her own words:

I am Lopamudra, the Divine, the beloved, the all-powerful. Because of my beauty, people see me for that. Because of my great husband, people forget that it is I within him. Because love is not of the intellect, people are afraid of what I represent.

I am passion, purity, and fire. I am the strength of desire, love, and unity, kindling each day to bring a greater wholeness. I am the love of the heart and desire of the body that together rise in the higher soul.

Agastya was a great aesthetic, filled with silence, moving the silence. And yet, the silence remained still. He sat in his cave day and night. He didn't eat, talk, or appear to do anything. He was breathing the totality of life, and yet it did not touch the world. With the power of my love, together we brought the silence to move on earth.

You might know this power as divine, the power of the Divine Mother. You might see this power as feminine energy and strength. It is all of that—and it is the power of love. For silence is silent, it is nothingness; it is still. Silence is beautiful as a flat frozen tundra in the dark of midnight is beautiful. There is beauty and peace in nothingness.

But the world and the oceans are not only nothing, for, in nothing, nothing exists. From nothing, nothing comes out. And yet, when you push and pull and knead silence like the fibers of cloth or the dough of a chapati, you find that it is alive. It is not silence but dynamism—awake, alive, and yes, passionate.

Some tell my story as a story of passion: a woman whose husband was ignoring her for his own pursuits and through her will and charm lured him back to her. That is one story and is one level of truth.

But the deeper truth is a truth of unity. To bring my husband back means to bring back our unity. Agastya was one of the greatest Rishi of all time. Living within him, with him, and through him, I bring softness, power, grace, and peace. I am the same all-powerful as he, and yet I bring the silence of his heart to life.

There is a saying that an elephant has two sets of tusks—one for eating and one for showing. One looks fierce but is mostly useless. The other does the work of chewing over a ton of food every day.

My story is like that of the elephant's second set of tusks—those for chewing. My work is not about processing food but about moving consciousness. When my consciousness moves, Agastya's consciousness moves with it. And when I bring him to me, I bring our subtlest natures to a level of unity.

Just like the work that goes on behind the scenes, my role in doing it was a role of a creator—creating my own destiny and that of the world. Silence is ever silent. But tickle the silence, and you find a world of possibilities. How do you tickle the silence? With the power of attention.

This is my message through the corridor of time: what you put your attention on grows stronger. Desire, and you shall receive. There is no limit to the power of your divine attention and love. You think of superpowers or superheroes, but there is one superpower inborn as old as time, and yet long forgotten: the power of love.

We as women have this power in our very essence. We think we need to be seen and heard to create. And yet, we are perpetual creators. The tusks for showing are just for show—the real ability to nourish the elephant comes from the hidden teeth.

When you think you want to move or create, never forget your power of attention in love. Desire quietly and let go. The beauty of your Being will radiate and attract the means to fulfill your desire or open new paths previously unimagined.

Using the Power of Attention

One of Maharishi's great contributions is the understanding that wherever attention goes, it connects mind and body. The nervous system carries impressions of past experiences. When the nervous system is connected, it brings healing. This is done through the power of attention.

Just putting attention on our bodies when there is fear, anxiety, grief, pain, or any other difficult emotion or physical sensation can start to bring healing. Negative or difficult emotions that we carry in our bodies can especially be softened through attention.

When attention reaches, life energy reaches. Perhaps you notice a feeling or sensation. Placing attention there increases coordination between the body and the mind. Lack of coordination results in abnormal functioning. We can experience this as fear, anxiety, jealousy, disharmony, or many other uncomfortable emotions that are a part of nearly everyone's experience at some point. Attention bridges the gap.

Attention in the body is an almost miraculous procedure to eliminate and balance any negativity. When attention is given, a person can be free from so much that is holding them. It is a self-healing mechanism built into each of us. This is the simple power of attention: where attention goes, that grows, especially in our own bodies and nervous systems.

Action Steps

Here are some reflections, ideas, and actions to absorb and experience this thread of wisdom:

1. Find the Good. There is a tradition in Sthapatya Veda (a Vedic system of architecture) that when you move into a new house you appreciate everything: the walls, the window handles, the doors, the carpet, the grout, the faucet, etc. Try doing it with something even for five minutes. You'll be surprised how much your perspective changes.

2. Make a Change. Acquiring a new habit with new attention requires at least 21 days. Consider which habit you want to put your attention on consciously until it becomes automatic. Choose something that is important for you, even if it is a small thing.

3. Reflect. Review your life from the perspective of the things you put your attention on and the results you got. What type of attention brought the greatest results? See how attention affects your health, relationships, spirituality, and professional success.

4. Remember. Review your life now in a simple way and see how attention is very important. Look at which areas of more attention brought you success and which areas you tried but were not successful. Was there a difference in your attention? See how putting your attention differently in different situations changed the result.

5. Use Attention. At any moment during the day when you start to feel anxious, nervous, or afraid, you can use the power of attention. Just sit or lie down and close your eyes. Gently focus your attention on the body. Perhaps your attention is drawn to a particular part. Just let your attention innocently move wherever it is drawn. Naturally, after a few minutes, the feelings will get softer as some sensation is released from the nervous system. (This simple practice of attention is from Maharishi Mahesh Yogi and taught in Facebook Live by Dr. Tony Nader, MD, Ph.D., MARR)

Self-healing reconnects every experience materially in pure happiness and totality.

Thread 8: Think Big

In the words of Pablo Picasso, *"Everything you can imagine is real."* Whether that is a fantasy land or the hand of God, the human mind is the great creator of possibilities. We can bring new possibilities to life. We started to see that in the last chapter.

Maharishi has also said that anything that has been imagined by the human mind is real, somewhere, in some level of creation. That doesn't mean that aliens will be landing in your backyard tomorrow or that your 10-year-old will be getting their letter to Hogwarts any day now. But it does mean that there are possibilities beyond our wildest imagination.

Thinking again of different levels of life, from the most surface level of speaking to the finest level of thinking, where intuition whispers, it is obvious that the surface of life isn't the only level of reality.

What we can see, hear, and smell around us in everyday existence is one level of reality. Beyond that, there is the equally real and vivid mental level of life. This is the world that lives within our thoughts and minds. It can be described as creativity, imagination, self-talk, or any other term to describe the constant barrage of millions of thoughts we all experience daily.

Likewise, the finest intellect or intuition is a different level of reality. When we hear that whisper inside, it is often without apparent logic. Some people describe a gut feeling. Others say they felt a tugging in their heart. Yet others say they don't know where the idea came from, but it was there. This higher wisdom or intelligence within us all speaks if we only listen. Those who are religious might call it the hand or voice of God.

Whatever term you use, these three distinct levels have their own reality. Have you ever talked yourself out of intuition? I certainly have. It is so easy to hear the voice of intuition whispering, "Do this, it's the right way." And then, when you look at the problem from the perspective of analytics and logic, your intuition seems wrong. Only later, you realize that your intuition was correct.

In these instances, when one person experiences the world, different levels of perception have different truths or different realities. What is true from the logic of the intellect is not always true from the level of intuition, as is it able to automatically calculate innumerable factors that may be hidden from the intellect.

Likewise, what is true at the source of thought is a different reality. From that unbounded, unlimited perspective, anything is possible. There are no limits to what we can perceive or what we can achieve.

If it can be imagined and experienced, it can be lived. This is the power of this thread of wisdom. If we allow ourselves to believe that the only reality is our most limited reality, then we miss out on unbounded power and possibilities. Call it the hand of God. Call it Natural Law. Call it Goddess power. Whatever name you want to give that "something bigger," the reality that there is something bigger is important.

This understanding also takes imagination and gives it validity. Knowing this, we can no longer think that because our perception or analysis on the surface of a situation makes it appear impossible, it must be so. Thinking big means recognizing that what we thought was impossible could be possible.

It also means surrendering some layer of control or the illusion that we were ever in control. To various degrees, we all believe we are the controllers of our destiny through what we do. We forget that the control of our destiny lies, before our actions, in our thoughts. And before our thoughts, our destiny lies in who we are.

There is a principle in Maharishi's *Science of Creative Intelligence* that summarizes this: *"Thought leads to action, action leads to achievement, achievement leads to fulfillment."*

It is not by desiring fulfillment that fulfillment is achieved. It is not only through action that achievement is guaranteed. It is the power and clarity of our thoughts that effectuate clearer, more powerful, and successful actions.

An architect sits and thinks and from her quiet contemplation designs a whole building. Before the foundation is laid, the building is constructed in her mind. The same is true of all of life. Before we lift a pen or take a step, we create a vision of fulfillment in our minds.

There is No Joy in Smallness

How do we create this fulfillment? Certainly, if all it takes is thinking, we would all already have it. What is the difference?

There is a common expression from the Vedic Literature that says, *"There is no joy in the finite, joy is in the infinite."* Maharishi would often remark, *"There is no joy in smallness."* The infinite in this case refers to infinite, unbounded consciousness, a field of all possibilities where anything can be achieved. The small or finite refers to anything less than that.

These expressions tie back to the feeling that there must be a higher purpose or something more in life. That higher purpose for each of us is to realize our unbounded potential. We can transcend limitations and boundaries. Anything less than our highest, unbounded potential is a boundary, a limitation on the greatest happiness. Joy in the infinite means finding joy in a level of existence without limitations.

Echoing this idea of joy in the great, Chinese philosopher Zhuang Zhou said, *"If you cannot do something great, become part of something great."*

Becoming great means becoming unbounded. Doing is an outside action. Becoming is an inner transformation.

It can also mean taking action, participating in that which you see as transforming the world for good. When we reach beyond ourselves, when even our individual sense of "I" or "mine" becomes unlimited, then we are able to be and do great for ourselves and for the world.

There is an expression in the Brahma Sutras (1.1.4) that says, *"Tat tu Samanvayat."* This can be translated as *"Summation, or unification, creates totality."* By finding unity, totality within ourselves, the biggest, most beautiful reality we can imagine is not far away. It is already within each of us. When Maharishi spoke of heaven on earth, he was speaking of each of us realizing our own highest potential.

And this reality in each of us is the summation—the unification —of all the realities and diverse perspectives of our vision, speech, thinking, feeling, intuition, and Being. And it is the summation and unification of the finest level of everyone else. It is the piece that holds everything together and makes everything possible. It is Being. It is really, really big. It is infinite.

This summation is experienced in the oceanic power of conscious-ness—the biggest, most powerful, and most peaceful level of ourselves. It is the same power of consciousness that creates the whirling dervish of forces and matter that create our diverse universe with billions of suns and galaxies, and yet remains, in essence, the quietness deep within each of us.

It doesn't mean that by thinking big we automatically become something bigger. On one level, it is our reality; on another level, we have to achieve or realize it.

Our minds are like containers. They can be big or small. They can be limited like a small pond or unlimited like the mighty ocean. It is only by allowing our minds to expand, to reach oceanic status, that they can become something bigger.

It is thought that leads to powerful action and achievement. The quality of thought depends upon the quality of the mind. A more powerful, holistic mind leads to more powerful, holistic, and fulfilling action. And the quality of the mind depends on its expe-rience of its unlimited, unbounded potential. This happens auto-matically when we transcend. Only unboundedness expands the vision to the unlimited.

All those who have accomplished something great in life throughout the ages have known this secret. The clarity of their thinking determines the quality of the results. It does not require belief. Belief is only useful if it has a path and is backed by action.

If there was a way to open the mind, systematically, to its unbounded potential, how great, how powerful we could all be. Everyone has unlimited potential. There is no end to the possibili-ties. By becoming bigger, wiser, and more expanded, we raise each other up.

There is a saying that a rising tide raises all boats. Individuals tapping into and reaching their unbounded potential, in reaching for something greater, raise up all those around them. Together, we create something more holistic and more beautiful than we could ever imagine.

Everything that we can imagine is real on some level. We can make the most beautiful world and life real now for all of us.

The Ego

Sometimes, believing in something bigger means faith. The power to have faith when we cannot see or perceive that which we believe in is one of the great human powers. When we believe in something, we expand our ego and desire to be right.

This melting of ego allows us to expand our hearts and consciousness. Ego, the desire to be right or be the best, is in fact a trick to limit the expansion of the heart and consciousness. The heart unifies. It looks not for what is best but seeks to melt with all that is loved. The heart rejoices in something great, something bigger.

Likewise, the field of consciousness is a field of unity. Totality is from summation—unification. It is a field in which all the apparent diversity becomes one. The power of consciousness is the power to perceive all the apparent diversity within unity. The one who is the best is the one who can be one with all.

This smallness of the ego is an enemy within each of us. We trick ourselves into believing that our worth is in any way derived from comparison. We judge ourselves by others. How our job is compared to others. How beautiful our house is compared to our friends' houses. How well we performed on a test compared to the scores of other test takers. How well our children do in school or sports compared to their classmates or children their age. How our hair, body, love life, friendships, income, awards, or you-fill-in-the-blank is compared to others.

Ego compares against something else. To be the best, one must be better than someone else. There is someone who is the best doctor at the worst medical school in the world. There is someone who is the best football player at a small rural school. There is someone who was at one time the best tennis player in the world and can no longer play.

Whether we are happy with our performance, status, bodies, or accomplishments, all too often depends on comparison to our own past performance or appearance, as well as to others.

The problem with comparison is that it depends on the performance of others, and it is constantly changing. This comparison is what feeds the ego. The ego does not seek ultimate unity, the highest knowledge, or perfect love. The ego seeks validation that it is worthy. The ego is an empty void asking the simple questions, "Am I good enough?" and "Am I loved?"

Once we see these comparisons for what they are—empty voids that need to be nourished and filled—some of the tricks of the ego stop. But the ego is a skilled trickster. It will degrade confidence privately while seeking outward validation. If you have ever felt that you didn't belong, or weren't good enough, while acting with outward strength, then you are familiar with the ego's tricks. But it is possible to transcend this small and limited ego.

Others will tell you that with an effort to raise others up and support your competitors, you can rise beyond the limitations of ego. While there is some truth to this, there are limitations. The mind and ego are like the body: you need to condition and train them. If you have not stretched to do the splits or trained to run a 5k, you may not be able to do it.

Of course, surface practice and conscious effort will make a difference. What you put your attention on grows stronger in your life. But what is far more effective is to open your mind to finer levels of thought where you can transcend the small limitations of the ego.

There is a shortcut to going beyond the small traps of comparison and feelings of inadequacy. This shortcut opens the mind to the universal mind and expands the ego to the universal ego. This is a shortcut to thinking big. When we transcend, as millions of people around the world have experienced, the boundaries dissolve and we experience a level of unity.

Some call it wholeness; some call it peacefulness; some just say they feel better. But all, day by day, begin to expand that small, limited ego that cannot comprehend either its full potential or its unified relationship with the environment.

The ego is opposed to unity. The ego, in its small and limited state, is the enemy of love. The ego seeks only to glorify itself. Love only has a purpose for the ego so far as it enhances its own importance.

Real love transcends the need for personal gain. It is no longer about the ego. When we can transcend beyond the limitations of the small ego, we start to feel freedom.

To believe in something bigger means to take the small ego of "I" and "mine" and make it a universal ego. This universal ego is the ego beyond the comparison traps of the small ego. The universal ego is like an ever-full ocean, unaffected by the change in waves or tides.

The universal ego is that reality of summation—of unity— described in the Brahma Sutras. It blossoms not through effort or affectation, but through an inner awakening no different from turning on a light in a dark room. To light the light of life and shine all possibilities is simple: it is from unification. When we find that the biggest, most powerful, and wisest version of ourselves is already inside, waiting to be discovered, anything we can imagine does, indeed, become possible.

St. Francis of Assisi

St. Francis of Assisi is an embodiment of transcending an individual ego to love God. St. Francis started innocently in love with his God. He wanted to be poor. He meant that he wanted to go beyond his mind and ego.

Born into a great family, tradition dictated that the young St. Francis would become a knight and go to war. On his way, he had an experience of melting with God, becoming one with God. In that experience, he felt God tell him, You have to be my warrior, not the warrior of the humans. That experience transformed his life. It is retold in *El Hermano de Asis* by Ignacio Larrañaga:

> *"All the chroniclers say that on that night Francis heard, in a dream, a voice that asked him:*
>
> *- What is this? Francis, where are you going?*
>
> *- To Apulia, to fight for the Pope.*
>
> *- Tell me, who can reward you better, the Lord or the servant?*
>
> *- Naturally, the Lord.*
>
> *- Then why do you follow the servant and not the Lord?*
>
> *- What am I to do?*
>
> *- Go back home and you will understand everything.*
>
> *And the next morning Francis returned home."*

After that, he had a Divine experience and visitation of God with deepest clarity of vision. He didn't go to war, but he did become sick for some time. This was all to the extreme disappointment of his family. After some time, St. Francis built a small church. Everyone wondered what he was doing, thinking it was ridiculous.

But then other people started to come to him. Many people started to feel that becoming "poor," going beyond the ego, was the way to experience heaven on earth. Maharishi said of St. Francis: You have to leave your thoughts, you have to leave your world, you have to leave everything and be innocent so then you transcend.

The whole accomplishment of St. Francis was to go beyond the ego. He didn't have a small ego. He was "poor."

This simple, poor man transformed the whole church. In seeing this, even the Pope began to cry, feeling that the spirit was lost in the church and that St. Francis was experiencing it. Finally, someone was in love with God.

The organization had become old and strict. A poor man who was not thinking about his ego was able to do the "biggest."

When you are not in the ego, you allow the highest to happen. Believing while aligned with the infinite power of natural law allows you to accomplish the highest. Infinite power of natural law allows you to become bigger and bigger, moving to infinity. St. Francis was this: moving in the infinite love of God. Becoming unbounded, anything is possible.

Yogic Flying

When I was 15 years old, I learned an advanced program of the TM technique, called the TM-Sidhi program. The TM-Sidhi program includes a technique called Yogic Flying. You must be thinking, "Flying?" But you've made it this far, so hear me out.

Yogic flying as taught by Maharishi Mahesh Yogi is based on the ancient teaching of Yoga by the seer Maharishi Patanjali. Yes, the same Yoga taught at Yoga studios, but much more advanced. And by more advanced, I don't mean more difficult. It is much, much easier than doing a headstand or even downward dog. More advanced, in this case, means it reaches finer, more powerful levels of life to create rapid transformation and evolution.

There are three stages of Yogic Flying described by Patanjali. The first stage is hopping like a frog, the second stage is floating or staying seated in the air, and the third stage is flying through the universe.

Even hopping like a frog from the level of the mind is impressive, but the power of Yogic Flying is not in the outward action. It is in the inner experience. When I first learned Yogic Flying, I didn't even notice my body was moving. It was hopping across the foam, but I felt so much happiness and inner lightness that I didn't notice anything else.

After that first experience, I looked forward to Yogic Flying as a highlight of each morning and afternoon. When I started to practice, I felt this tremendous power beyond myself filling my physiology. It was like being charged to an unlimited source of energy.

And it was fun! Sometimes I would laugh and laugh, other times I felt such powerful bliss that I couldn't stop smiling. Sometimes, there was a perception of golden light flooding my body and inner vision.

The experience of Yogic Flying is better than any amusement park ride. Others have compared it to surfing consciousness. I would say it is like connecting to—and feeling—the power of who you are in your deepest of consciousness for the first time. It is a physical reality of finding that something bigger we were talking about. It is like being super-charged.

Yogic Flying accelerates the benefits of Transcendental Meditation. It trains the mind to think from the field of pure consciousness and creates maximum mind-body integration.

While you will hear people talking about TM, you almost never hear about Yogic Flying in public promotions. Some people are afraid that it will be too weird or out-there. On words alone, they are probably right. But in reality, it couldn't be more integrating and powerful for life!

It seems like nearly everyone is practicing some version of Yoga. If doing a headstand could surcharge your body with energy and your mind with bliss, everyone would be doing it. That is the power of Yogic Flying. For the seeker of enlightenment, or even a seeker of more energy or happiness, Yogic Flying is revolutionary. Doing it in a group multiplies that effect.

This book recounts many turning moments on my path of spirituality, but there is one important dividing line: before and after learning Yogic Flying. You'll remember earlier I talked about experiencing a cushion of softness or peace. Yogic Flying brought a new dimension of bliss and experience of finer levels of life. Afterward, my physiology felt lighter, my perception deeper, and my concept of bliss so much bigger.

The idea of "something bigger" no longer required belief. Being unbounded was not an abstract concept. I could see, feel, and experience it daily. I wish I could give each of you even one drop of happiness from the best moments of Yogic Flying. Even one drop would change your ideas of reality forever.

The Universe is Tiny

Beyond the experience of Yogic Flying, there have been a few moments in my life when I saw the huge expanse of consciousness. I'm not talking about feeling big; I'm not even referring to the feeling of unboundedness in transcendence. This experience was so enormous, so far beyond what I thought of as "big." I'll do my best to try to describe it, but there are not enough words to capture this reality.

The first time it happened, I was sitting, meditating in my room. All of a sudden, something shifted. It was like I was being physically propelled by bliss (although I don't think I actually moved). I was filled with golden light. It kept expanding my inner vision, bigger and bigger, until I was in a giant, unbounded space.

I could see our universe like a small dot in this vastness. After looking very carefully, I found Earth there. It was smaller than the smallest pore on your skin set against a backdrop of not just our universe, but universes. It was so tiny, so insignificant, that I started to laugh.

It was a combination of two feelings: First, being so suffused with bliss that I saw in that moment that the very structure of who I am is bliss. Second, the realization that everyone and everything that had seemed so important was like a tiny pinprick in infinity. The reality of who we are on Earth seemed minuscule. And in that moment, it seemed like a punchline to a joke. "This is it?!"

I kept laughing in this blissful ecstasy. It lasted for more than an hour and a half. There was a feeling of light physically moving through my brain like a comb weaving in bliss. The perspective was life-altering. This experience contained the answer to my question, "Is this it?" It was also a new perspective on what it means to think big.

The Story of Maitreyi

Maitreyi was one of the two wives of the great sage Yagyavalkya. While Yagyavalkya is world-renowned, Maitreyi herself is renowned and revered for her purity and dedication to the highest wisdom. Maitreyi is a model of love, devotion, and sacrifice for the highest, along with an inquisitive pursuit of wisdom. Here is her story:

> *The hall was decorated with flowers. Garlands of marigolds were strung along the walls, and fragrant jasmine sat in bunches and on bushes lining the walk. The delirious smell of champak wafted in from the trees in the meadow and the ylang ylang underscored the heady scents. There were pedestals with fresh golden cloth laid out for each of the scholars.*
>
> *At one end of the room, I could see the stacks of books and volumes surrounding the wise commentators who were to judge the contest. They sat on richly-woven red and gold carpets, piled high with silk and cashmere. Fragrant sandalwood and frankincense created billows of smoke above their heads.*
>
> *There were lanterns ready, for the debate would surely go into the night. But just now, I could see the tender peach and pink of the early dawn creeping onto the horizon. It was the day of the great debate.*
>
> *My husband, known to most as Maharishi Yagyavalkya, was famous for his debates. He attracted the most learned scholars*

and visionaries. Usually, they fell into one school of philosophy or another. He delighted in watching them play with reality, twisting in their minds all possible resolutions until, after days or sometimes weeks, he would step in with the answer as if it had been sitting on a tray in the center of the room all along.

The moment the words come out of his mouth, everyone can hear the truth. While Yagyavalkya is known for his brilliant intellect and vision, his real strength is in the vision to see the truth, Brahman, the highest unity of life and the true purpose of all souls. This means he could find unity in the most contentious or opposing viewpoints. He was a great unifier.

That skill of unifying the opposing irascible factions was like that of a gentle father and guide. He lets even the most Himalayan intellects of his age play with their logic as children play with toys. The play was part of the fun.

After a time, Yagyavlayka brings another vision, another element. It is like a light being turned on in a room filled with darkness. Intractable problems and irreconcilable differences are at once rectified and unified.

Of all the things I love and admire about Yagyavalkya, this is what touches me the most. He does it not for fame or glory but to show others that there is never just right or wrong. He is skilled at opening the eyes and inner vision of others to the truth of life.

Some might call him a boundary-breaker or a free thinker. But it is beyond that. He is able to perceive, to feel in his skin and in his eyes and heart, a fundamental unity. He is able to see what others do not. But this is not a story about him. This is the story of how I also realized the supreme reality and unity of life. This is the story of how I kept thinking big and desiring the highest until I became unbounded.

From a young age, I followed the debates with interest. I learned his logic and his arguments, but I still was not living his vision.

The logic made sense, but I couldn't feel the tingling dance in my skin or the voice, as if speaking from within, guiding the way. I was able to challenge him with my intellect and love him with my heart, but I couldn't feel what he was talking about when speaking of Brahman (supreme unity of life).

Day and night, I organized the details of the household, oversaw the servants as they prepared the pavilions for the debates, and cooked lavish banquets of the richest, freshest foods. Mundane tasks often filled my days, but the deep longing tugged at my heart: the feeling that there was something more, something just beyond reach, something that I was destined to do or be.

One day in old age, Yagyavalyka came to me and told me that he wanted to enter the phase of life of an ascetic. He planned to give his enormous riches to me and the rest of the family and wander the forest living off whatever he found or was given to him.

He assured me that his wealth could protect me forever. I could live in a beautiful palace with many servants, the best foods, beautiful silk clothing, plush woolen carpets, and fine furnishings of cashmere, wood, and silk.

But I asked him, "If this whole earth filled with wealth belongs to me, will I be immortal then? Will I realize the supreme reality?"

For me, to see the unity of life, to feel it percolating deep inside as an all-time reality—to feel the deepest happiness and peace was worth more than any luxury. I knew there was no joy in the small. I craved joy in the infinite.

"No," said Yagyavalkya. "As is the life of the wealthy, so would be your life. There is no hope of immortality through wealth."

I felt his statement was like a blow to my heart. Having known the life of opulence and comfort, I knew of its beauty. But I also knew its emptiness. And so, I continued, "What should I do with this wealth which will not make me immortal? I want to have your supreme wisdom and teaching of immortality. I want to be unbounded."

And thus, Yagyavalkya began to expound the reality to me and unfold, petal by petal, the threads of wisdom in my heart and experience. At first, they seemed just like words, ideas, or phrases. Many were phrases I'd heard hundreds of times before. Many were his favorite sayings.

But gradually, my own experience dawned. With practice, I began to feel so much joy and fullness inside that a new reality came into focus. I started to feel the unity of life pulsating inside of me.

As I began to see the reality, I pressed Yagyavalkya for the truth. In our tradition, it is said that "Atma," the individual self of everyone, is "Brahm," the supreme unity of life. It is like saying that the small individuality is already unbounded.

So I asked, "If Atma is the self of every individual and Brahm is the totality, then is Atma not the same as Brahm? Why the pursuit or path if we are already all Atma, which is Brahm?"

Yagyavalkya smiled at me, his eyes sparkling with joy. "So now you see that you were already at the goal." And he began to laugh.

I felt a rush of emotions merging and melting: elation and peace, frustration, and confusion; but through it all, I felt happiness. So much happiness. This was it. This was the thing waiting for me, pulling me, calling to me. This was the destiny I was searching for.

It is unbounded and yet intimately familiar. I am the self. Both small and big, as are you and as is everyone. We are born to live this reality, and yet we find a billion paths to realize it—and just as many reasons to hide from it.

We think, we do, we decide, and we act; but ultimately, it is the destiny within each of us, pushing us on to reach greater heights, that calls and pulls on one path or another.

I began to realize that even when we appear to be selfless—such as in selfless love—it is all ultimately for the higher, unified reality of the self.

To love another is to love oneself. To give to another is to give to oneself. To harm another is to harm oneself. Seeing the self in all makes all intimately dear, and yet it makes the idea of self so much bigger. We become the source and the goal—the like or dislike, love or hate, unity or diversity.

The story of Maitreyi is the story of becoming unbounded and believing in each person's unbounded potential. Maitreyi lived in a time when women managed houses, and yet she sought, and realized, the highest wisdom of life to open all possibilities. She had the opportunity for vast wealth, yet she chose something even bigger.

Vast wealth and prestige might seem big, but in cosmic glory they are small. When we choose the joys of the ocean over the joys of the small stream, the stream is not lost to us. It becomes one with the ocean.

This is not a story against wealth or maintaining a home. This story is a reminder to follow YOUR truth and your vision, whatever that is. And it is a reminder that we are all rarely one thing. You can have wealth, a home, and enlightenment, as did Maitreyi. You choose your own path and add the layers that bring you joy. And everyone, on every path, is destined to be unbounded. Transcend, think big, and act.

We can have many truths and many destinies. There is no reason to neglect one for the sake of another. When you go for the highest, that is what you become—all that you can imagine—and so much more.

Action Steps

Here are some reflections, ideas, and actions to absorb and experience this thread of wisdom:

1. Reflect. What was one moment in your life when you felt connected to something bigger than yourself? What did you feel? How did it change the direction of your life or your understanding? How did that become part of yourself?

2. Be Unbounded. When in your life have you felt unlimited or unbounded? How did you feel? How did it happen? How did that experience change your perception or action?

3. Remember. Think of something that looks impossible to you now. Now see yourself five years from now having accomplished it. What has happened? Can your future self that has achieved your goal give a hint to you now?

4. See. What you think deeply in your heart and believe in without questioning materializes. Discern what you think deeply in your heart and believe in without questioning and see how that relates to what has materialized for you.

5. Reflect and Write. Connect the strength of a decision and its belief to the power of your action for accomplishment. Now compare it to another decision or belief that you felt mixed about and that produced mixed results.

How did the different results appear in your life? See that
the deeper a conviction resides in your heart, the more
power you have to accomplish, regardless of the obstacles.

*Supreme heavenly reality, eternal enlightenment, manifests pure
holistic
Absolute Totality that becomes a living reality.*

Thread 9: What You Put Out— Comes Back to You

As you sow, so shall you reap.
~ Maharishi Mahesh Yogi
Also in Galatians 6:7
"for whatsoever a man soweth, that shall he also reap."

This thread of wisdom—what you put out comes back to you—could be called the law of karma. This is not the simple equation of effort equals results, but a deeper action and reaction within nature. We talked about karma in the chapter on happiness, but now we're going to take a deeper dive into action and reaction.

It says in the Bhagavad Gita, often referred to as the "concise index of the entire Vedic Literature" that the realm of karma is unfathomable. No one can know or calculate all past actions and their effect on future outcomes. In that sense, there is no need to know.

But even if you cannot calculate the exact effect of every action like some sort of mastermind, it doesn't mean the laws of karma don't apply. What you put out does come back to you. What you don't know is when or how it will come back. It might come back five minutes later, or it might come back 20 years later.

That mystery and unknown is a challenge to our idea of control. There are no guaranteed results. You cannot control karma. But you can create the best circumstances for good karma to come back to you.

There are universal laws of action expounded in every religion and every culture of the world. Ideas like the golden rule, *"Do unto others as you would have them do unto you,"* can be found throughout the spiritual texts. This is because the energy we put out comes back to us.

Kindness, compassion, love, and grace put out into the universe all come back to you. Anger, hatred, pride, and jealousy will also come back. Things as simple as letting someone get ahead of you in traffic or smiling at a stranger are small acts of kindness put out into the universe.

Just as in physics it is said that energy cannot be created or destroyed, the energy of feeling, thought, intention, and action also continue to be transferred from one state to another, from one person or feeling to another. It is like throwing a basketball at a wall. It will bounce back. When and how this ball bounces back are unknown.

Knowing that our actions, feelings, and intentions come back to us does not mean we can know when or how. For example, expecting one person to be nice to you because you were nice to them can be a formula for disappointment. Consider being kind, gracious, and loving without expecting anything in return.

How to Give

In the Vedic tradition, a gift is only considered a gift if it is given without any expectation of return. In the western world, many people get caught up in some type of balancing or matching: "She gave me an expensive gift for my birthday, so now I have to give her one for her birthday" or "I helped him out with his business deal, so now he should help me with my business deal." These sorts of trades are not gifts. It is a sophisticated form of bartering.

A gift is usually not judged by its value; it is judged by its intention. That intention is only known in truth to the gift-giver. A billionaire could give someone a new car, and it might have no meaning or value for her. With her wealth, she could hire an assistant to arrange the gift of the car and never even notice that she gave it. Or it might be something she has thought about and planned as something important for the recipient. In this case, the gift could be a special act of giving.

A gift is not about monetary value. It is about the heart value. Any gift given with love is precious. It could be a single flower, a batch of cookies, a well-timed hug and kiss, or any other offering of love that comes from deep within the heart—the desire to do and give good without thinking.

In the process of giving, energy and feeling are transferred. This can be any type of feeling depending on the type of gift—love, sympathy, compassion, gratitude, happiness, etc. The energy we put out is received by the recipient.

But more than an almost scientific process, the process of giving is a mechanism of building bridges toward unity. In giving, we become, even temporarily, unified with the heart of the recipient. To give is to reach toward unification.

> *"Generosity is giving more than you can, and pride is taking less than you need."*
> ~ Khalil Gibran

Isn't it incredible to think of giving more than you can? Taking less than you need can also be seen, in some cases, as a type of giving. Can we not all reach beyond ourselves a little more each day?

The Source of Giving

We can only give from what we have. Only a full cup can overflow. The results of giving will always be limited by what we are able to give. If you want to be able to give without limitation, you need a source where all the best qualities of life are available to you now. There is a source of all friendship, kindness, all love already with you. It is the deepest essence of every person in unbounded consciousness.

This is unbounded consciousness we've discussed in the previous chapters, but it is worth mentioning again. While conscious effort to give is good, with an unbounded reservoir of happiness, love, and kindness, giving can be truly unlimited.

Fortunately, this is easily available to every person. When we transcend, when we go beyond the limited levels of the mind and thinking, we reach unbounded consciousness. This is an unlimited source of giving within each of us. If we want to sow all good, we must reach and experience the source of all good.

Energy Transformation

The process of *"as you sow, so shall you reap"* works through transformation. To take a simple example, energy transformation is seen in nature. Energy is not created or destroyed, but it takes different forms. Water freezes and becomes solid ice or boils and becomes vapor gas. The essence of the water remains the same. Water "gives itself" to become vapor or ice. Of course, it is a chemical process, but the idea that energy is given in transformation is seen throughout life.

The same is true of all of us. Our essential nature is consciousness —unbounded, unlimited, and eternal. And yet, we take different forms. We "give ourselves" to become the individuals we are. We may appear young or old, short or tall, wise or foolish, happy or sad, kind or selfish, or any other possible combination of what makes us unique. But these characteristics are the covering, the appearance.

> *"Just as a mountain of snow is nothing but water,*
> *so also the whole universe is nothing but bliss."*
> ~ Maharishi Mahesh Yogi

Whether solid, liquid, or gas, the substance we call water is the chemical compound called H_2O. It transforms appearances but maintains its structure. We are the same. Throughout our life-time, we transform our appearances, our viewpoints, and our desires, but the essence, consciousness, remains the same.

In this quote, Maharishi takes this one step further. We are not just universal consciousness but also the nature of consciousness, bliss. Not just each human, but the whole universe. From this perspective, we are already unlimited bliss; we also have unlimited capacity to give.

Science has led us to believe we can classify all diverse qualities—water, ice, vapor, table, mountain, ocean, tree, hydrogen, carbon, proton, neutron, dark energy, and on and on. All of these diverse expressions of life are pure energy being transformed. More deeply, looking at energy, we can see layers of energy within human existence.

Evolution

We transform from one life to the next. Science says life evolved from single-celled organisms. That is true. And we are also the same consciousness, ever-evolving and transforming, taking different forms in life after life to reach this moment.

We take these forms as a process of evolution, building in layers of experience of consciousness, from a most primal, self-centered need for food, shelter, and space, to the ability to dream, build, and create. And from there, the ability to dream bigger, love, connect, expand consciousness, and even encompass the whole world and universe in our vision and reality.

The process and flow of consciousness are continuous. It is easy to think of consciousness as a higher ability, as in "higher consciousness," but it is the same consciousness flowing and evolving from a simple organism to a complex being.

The same consciousness is in the single-celled organism and the enlightened seer. Consciousness is consciousness. Supreme consciousness is consciousness awake to its own nature—aware of itself. But even in the deepest depth of ignorance, consciousness is there, pervading everything as the sap pervades all parts of a flower.

The flow of consciousness appears natural and automatic. But there is also the karmic action and reaction that takes place in this process of evolution. Just like in a rose, there are petals and there are thorns. Every part of life has a possibility for growth and evolution. Every part makes the whole. All pave the way for future possibilities.

You can choose to take the role of the thorn and prick everyone who comes near. Or you can choose to take the role of a soft petal, giving off a sweet fragrance. Both are important parts of the flower; both are valid.

But what comes next? The role of the thorn brings more of that quality—hurt, harm and pain. In the same way, the petal brings more of that quality—sweetness, beauty, fragrance, and softness.

We build on what we are. From day to day, week to week, year to year, and even one lifetime to the next. We create from what we have, and then we renew ourselves. What we put out, comes back to us.

In the Vedic Tradition, the process of death is described as analogous to throwing out old clothes. Just as clothes become worn and no longer useful, a body becomes worn and stops serving the process of evolution for more happiness and more expansion of consciousness. And so, the body is put aside and a new body is taken. It is as simple as throwing away your favorite pants that are falling apart and getting a new pair.

In the case of the body, consciousness, continues to a new life and a new body. Individual consciousness continues, from one body to the next, just as you continue from one pair of pants to the next. There is a continuity of awareness. This is the consciousness that evolves.

Unbounded Consciousness vs. Individual Consciousness

There is a part of consciousness that is unbounded and unlimited —the source, course, and goal of all things that we've been referencing throughout this book. Then there is individual consciousness.

In the Vedic tradition, this individual consciousness is described as a drop taken from the ocean. It appears to be separate but is nothing other than the ocean. Let it go, and it will merge again with the ocean. The ocean, in this case, is unbounded consciousness, unlimited and eternal.

This individual consciousness is called *"jiva"* or *"Atma."* The individual quality of consciousness is that which can evolve. It is making its way back to remember that it came from the ocean. It has lost its memory.

This is the reality we are all living. We have unlimited power, but due to a loss of memory, we believe we are limited. We analyze every action, (will saying this or doing this have the effect I want?) when we are already the source of all actions.

It is a big idea, I know. It is also another way of saying you are so much more than you imagined—so much more than one action or reaction. You are also, at every moment, ready to open that memory of all possibilities.

> *"Your children are not your children.*
> *They are the sons and daughters of Life's longing for itself."*
> ~ Khalil Gibran

We are all the children of life's longing for itself. We are all the children of our own destinies and our own longing for enlightenment. Some see it and move toward it, others are carried away only to find a faint memory at the end of life, remembering "this is why I am here" and "this is who I am." We are the creators of our destiny and the creators of our desires.

We are drops from a mighty ocean, longing to merge once again with it. We create the play and display of life with all its facets that appear to be real, and we merge, ultimately, with our highest essence.

We become the love we desire. We become the beauty we want to see. We become the compassion we want to be shown when we show it to others. We become the power, intelligence, and peace to move the world.

What we have already put out we receive each day; what we create now we receive the next moment, and beyond.

Let Us Be Together...

In the Upanishads the idea of putting out the best is expressed in a common invocation:

सह नाववतु
सह नौ भुनक्तु
सह वीर्यं करवावहै
तेजस्वि नावधीतमस्तु
मा विद्विषावहै

"Let us be together
Let us eat together
Let us be vital together
Let us be radiating truth, radiating the light of life.
Never shall we denounce anyone; never entertain negativity."
~ Introductory verse for Upanishads of the Taittirīya Saṃhitā of
Yajur-Veda

While this appears to be a guidance of behavior, it is in essence a path for the drop to return to the ocean. To be together, to eat together, to be vital together is to realize the infinite power we all are as one.

When we are the ocean, every wave, every movement is in togetherness. A wave appears, but the whole ocean moves with the swell. What you put out there is not just an individual activity. We are all interconnected.

How we are together, what we radiate, and how we express opinions about others affect not only us but sends ripples through the environment. When the truth of life radiates as an effortless beacon of unity, the power of togetherness amplifies the good we put out.

What we do as individuals affects the whole universe. While we may only be one, together we are mighty. What we do together can change the world. This verse is the power of togetherness.

Millions of lights, each lit on their own, can illuminate everything. Moving together, being together, and radiating truth and light together can bring about a powerful transformation much more quickly and completely than one alone.

When many drops join together, they are the ocean. They can become a mighty river rushing toward the sea. Together we can create a flood and change the trends of time.

Choose light. Choose good. Choose happiness. Be the happiness and joy you want to feel and radiate it out into the world. Reach your unbounded source of these qualities to be able to truly give and be together. What we put out comes back to us, and what we put into ourselves and those around us builds the foundation for all good to come in life.

The power of karma makes us believe we are just a drop and not the whole ocean. The power of this thread, that what we put out comes back to us, is the path for the drop to find the ocean. And as many drops together, we can join hands and join hearts to transform not only our lives but the lives of everyone around us.

When we put out fullness of life, the path is fulfilled as the drop merges with the ocean. Life finds fulfillment in taking individuality and becoming the power of the infinite ocean.

When together we rise up, we transcend our individual karma and destinies and reconnect with our source, the field of consciousness which is the goal of all destinies and the path to all goals.

Tajabone

The story of celebrating the new year in Senegal is the story of a very traditional way of fulfilling desires. The community together creates greater happiness and connects their traditions and community life to the divine. Here is the story of the Tajabone festival, told by eight-year-old Mariama:

> *On the last day before the new year, we run home early, dust flying in clouds behind our pounding feet. I can see mother has the paper ready to prepare the drums. She is standing outside, stirring the millet that we will have for an early supper. We always eat early to prepare for Tajabone, one last feast before the new year.*
>
> *I scurry behind the brightly-colored curtain with my younger brother, Amadou, and find our older sister, Aissatou, already there, starting to cut and roll the paper. The three of us sit cross-legged on the dirt floor, building the drums.*
>
> *We hear our grandparents enter the house, and the rattling of grandmother helping our mother to prepare the final dishes. They call us to sit together outside in the soft afternoon sun. I feel its soft warmth on my skin, the light shining orange above the horizon as we eat Tajabone supper. We are many more now, as my father's sisters and their families have all arrived to celebrate the new year.*

After dinner, the adults prepare the prayer, and I run with my cousins, Amadou, and Aissatou to the festival of Tajabone. We grab the clothes our grandparents brought and giggle as they hang off our bodies. I put on one of my grandfather's blue shirts, then helped Amadou into one of my grandmother's pink shirts. On Tajabone, all the girls wear something blue from their grandfather, and the boys something pink from their grandmother.

Finally, it is time for the festival. We sing and play, dancing in the streets and laughing until we can't stand up. We meet with other children from the village and go together, house to house, playing our drums at each house and requesting sweets and cookies from the adults.

We fill our bags and our hands, giggling with delight at the sight of the sweets. After we've visited every house, we take our sweets home and all of us climb onto the bed to sleep. As I drift off, I look at the bags of sweets piled together in the corner and feel the soft breath of Amadou on my ear. I wrap my arms around Aissatou and slip into sleep.

The next morning, when the sun is just peaking above the horizon, my grandfather leads a collective prayer. We hold hands and each say a prayer over the dish that we used last night for eating. We join in songs of prayer, filling our plates with sand and then pouring the sand with our desires into the earth.

Then we look to the sky, to holy heaven, and all together we see the presence of an angel, Abudhu Yambarr, in the sky. He lets you see to the eye of the soul. Angel Abudhu Yambarr makes you feel his blessings for fulfilling your desires. Watch the eye, you will see it, too. It is our own inner angel that is available to us and allows us this transformation.

We all saw the holy eye and felt the power of the presence of the angel within us. Then we sit in silence, stirred by the power of higher blessings.

After a little while, Aissatou opens her palm. "Look," she whispers as she shows me the cookie closed in her palm. She holds it up to my mouth for a bite, and I cannot resist the buttery-peanut flavor. I ran to the bedroom with Amadou where we saved the Tajabone presents of last night and spread out our treats. We sit and fill our mouths with cookies, bread, and sweets until we cannot eat anymore.

As we eat, we feel the Angel still with us. There is joy so big. We sing to Tajabone, laugh, and play. It is the happiest day of the year. Every year starts the same: with prayer and vision of the eye of the soul, the blessings of the Angel Abudhu Yambarr, and the sweets of Tajabone.

The festival of Tajabone is one of joyfulness, happiness, and divinity after the period of fasting that reminds us of who we are and who we are together. When we put out joy and surrender to the divine, all gain and none lose. What we put out, comes back to us.

The celebration fulfills the desires of all the children in the village and connects the community together. It is a reminder that we can fulfill everyone's desires at once. What you put out comes back to you. And when it is connected to the divine power within each of us, it becomes something greater than our individual desires.

Action Steps

Here are some reflections, ideas, and actions to absorb and experience this thread of wisdom:

1. **Connect.** What can you organize for your family or community that will bring joy to everyone? Organize

something (manageable) that will make you and those around you happy. Involve them and make it an event together!

2. Find the Good. Avoid entertaining negativity. Watch for the good and see the good it brings to your life. This week, take time to find the good in any situation, even those that you usually don't. There is always something good.

3. Reflect. Review recent events of your life and see when you received things or situations that were unjust or unfair. Note two or three in the last six months to one year. Then, connect that to what you could have done or offered differently. *As you sow, so shall you reap.*

4. Remember. Review the five things you got in your life (i.e. that happened to you) that you liked least and see how your actions (doing or not doing) created that outcome.

5. Reflect and Write. Look at something important that didn't go well—such as a relationship or your profession. See what you have done that you could have done better. Instead of blaming the other(s), see what you sowed.

Self-healing reveals enlightened experiences, purity, holistic action, and thought.

Thread 10: Don't Be a Football of Situations and Circumstances

योगस्थः कुरु कर्माणि
"Established in Being, Perform Action"
~ Bhagavad Gita 2.48

Perhaps the most pivotal verse in the entire Bhagavad Gita, the concept of *"established in Being, perform action,"* could also be said as "established in consciousness, perform action," or even "transcend through TM and act."

Maharishi has highlighted this verse repeatedly over the years because he said it encapsulates his whole message: transcend and then act. It also encapsulates the whole message of this book. All the great, glorious things we want to accomplish can be achieved by first transcending and then acting.

Action alone is not enough. Transcendence alone is also not enough. The combination of meditation and action, or silence and action, pave the way to all possibilities. It is also the secret to this thread of wisdom.

One of the 16 principles of the Science of Creative Intelligence is *"rest and activity are the steps of progress."* It is so simple and yet so profound. To offer a simple example, when we walk, one foot "rests" while the other is active. Likewise, rest, through TM, and activity, just as described in the Bhagavad Gita, are the steps of progress.

How do rest and activity relate to this thread of wisdom? They are the path to avoid being a football of life's situations and circumstances. The phrase "Don't be a football of situations and circumstances" was an analogy Maharishi used to make this experience clear and connect practical experiences to abstract expressions.

What it Means to Be a Football

If you've played or watched sports, you've heard coaches yell things like, "Control the ball!" The ball never controls the game. The players control the game. To be a football means to be kicked around.

To be a football means to let life control your destiny and make you suffer because you don't see an alternative. We all have, knowingly or unknowingly, been a football of our situations and circumstances.

We might feel controlled by circumstances, controlled by others, or controlled by the winds of time—like a global pandemic. It means to have lost control in a negative sense. This is not control on the level of trying to control. It is about not losing a fundamental basis of who we are.

You can protect yourself from being a football and still be flexible, adaptable, compassionate, and giving. When you allow these qualities to open up from you while you are centered in yourself, in the essence of who you are, then they do not control you. When you have lost your basis, your feeling of centeredness, the quality of being a football takes over.

Women are particularly susceptible to this as the demands of children, spouse, work, and home pile up to such an extent that you seem to have lost yourself. I've had friends confess that they have lost themselves in the pressure of life. I've felt the same at times.

This is not anyone's fault. It is the reality of life. If you are constantly giving, without taking time to recharge and nourish yourself, one day you will find nothing to give.

Some people will interpret this to mean you should stand up for yourself. But the analogy of not being a football goes much deeper than that. It means that we can reach a level where it is easy, even automatic, to guide the destiny of our lives and continuously replenish the reservoir of giving.

In childhood, we had control of very little of our lives. Our control was limited to our toys and which clothes we wore, from a selection we received from our parents. As we got older, that control increased to include independence in friends, clothing, after-school activities, completion of homework, etc.

As adults, we have a great deal of autonomy. We make decisions about our work, family, friends, diets, lifestyles, and beliefs. What we miss is that those choices are within the boundaries of the best available option.

We choose a job because it meets our basic criteria and is better than another option. We choose our family, but even in that choice, divorce, death, and other circumstances can cause undesirable changes. We choose a lifestyle, but economic circumstances, pressure from family and friends, or any other number of personal situations can limit or change it. In other words, we have freedom, but we have freedom within boundaries.

Just as when we were small children selecting the clothes amongst the ones our parents already purchased, now even with bigger boundaries and a greater range of influence, we are still living in boxes created by circumstances.

Some people—referred to as privileged—have fewer restrictions. These are people whose country of origin, economic background, race, gender, professional qualifications, and luck have afforded them more opportunities. But even the most privileged of the privileged are living within boundaries and limitations that are often only uniquely visible to them. It is as if we are each living within a glass cage of our own limitations and possibilities of what to do in life. This is what it means to be a football of life.

"But wait, I'm happy!" you might be saying. If you are, enjoy every moment of it. If someone is fortunate, there will be times in life when they feel completely happy. It might be a few months or even a decade. But life is always changing.

You can take a snapshot of a person's life at one moment, and it may look "perfect." They may be happy and have everything they ever dreamed of. Another snapshot of the same person's life could look completely different in five or ten years.

We cannot know exactly what life will bring our way, which is why, without a way to guide our own destiny and secure ourselves beyond limitations, we will always be a football of life's situations and circumstances.

Go to the Source of All Solutions

Life is ever-changing. The winds of time will sometimes blow fierce and strong and other times soft and gentle. You want to be wind-proof.

To transcend is to go beyond. Transcending is like diving to the depths of the ocean where you don't feel the crashing waves of the surface. And, as we have all experienced, the waves of life can really crash down on us sometimes.

To transcend means to "go beyond." You go beyond surface thinking; you go beyond the ever-changing reality of life; you go beyond limitations. To transcend, in the highest sense of the word, means to go beyond all the limitations you were consciously and unconsciously putting on yourself to a level where you—the same person who believed they were limited —become unbounded, unlimited, and all-powerful. It is from this level that every person is able to rejuvenate, nourish, and center themselves beyond situations and circumstances.

The application of this experience is simple and natural. The best way to change the ever-changing level of life is to go beyond it. Go to the source of change. From the source of all change, a transcendental field where anything is possible, you are rooted beyond the changing winds of life.

One of Maharishi's 16 principles of the Science of Creative Intelligence is, *"The field of all possibilities is the source of all solutions."*

This means that when you experience a field that is unlimited and unbounded—and thus has all possibilities—new solutions can pop up in the most unexpected ways. It is no longer your job to control or break the boundaries. The unlimited field within— your own inner power—will help you to see or realize new solutions. It is so simple and yet so effective.

There is an analogy to explain how something so simple can work so well—how the field of all possibilities can be the source of all solutions. Suppose you are in a room that is completely dark. There is not even a faint glimmer of light. It is a room you have never been in before, so you don't know if it is a kitchen, a living room, a bathroom, or a barn. You can see nothing.

You start to feel your way around the room and guess at objects. In that environment, if someone asked you to prepare a meal in 30 minutes, it would seem like a joke. You would have to laugh.

Now suppose someone turned on the breaker and the lights came on. You found you were in a fully-stocked gourmet kitchen. Now preparing a meal in 30 minutes would be much easier. You have some work—but the circumstances and ability to use your surroundings have changed. What was difficult becomes simple.

We live in a universe that is continuously conspiring in our favor. We can do our part, not through more action, but through silence. We can go beyond and allow nature to work for us.

This is the secret of consciousness, summarized by Maharishi in describing his role in the world, *"to make the difficult easy."* To not be a football of life is to make the difficult easy. Instead of being kicked around by life, your surroundings can work to help you.

How does this happen? It is because this transcendental field is nothingness, but it also contains all possible actions and their derivatives. That is what is meant by *the field of all possibilities is the source of all solutions.* By associating with a field that contains all, that is also our own inner intelligence, we are able to make decisions and take action that will bring about maximum evolution.

An engineer may have a thousand different bridge designs but will choose the best one for each location based on external factors, calculations, and internal inspiration or intuition. The same is true for all actions. When we transcend, we experience a level where all solutions and their outcomes are there—and we will more spontaneously choose the right course of action in all situations.

By transcending and reaching beyond, we are glorifying the teaching of every religious and spiritual teacher throughout time. We are realizing the highest ideals of those teachings.

Christ said, *"The Kingdom of God is within you."* ~ Luke 17.21. The highest ideal was not to suffer. The highest ideal was to reach the kingdom of God within. When knowing and being the highest qualities of Christ—love, humility, compassion, and self-less service—we live the reality of the religious teachings.

Likewise, in the Muslim religion, Imam Ali said, *"You presume you are a small entity, but within you is enfolded the entire universe."* This truth whispered from a different culture and a different religion, speaks of the same highest truth. The entire universe can be understood here to mean not only the physical universe but also the inner world of transcendental consciousness. *"But within you is enfolded the entire universe"* is a different way of saying, *"the Kingdom of God is within you."* These great expressions of wisdom describe the transcendental reality, the unlimited field of life that has enfolded within it the source of the whole universe.

Christianity calls it the Kingdom of God; Imam Ali says the entire universe is enfolded in you. What if they were speaking of the same reality that is more magnificent than any description?

When Imam Ali speaks of *"within you is enfolded the entire universe,"* he is referring to the same field of consciousness—of all possibilities—that Maharishi spoke of over 1,300 years later. This level of consciousness is a silent, unlimited, powerful level of ourselves—the level where we can go beyond our own limiting beliefs, situations, and circumstances. From this field, in which the power of the whole universe is enfolded, we can do anything. We are no longer the football of situations and circumstances. We are the masters of our own destinies.

Socrates of ancient Greece advised, *"Know thyself."* In two words, Socrates summarized the whole truth that within ourselves we can find the highest ideals that we are searching for outside. What appears as who we are is just a small percentage of our full potential. By going beyond, by turning on the light, by diving below to the depth of the ocean, we can finally know ourselves.

All these whispers of truth, echoing through the corridors of time, are reminders that it is not our nature to suffer, nor is it our destiny. It is not a *fait accompli* to live a life kicked around by situations and circumstances. We are not destined to be footballs of life. These teachers and others show us that we can go within to become one with supreme intelligence. We can have liberation from where we are.

We are all destined to know ourselves, to find the kingdom of heaven within, and to find the entire universe enfolded within us. We can be masters of our own destinies. We are destined to be creators of our own lives.

When we begin to transcend, the process of changing our lives accelerates. Most people notice gradual improvements, like a spring of water appearing in a dry lakebed. What was once empty starts to become full.

With the experience of a level that is unlimited, unbounded, and all-powerful, our perception begins to change. We begin to see opportunities where there were none. We begin to have ideas and perceptions as never before. Impossible dreams become possible. This is not an intellectual process. The experience itself brings greater support from life to create favorable situations and favorable outcomes.

The Elephant

There is a story in the Vedic Tradition about an elephant. This elephant was a great devotee of Vishnu, a form of God in the Vedic and Hindu traditions. One day, the elephant was splashing happily in the water when suddenly a crocodile took his leg. The crocodile started pulling the elephant into the muddy pond to eat him. In a moment of desperation, the elephant prayed to Vishnu to save him. At the last moment, just as the elephant was about to be swallowed by the crocodile, Vishnu appeared like a mighty eagle and lifted the elephant from the grasp of the crocodile, saving his life.

While there are layers of symbolism in this story, the simple truth is this: no matter how life seems to be swallowing us up at any moment, there is a chance to be free. It doesn't have to be Vishnu swooping down as an eagle. Vishnu is an expression of focused dynamism within each of us. We can choose to focus on our own intentions and take recourse, even in the last moment, to embrace our unbounded potential and still be saved from our own crocodiles of life. The Grace of God is unlimited and always available. Whatever name we choose for God, every spiritual tradition has the same message: God is all-merciful and almighty, it is never too late to be saved.

This is the power of reaching beyond the relative, ordinary levels of life where everything changes and where a change in perception can change a whole situation. Going to the source of thought— which is also the source of power, creativity, and intelligence— means reaching a level where the ever-changing reality and perceptions of life can no longer disturb and distort our happiness, success, or self-worth.

Everyone Can Fulfill Their Destiny

To not be a football means that the ever-changing reality of situations and circumstances cannot derail our lives. It means that we can be the masters of our own destinies and that those destinies, all eight billion for each unique person in the world, can be mutually beneficial and enriching.

For me to fulfill my destiny, you to fulfill your destiny, and for every other person on planet Earth to fulfill their own destiny is the real plan. That is where we are all going. One person's destiny is not in contradiction with another person's destiny.

That is the brilliance of nature—it is like a cosmic computer that can calculate the highest good, greatest happiness, peace, and fulfillment for every individual in the world—without taking it away from another.

Perhaps an even more important reason to take recourse to our own higher intelligence is that by fulfilling our destiny we bring the greatest good to those we love. Nature automatically calculates the greatest good for everyone in our environment. How many times have we been trapped between trying to make one person or another happy? It is no fun to feel pulled between several people we want to help, whether it is children, a partner, friends, or colleagues.

To not be a football means we are no longer caught in the trap of impossibility, trying to decide between two disappointing outcomes. To not be a football of situations and circumstances means we are finally free.

"I love you when you bow in your mosque, kneel in your temple, pray in your church.
For you and I are sons of one religion, and it is the spirit."
~ Khalil Gibran

May we all find the spirit, which is beyond the changing circumstances of life, to carry out our destiny. By whatever name and in whatever language we speak of it, may we find that divine spirit. May we reach—and be—the spirit where we are all one. In temples, mosques, and churches, or with or without any religion, in our hearts, we are sons and daughters of one highest destiny.

To be great doesn't refer to outside accomplishments. It is a level of consciousness that is beyond suffering, a state of permanent bliss. On this level, the different phases of life play out without shaking the underlying bliss. This is the essence of this thread: by accomplishing the level of consciousness that is unshakeable bliss, no change on the outside can harm. You are beyond suffering. Even a step in this direction can bring great peace.

The Compassion of Life

In the Vedic tradition, there are two principles related to action and their results. One, discussed in the previous chapter, is *"As you sow, so shall you reap."* That is the principle of karma—of action and reaction. But there is a second, equally powerful principle in nature: it is the compassion of life to give us more than we deserve.

This is available on two clear levels. One is what we've been discussing here. By transcending, going beyond our individual limitations, we engage the almighty power of nature to help us accomplish action that is evolutionary and productive. From this level, we are able to do less and accomplish more. Maharishi used to say that we engage the infinite power of natural law to work for us. That is to say, we find solutions, insight, and opportunities that we may not have found otherwise. It is the principle of transcending, going beyond limitations, and then acting that has been the theme of this chapter.

But there is a deeper level available in the compassion of life. It is in a Vedic technology called Yagya. The principle of Yagya is the principle of offering and creating. In simplest terms, Yagya is a means to engage the power of nature to give someone more than they deserve. The specifics of Yagya—how it was lost and how it was revived by Maharishi with some of the great custodians of this knowledge in India—could fill an entire book or books.

It is enough to know that Yagya works on frequency. Everything can be reduced to sound or sound waves. What we see as solid around us, according to physics, at fine levels is frequency. Yagya works to create more favorable circumstances through the technology of sound and engaging the fine levels of nature to work for us.

It can be visualized like a sine wave.

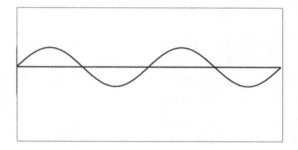

We said before that every action creates a result. That returning karma can be imagined moving back toward us like a sine wave. The Yagya creates the balancing frequency—a cosine wave—to neutralize the negative result.

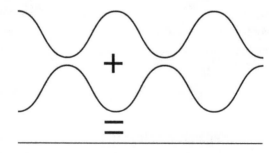

It is a way to avert the danger that has not yet come, and neutralize past negative actions to gain a better result in the future. But the principle of Yagya is not 1+1=2. The power of Yagya is to give people more than they deserve.

It is on the basis of this principle that we say we can create "all good for everyone." This is an additional, powerful tool that anyone can use to protect themselves from being a football of situations and circumstances. The compassion of life is to give us more than we deserve.

The Dreams of Allira

The Australian aboriginal cultures are some of the most ancient, sharing many of the same teachings and wisdom discussed throughout this book, including the concept of one-ness and interconnectedness of all beings. With the arrival of European settlers, these sacred cultures faced extreme challenges and persecution. But, like any expression of truth, these cannot be permanently snuffed out. Nature finds a way to restore and re-enliven expressions of truth, generation after generation.

The Murrinh-Patha of the Northern Territory of Australia is one such community. It is still growing and thriving today. Young people are learning the language, so it is one of the only aboriginal languages that does not face imminent extinction. This story is not of the modern Murrinh-Patha, but of a girl named Allira who was born in northern Australia in 1900. She and her community roamed in the desert. This is her story:

I was 10 when the drought began. The soil, already a rich red and soft like a cow's hide, started to get dry and crack. The drought brought worry. The parrots, finches, and doves called it on the wind. The wallaby and kangaroo thumped the earth as if demanding rain. The watering holes dried up. The deep wells under the earth were farther and farther to find.

The tribe moved inland, searching for Mother Earth. The elders started to visit dreamtime and go on more walkabouts. They spoke to their ancestors and prayed for protection. I, too, visited dreamtime more often. But all I saw was drought and misery.

One day, on the edge of the village, half-hidden in the bushes, I saw the first white man. He looked so foreign, with his strange clothing and hat, carrying a large metal object. I knew not to trust him, but he looked so thin and so helpless. Knowing that an enemy in confidence is often better than an enemy roaming the bush, the elders brought him in. They gave him sacred sips from the water of a deep spring we'd found.

He told us that he was lost in the desert, and without our help, he could not survive. We told him we are all one. The survival of one is the survival of all. The stars, the sun, and the sky all move as one, as do we on this earth.

Without water, we do not survive. But the water is a gift from dreamtime and a message from the stars. The elders performed many sacred rituals, constructing special tents that I could not enter. But I could hear the voices from outside, low, melodious, and keening. They spoke of all since the beginning of time and all that was to come. They continued day and night for seven days and seven nights.

The white man wanted us to move on, to go toward another territory. But the elders knew the truth: to move man is not to move the stars. All the destinies are intertwined. We are not the source, nor the goal, and yet we are all one.

In the soft glimmer just before the sun rose on the eighth day, the rains started. I jumped from where I had been sleeping and ran with the other children. We laughed and thanked the Rainbow Serpent, the creator of all. We thanked the ancestors and the dreaming and the oneness for its blessings. The stars had moved, and balance was reset.

The elders later told me that the prayers and rituals of dreamtime had restored balance, but so had the white man. By entering the tribe with respect, he did what few others did. We saw his unity and oneness. We know we are the creators. We come from the ancestors and the Rainbow Serpent to bring blessings to the earth and all. We accepted him as one, and he us.

This story of Allira is a reminder that even in the most extreme situations of danger, we are not alone or without recourse. Even when the enemy appears at the door and natural disaster surrounds us, there is hope. The compassion of life can give us more than we deserve. Taking recourse to the oneness of life, the eternal field of consciousness described clearly in so many ancient traditions, we go beyond our individual destinies and connect to a higher one. This is the essence of not being a football of situations and circumstances.

Teaching Transcendence: Guyana

Shortly after becoming a teacher of Transcendental Meditation, I had the opportunity to travel with another TM Teacher to Barbados and Guyana to teach. We started in Barbados as a waiting base until we could create a project in Guyana.

I taught my first person on August 31st in Barbados. Even though I'd heard my whole life how simple and automatic learning the TM technique is, it was so special to see it for myself. It was simple, easy, and automatic. I could see the brightness in her eyes. Or perhaps it was the change in me that I felt.

A week later, we arrived in Guyana. We were there to create a group of invincibility equal to, or greater than, the square root of 1% of the population of the country. This is another way to give the people more than they deserve, to create a better destiny for the country with greater prosperity, stability, and progress.

For Guyana, the square root of 1% of the population was only about 100 people, although we wanted to teach at least 300-400 people to meditate. Maharishi would often explain that a good engineer builds in a safety factor. Having more people practice TM together would be a safety factor to create more positivity in the country.

Guyana was in political turmoil at the time, with strong cultural divides and conflict. It had high levels of violent crime and one of the highest murder rates in the world. We were staying in a hotel that had an enormous metal fence, topped with barbed wire like a prison. There were guards posted around all the entrances. That was common for the "good" hotels.

We had one contact, a 95-year-old man named Jodha. He could work from early morning to late into the night. He was more vital and focused than most 20-year-olds. He had met Maharishi in the 1990s. Maharishi had charged him with making Guyana "invincible."

A simple definition of that would be all good for the country— the removal of problems both within and from outside. Jodha was determined to bring Maharishi's vision to life. He saw it as his mission. Even though he'd been busy in his career in the 90s, he felt personally responsible to create a better life for the people of Guyana in his lifetime.

He visited school after school, arriving with pamphlets, unannounced. Jodha would ask to meet with the principal and tell them how they needed to learn TM and its advanced programs to reduce stress and improve academic outcomes. He was passionate about making his country better in every way. He would also speak of political stability and harmony for the country.

With the purity of his intention, people started to respond. His simple determination and one-pointed focus to help his country rise above becoming a football of situations and circumstances bore fruit.

Once a principal agreed to a meeting, Jodha would call us enthusiastically and tell us they wanted the program. What he meant was that they were willing to meet with us. But it was a start. We met with principals of Catholic, Christian, and Hindu schools. We also met with the national dance company, the secretary of education, and state education secretaries.

Shortly after we arrived, a school with two campuses was ready to start. There were about 200 students in the upper school and another 200 students in the lower school. We taught them all in about five weeks. The principal and a few teachers at the upper school also learned. Their innocence and enthusiasm were infectious.

The principal at that school, Ms. Keshari, was a woman in her late 50s who was full of wisdom. She guided the children like a grandmother. In a country full of violence and chaos, she stood as a pillar of peace and compassion. It was her dedication that made it possible for the students to practice twice daily in school. When Ms. Keshari learned to meditate, she commented that this was what she had been looking for her whole life. She wanted her children and grandchildren to learn, as well. She recognized the power of this simple technique—to give the students something more and to be something more in life.

When we taught the small, four-year-olds their word of wisdom, it was a mix of utter chaos and deep joy. I will always remember one little boy in the kindergarten class. His teacher told us that he was on the autism spectrum and wouldn't speak. But, he could understand so we should teach him. When he learned his word of wisdom, I looked into his eyes and saw them light up with surprise and recognition.

The next day, when we were checking the children to make sure they remembered how to do their word of wisdom, I asked him if he remembered what he'd learned. He looked into my eyes, nodded, and then whispered his word of wisdom to me. The look of deep understanding and care for this technique made me feel he would treasure it and that it would change his life.

I told his teacher he had spoken, and she looked surprised and happy. For that boy, a way to go beyond created immediate new strength and unexpected possibilities in his life. Usually, it is cumulative practice. But that little boy stands out because the effect on him was immediate.

The oldest students in the upper school were 15 and 16 years old. They were under tremendous pressure from exams for national rankings and college entrance. They were stressed. After they learned TM, they became bubbly and happy. They asked creative and interesting questions about how TM connects to past lives (it doesn't), what their dreams meant (we aren't dream interpreters), and why they felt so happy after meditating (inner bliss!).

We were in the country for only two months. But in those two months, I saw the power of Maharishi's knowledge to uplift people in difficult circumstances. The outer didn't change, but the inner became a rich resource of peace and happiness.

In total, we taught just under 400 children, teachers, and administrators between those schools, another school, and an orphanage. Guyana was an opportunity to see the effect of "don't be a football of situations and circumstances" in action. We saw its living proof in the children and teachers even in a short time.

The name Guyana comes from the same Sanskrit root *Gyan*— pure knowledge There is ancient wisdom in the land and in its people. It is a land of knowledge. Knowledge of transcendence has the power to transform situations.

Jodha's purity of focus, even now at age 99, and the people of Guyana make me feel the deep meaning behind this country's name. The country is filled with people of beautiful hearts and, within each of those hearts, deep knowledge, Gyan. The power of knowledge and transcending to transform lives was lived by many first-hand in Guyana. May many thousands more will have this opportunity as the experience brings all good for everyone and far more than we deserve.

Action Steps

Here are some reflections, ideas, and actions to absorb and experience this thread of wisdom:

1. **Reflect.** Revise three events that were disturbing in your life—professionally, emotionally, etc. Instead of blaming the person who brought that, see what you could have done differently to get a better result. You are the center of whatever happens to you. Any situation in life, even if it is very hard, has to do with a seed you planted earlier. That means you blame less the person who delivered the result. After seeing how you are the center of what you create, transcend and create better seeds for future karma. *See life as an opportunity to give so you can receive more.*

2. **Transcend.** Become unbounded; experience transcendence. Unbounded consciousness allows us to better deal with the point values of life. The only way to get beyond the changing field of life is to reach the non-change within.

3. **Find Peak Experiences.** The psychologist Abraham Maslow says that in every person's life there are a few experiences of total functioning that are called peak expe-

riences. They are characterized by giving a person a sense of unboundedness and use of their full potential. It could happen in so many ways—by looking at a landscape, with intuition for a project, in a deep relationship, while composing a song or painting, while playing sports, etc.

4. Reflect and Write. Remember a moment like that in your life and see how in these moments you were not a football of circumstances. In these peak experiences, a person structures something invincible because they are connected to their own source.

Everyone has a moment or two or three in life when they experience their full potential. Imagine you can do that daily and make the best work through you.

योगस्थः कुरु कर्माणि

"Established in Being, Perform Action" ~ Bhagavad Gita

Self-healing reveals enlightened experiences manifesting all possibilities.

Thread 11: Just Let Go

चितिशक्तिरिति
"Power of consciousness alone is."
or
"The power of consciousness is infinite."
~ Yoga Sutras 4.34

This essential thread of wisdom is encapsulated in a Yoga Sutra. *"The power of consciousness alone is."* That means that we can try, plan, and navigate life; but ultimately, life will take the best course for evolution through the almighty power of natural law, structured within consciousness. This is a thread of surrender.

Because the power of consciousness alone is, it is consciousness, unbounded and unlimited, that is far more prepared to protect and uphold evolution and fulfill our desires. Many great accomplishments come not through pushing but in surrendering to the power of the unlimited to accomplish that which is difficult to do within limitations. Another way to say "just let go" is to say go beyond.

Sometimes, even with the best efforts and intentions and the best plans and credentials, everything still seems to go wrong. You try your best, you show up, you do the work, you're grateful...and nothing. Life hits you in the face, knocks you down, and then laughs while you're hurt. Yes, I've been there, too.

Or sometimes, you have a dream or desire so big that you don't know how you will ever achieve it. In both cases, the formula is the same: just let go. Go beyond the limitations of how and why, cause and effect, effort and intention. Go to the transcendent from which anything can be accomplished—and leave your desire there.

Letting go is different from giving up. Giving up means shrinking back within yourself, feeling so small and unimportant that you'd rather hide in bed than face the world. I've had plenty of those days, too.

But letting go means being bigger. It means saying to nature, God, or the universe that you know there must be a higher plan, and you will let he/she/it take over. Letting go is like taking the most precious petals of your heart and setting them into the wind to see where they are carried.

In the words of Khalil Gibran, "*If you love somebody, let them go, for if they return, they were always yours. If they don't, they never were.*"

This goes not only for people but for desires of all types. Let the desires and expectations go free. If you want to travel or change careers or have your teenagers love you more—let them go free. Let the vice grip of desire in your heart and the endless hustle go free. Let your mind and intellect, with their creative ploys, go free. Settle and be.

Depending on your personality, this can be the most difficult and counter-intuitive action of your life. Letting go means accepting that you do not control your destiny. That you are not an all-knowing God who can see into the future and divine the best path for all, or even for yourself.

Letting go is not a failure to act. It is simply the act to stop chasing something out of your control. Letting go means letting go of the illusion—and it is an illusion—that if we hold on tighter or do more, we will get there. And "there" could be anywhere.

If you want to achieve all you have ever desired, let go. This does not mean letting go in the middle of a difficult run or meeting. It means looking at the bigger picture of what you want to achieve. If you find yourself pushing and desiring, and it feels like all you are getting is pushback, that is the time to examine if you are forcing something.

We all do it. This week, I've watched someone push unreasonably about a book they want to publish. Someone else pushed to give a presentation that turned out to make her look bad. A third person pushed to do something that would have inadvertently hurt someone else.

What happens when you let go is one of two things: either you give the Almighty (by any name) enough space, without the pushing, to find a new path to work it out for you and give you what you wanted all along, or you find a new different opportunity that you couldn't see before because you were so attached to what you thought was right.

Here's an example: In the case of running, letting go doesn't necessarily mean to stop running. It means that if you have tried your best to achieve a time and still couldn't reach it, let go of that time goal and start having fun. Eat more or train differently just for the fun of it—and see where it takes you.

There is a delicate balance between the psychology of *"no pain, no gain"* and letting go. This chapter is not advising laziness or indifference. The key is to find the delicate balance between doing your very best and stepping back to let nature do. It forces us to consider that not everything we want is meant to be. And yet, if we can step back, something far more beautiful is often waiting around the corner.

That is the advice of Khalil Gibran from over a hundred years ago, and it is my hard-earned advice of today. If, like me, you think that you can work harder or smarter to find a solution, here is the vital lesson: Nature will keep pushing you harder and harder without what you desire until the only solution is to let go and see what comes.

Letting go also means letting go of what others think of you and what you think of yourself. All the ideas such as, I should have accomplished or bought x, y, or z by whatever age, are useless. If you are destined to accomplish those things by that age, you will. If not, they will come in time—or not.

Charting Your Own Path

There is no set path or outward trajectory that is the right path or the only path. Each person must chart their own path. Sometimes those paths converge, or at least appear to, for some time. But no one can know the full inner reality of another.

For that reason, measuring your life, your worth, or your happiness on any outward criteria is a definite path to misery. Even if you can check all the boxes that you think you should, you may reach the end of the list to find that your inner feeling is still lacking.

While judging your life by outer accomplishment is a sure path to misery, judging your life by other people's opinions of you is also a misery trap. Falling into this trap only leads to suffering, so it's best to avoid it altogether. Your friends know the real you— everyone else doesn't matter.

Different Lenses

Everyone perceives from their own level of consciousness and understanding, meaning the same behavior is interpreted through different lenses. Someone wearing red glasses will see your actions as red. Someone wearing green glasses will see all your actions as green. While this is a simple overgeneralization, the difference in perception is just as real.

The statements and observations people make about you are usually more about them than they are about you. We create for ourselves a personal echo chamber. Often, we put out observations about others that are reflections of something we are facing ourselves.

I've sometimes been surprised by the assumptions other people have made about me. Granted, my life is a bit atypical. I chose an unconventional educational path and to step outside the norm to work for the vision I want to create in the world of all good for everyone.

After finishing my Vedic studies with a BA, MA, and Ph.D., I went on to earn an MBA from Maharishi International University while continuing to work on projects dedicated to bringing knowledge of Maharishi, including Transcendental Meditation and its advanced courses and programs, to people around the world.

I have friends all over the globe and love connecting with people from all cultures, religions, and belief systems. My friends are young and old, men and women, married and unmarried. I am so grateful for this extended family of people working to create a better world.

But people like boxes, and much of my life has been out of the box. From the moment I started asking, "Is this it?" I knew that to realize my goals of enlightenment and creating a better world, I might not follow a conventional path. Some people are puzzled that I'm not married or that I can be both outgoing and reclusive. That can lead to some funny conclusions to put a life "out of the box" into a box.

Here are some of the assumptions acquaintances have made about me over the years:

- That I am a lesbian because I walk and dress like a lesbian. (How do lesbians walk or dress?)
- That I was having an "affair" with a single man. (That is called a relationship. In this case, he is a friend.)
- That I was in love with and/or a mindless servant of a married man. (Excuse me? Do guys have to put up with this?)
- Because I care about education and opportunities for women, I must hate men. (Can they please decide: do I love men or hate them?)
- That I am a friend's secretary because I helped him. (Why do women automatically have to be secretaries?)

While none of the above statements are true, I choose to list them because this is what the rumor mill churned up and kept going. I am not a celebrity. I do not have a large social media following. In other words, this is the kind of nonsense being churned out about all of us.

We can choose to give it power or we can choose to let it go. As my mother used to say, *"Water off a duck's back."* Depending on the special variety of rumors you get—they could be about you, your children, or your spouse—the reaction can range from a desire to fight back to the feeling of questioning, "Do they think so terribly of me?"

But whatever the reaction, the best choice is to let it go because does it matter? Water off a duck's back means don't let it stick to you. Don't let it hurt you or penetrate your heart or confidence. Let those comments roll off like they were never there.

Cream Always Rises

My mother's other favorite saying was, *"The cream always rises to the top."* Let me explain: the rich, fatty cream of unhomogenized milk will rise to the top of a milk jug in a matter of hours. This cream ranges from extra-rich milk to solid buttercream. This is the best part of the milk. You can pour it on cereal, into tea, or dip your finger straight into it. Generations of people can't be wrong in classifying the cream as special or in some ways superior to regular milk because it is richer.

The cream always rises to the top means that if you are doing what you believe in, with your whole heart, and acting in a way that is kind to others, that will shine through. It might take years, but in the end, purity rises and is seen.

It also applies to every other area of life. Perhaps you believe you are the best and aren't getting recognition. If it is true, eventually it will be recognized. This could be in any area of life—a job, a skill, or anything. Again, it might take years. But that which is the best—in quality, in performance, and in intention—will shine through.

This makes letting go that much easier. Who are we to control whether the cream rises now or in an hour? Who are we to control whether the recognition comes now or ever? What is the lesson we need to learn? What is nature trying to tell us? First, it is telling us to let go.

To let go means surrendering to a higher purpose and a higher power. It means recognizing that not knowing all the answers doesn't make us weaker, but stronger. Because in learning to surrender, to melt, we regain our real strength.

It also means acknowledging that there might be something more than we ever imagined. In letting go, we can still go for it. We can accomplish something magical and beautiful.

How many of us have deeply desired, craved, and yearned for something only to find that it doesn't meet our expectations or falls short? There can be unexpected consequences we missed or other complications. Letting go removes the need for control and calculation.

Letting go means letting the best come and not knowing what that is. It means doing our best and giving our best each day and then accepting what happens, what comes, and what we find on this unfathomable path of life.

The Car Accident

When I was 19, I took a day trip to the nearest ski area in Iowa with my dad, uncle, and seven-year-old cousin. There aren't very many hills in Iowa. The ski place had about five runs that each took less than two minutes to complete, but we loved it. It was about a three-hour drive from our town.

As we were returning from that trip, and only about one mile from home, my uncle fell asleep while driving our minivan. The cruise control was set, and we were on an empty Iowa highway. The car pulled to the right and catapulted into a 20-foot ditch— still with the cruise control set to 60 miles per hour.

It is amazing how in moments of extreme danger every second has the clarity of many minutes or hours. I was lying down on the farthest-back bench of the van. When I first felt the car leave the highway, I thought maybe we were home. But then the car started to tip. It tilted up on two wheels until we were at about a 90-degree angle from the hill.

I wasn't afraid at that moment, but one thought entered my mind as if from an emotionless observer: "If this car flips, we're all going to die." I started to pray, but as soon as that thought finished, I saw a brilliant flash of golden light. I am not sure whether it was inside my vision or in the car, but the brilliant light seemed to be screaming one word: "NO!"

With the word "No," the car came crashing back down onto four wheels, sped down the hill, and jumped a creek before my uncle was fully awake and hit the brakes. Miraculously, other than being a little bruised and shaken, we were all fine.

The voice of the "No," accompanied by light, was so overwhelming, that I knew it was a window into something bigger. I cannot say whether this was angels, God, devatas, or some other force, but it is clear to me that there is a plan beyond any of us. What was meant to be and what was happening at that moment were not aligned and needed a push, fast.

The feeling that came over me as the car landed on four wheels was that my father and I had something more to do with Maharishi. At the time, what that was or how we would do it was not obvious. But the realization of something bigger, more powerful, and all-knowing guiding us was undeniable.

I've chosen this story for this thread of wisdom because there were three ways to look at it. One is that it was dangerous. Another is that it was nearly a dangerous tragedy—but with gratitude that we were all okay.

The third way to look at it is that it was part of the plan all along. We were meant to be in an accident, and we were meant to be saved. The control we think we have over our lives is a small drop in the ocean. We have the power and creativity to make so much more happen, but only with Grace. And for that, we just let go.

We are all part of a whole so enormous. What happens when, to whom, how, and why are questions for the divine, the universe,

God, or whatever form of a higher power you believe in. Life is 100% free will and 100% destiny. Destiny takes us where we need to go; free will allows us to choose how we respond, the path to take, and how to set the pace.

From that moment in the car, I knew I had a purpose greater than what I had imagined for myself. My father and I both have since become international administrators for Maharishi's worldwide organization, although that also might be just a step on the path.

To be and become is a constant journey. We show up each day, do our best, and see what Grace provides. There is always a safety net, even if we don't see it. This life, this moment, is but a drop in eternity. Who we are now and who we can become is like a flower bud waiting to blossom.

Lotuses are said to have a thousand petals, representing an infinite number of qualities. Which petal we unfold today, and how we blossom into who we are destined to become, is the power of letting go and letting the Divine carry us. Trusting that we are each destined for the highest—and loving that destiny and path—will unfold new petals, new opportunities, and new vistas of possibilities.

In the Vedic tradition, the saying is, *"Truth alone triumphs."* The power of purity will shine through, the power of that which is truth is real power. So, all we have to do is do what we know to be right—and let go. As they say in the Christian tradition, *"Let go and let God."*

The Story of Queen Chudala and King Shikhidhvaja

The story of Queen Chudala and King Shikhidhvaja is from the Yoga Vaishishta. Queen Chudala was a wise, enlightened Rishi married to the pious King Shikhidvaja. King Shikhidvaja was a great seeker, devoted to his meditation and spiritual practices in the pursuit of higher wisdom. Here is their story, told by Queen Chudala:

My husband came to me distraught. He could stand it no longer. He said he had tried everything but could not find peace. No amount of meditation or spiritual offerings seemed to bring the peace he craved.

He was a great king, kind to his people; but he saw that he was not beyond the cycle of birth and death, any more than any other person. He ruled with justice and wisdom but was overcome with the need for enlightenment and the feeling that he was missing the essence of life. To be a king is not to be enlightened.

He knew of a saying from the Vedic literature, "Peace follows renunciation." Desperate for peace, he decided first to renounce the throne and kingdom. He came to me and asked me to perform the duties of the king.

I saw immediately that his idea of renunciation was misguided, but he saw me simply as his wife. Because of that, he was blind to my inner vision and the enlightenment cultivated by my master.

I agreed that if he wanted to renounce the kingdom, I would rule in his name so he could go to the forest.

He gave up the soft silks, fine cotton, and luscious cashmere he was used to wearing. He left behind the cushioned beds and sofas and the rich foods of the palace and set up his place of renunciation in the forest. He wore bark and slept on a straw mat on the ground. He ate berries and leaves he gathered in the woods and washed in the frigid stream.

While I stayed behind and ruled the kingdom, I watched his progress with my inner vision. The hard earth pressed on his soft skin and the rough bark left scratches. He shivered in the cold nights.

The more he gave up, the more agitated his mind became. Instead of thoughts for his kingdom and subjects, his thoughts were occupied with his comfort and where to find food. His mind was even less peaceful than in the palace.

But the great King Shikhidhvaja was a true seeker. He did not stop or return to the palace. He decided that if the renunciation had not yet brought peace, he must renounce more. He started to eat only every two or three days. He slept without any covering on the cold ground. And still, his mind became more agitated while his body wasted away.

Finally, I could stand it no more. I had waited patiently for him to see the truth; but since he had not, it was time to use my divine power. I knew he still simply believed me to be his wife, ruling the kingdom, so I took the form of an ancient Rishi called Kumbha and appeared in the forest before King Shikhidhvaja.

"How are you?" Rishi Kumba asked King Shikhidhvaja.

The desperate king recounted his woes and agitation and pleaded with the great Kumbha to help him find peace. Rishi Kumbha replied to him only, "Peace follows renunciation."

In desperation and true dedication, the confused king gave up more and more until he built a great fire and was ready to sacrifice his own life. He threw his hut into the fire, his water pot, and his loincloth. As he stood naked, shivering in the cold, ready to throw himself into the fire in a misguided idea of renunciation, I appeared again as Rishi Kumbha.

I grabbed his arm to stop him from jumping into the fire as I called, "Stop! This body is a gift from your parents, it will anyway one day return to Mother Earth. If death was enough for peace, all those who were gone would already have peace. The body is not yours to renounce. Where is this idea that a hut or a palace was what you were to renounce? Peace follows renunciation. Renounce the idea that you are small and limited. Recognize your unbounded consciousness. Your Self is unlimited. Renounce to the boundaries of the small 'I' and 'mine' and then you will surely find peace. Live the life you were given. Follow your dharma and renounce the notion that you own a body or a palace or are limited by those things. You are unbounded, unlimited consciousness. You have all possibilities. See the reality, which is bliss, and then you will have eternal peace."

In an instant, the great King Shikhidhvaja saw the reality and gained the peace he so desperately craved. The Rishi Kumbha disappeared. When King Shikhidhvaja returned to the palace, he found me waiting for him with the softest silks, sweetest fruits, and garlands to celebrate the real renunciation that brings peace.

The story of King Shikhidhvaja teaches that renunciation is not necessary. When we go within to become one with our supreme consciousness, we live the benefit of this association, making our life excel in all possibilities. We can have liberation from where we are, on our own paths. The infinite power of nature is ready to help us live all that we imagine and more. To let go means to go beyond limitations.

Like this thread of wisdom, King Shikhidhvaja had to learn that to let go is to remove the notion of individual control so that the higher power of nature could take over. To just let go is not to run away from desires, or the world and responsibilities. To just let go is to let go of the notion that we are small and limited and see the unbounded possibilities waiting already inside each of us.

> *"When I let go of what I am, I become what I might be."*
> ~ Lao Tzu

The power of consciousness is infinite. Consciousness alone is infinite peace, and it is always available within each of us, ready to fulfill desires, both inner and outer.

Action Steps

Here are some reflections, ideas, and actions to absorb and experience this thread of wisdom:

1. Pause. When something isn't working, take a break for meditation, a walk, or a new perspective. Leaving something often presents new solutions, especially after meditation.

2. Use Attention. Pray from a deep level of feeling. Think of a desire as a tender impulse of your heart—and then forget about it. It helps to put it out there softly, from the inside, before letting go.

3. Connect. Surrender to nature. The forest, oceans, mountains, grass, desert, and fields all have a revitalizing quality. When you feel blocked by your desires, or without recourse, connect with nature. Be sure to also connect with yourself (through meditation or spiritual practices).

4. Reflect and Write. When have you seen something that needs to change but waited to respect the timing and growth of others, as Queen Chudala did? How did it make you feel? What was the result?

5. Reflect. When have you felt afraid to let go? What were the results? What might have happened in that situation if you had allowed yourself to surrender to what was happening?

Having rediscovered enlightened eternity, miraculous potential healing awakens transcendence.

Thread 12: Start Where You are, but See the Goal

अल्पकाल विद्या सब आई
"Total knowledge gained in a short time"
~ Rama Charit Manas, Bal Kand 203.2

Another way to say this would be: with the first step, you already have the vision of the goal. It is the concept we discussed at the beginning of this book that every step on the path has the fulfillment of the goal. But it goes beyond that.

It is a technique of accomplishment. Seeing, feeling, and tasting the goal—you can then move forward with greater support from nature and the environment to achieve it. That is not to say that you will know all the steps, but even from the beginning, just a glimpse of the accomplishment is enough to structure the steps to fulfillment.

I realize that may sound confusing or theoretical. How do you practically do that in daily life? It is simpler than you might imagine. There is a proverb in India, one of Maharishi's favorites, that provides the answer:

. . .

*"Success of action depends on the purity of the heart,
not on the means of accomplishing it."*

It is the purity of heart and the intention that carry action to success. Purity of heart comes from association with our own highest potential and loving nature. When the intention is pure, nature supports it. You have the right thoughts and intuitions that allow you to conceive the goal and accomplish it. It is not only by thinking but by thinking with a pure intention that nature will then bring support.

One way to increase association with our own highest potential, the intelligence of nature, is with the practice of Transcendental Meditation. The brain becomes accustomed to thinking from this level—intuition becomes more awake—and we are more easily able to accomplish our goals.

How does nature organize? The example is of water on the top of a mountain. The water will find the best path to reach the bottom —nature calculates it automatically. Nature knows the way, with minimum effort, to reach the goal. The same is true for all aspects of life. That is why this expression does not put emphasis on the means of action. The means are organized with the purity of intention. Start with the goal and a pure intention, and the steps to success will reveal themselves.

Success depends more on this principle of purity of action than anything else. You must have experienced this at some time, perhaps at the best moments of your life. In those moments, everything seemed to fall into place. It may have been like all actions were moved by something more—automatically calcu-lating the best results. When we can systematically open the full potential of consciousness, and with the compassion of life to give us more than we deserve, great accomplishments can start with soft intentions.

The First Step

"You can't cross the sea merely by standing and staring at the water." ~ Rabindranath Tagore

Sometimes, the first step, the first word, or the first second is the hardest. Inertia is difficult to overcome. Vast arrays of possible excuses are enticing. It can seem easier to say, "I didn't feel like trying" than "I failed." But to start doesn't mean to finish. To start, in and of itself, is an accomplishment.

Every time I sit to write, I could give you 10 reasons why I'd rather not. Yet once I start, I never want to stop. The same is true of exercise, meditation, and so many other things in life. Before you start, it seems impossible. Once you start, it builds its own momentum.

Those are small examples. What if, instead of writing a book or taking your daily run, you were trying to gain enlightenment or spiritually regenerate the entire world? The solution is the same: start.

Whether your goals are enormous or minute, whether you feel confident or unqualified, the best place to start is where you are. Once you start, the path you're on will lead to the next steps and new paths.

In the words of Lao Tzu, *"Great acts are made up of small deeds."*

Paint What You Can

The painter for Maharishi recounted to me how, tasked with painting his vision of the Vedic Tradition, she often didn't know where to start. She often felt Maharishi had given her impossible instructions. She didn't even know how to begin. Then the only thing to do was to sit there and think until she could find something she could do, no matter how tiny. She just had to find a place to start. This strategy worked for her, and it works in all aspects of life.

Maharishi was fond of saying, *"God helps those who help themselves."* That has been my experience over and over in life. Whenever I wanted something, I had to act, to move in some way and see how the environment responded. Sometimes it was fantastic. Other times, it was like hitting a brick wall. But it was never just thinking—always there was action.

While Maharishi would talk about thinking and accomplishing, he did not literally mean sitting and thinking and doing nothing. That seems to be a trap for many spiritual seekers, sitting and wondering why their desires haven't been delivered.

It is true that powerful thought can move mountains. Those who have clear thinking can have the vision to perceive what others can't see. Those whose thoughts are so powerful they can move nature can certainly create more favorable circumstances. I've seen it countless times with Maharishi and others. But I have never seen them think and fail to act.

> *"All difficult things have their origin in that which is easy,*
> *and great things in that which is small."*
> ~ Lao Tzu

Follow-through

Like a good golf or baseball swing, you need follow-through. The initial impulse isn't enough; you must follow the momentum. What does that mean in practical terms?

It means that whatever your first step, take another. When you have an "a-ha" moment, run with it. And whatever you do, when you are in the flow, don't try to stop it. One step leads to the next. One impulse leads to the next, and one goal leads to the next.

That doesn't mean you have to believe you can do it. You might not believe you can accomplish great goals or see opportunities where others do not. You might feel like the smallest, most shallow, or incompetent person in the world and still at that moment believe in your divine potential. You can still move toward something great and something higher.

You can feel hopeless and lost and still have the chance for hope. You can believe in an enormous dream or no dream at all. But if there is life, there is hope. You can think, and you can act.

If that seems to be too much, see what step you can take today. There have been days of my life when getting out of bed was an accomplishment. There have been days when not eating two liters of ice cream was something I "did." There have been days when I felt so broken-hearted, from myself or others, that all the inspiring things I've written in this book seemed like a joke.

And on all those days, I got up and did what I could. I ate only one liter of ice cream, or got out of bed for an hour, or lay there staring at the TV because it was the only thing I could manage. But I did it, and one day I could do more.

That is the essence of this chapter. Start where you are. If you want to run 100 miles and can't take a single step, you are not a failure. You are already a success for believing in your goal. Or not even believing, but at least not closing the door on the possibility of someday. To even start—to have the courage to try—is the greatest triumph.

We are not defined by our easy moments—the ones where the right thing to say at the right moment jumps onto our lips or a task practically completes itself. We are defined by what we do in our unlucky moments. The ones where everything goes wrong, when instead of believing in ecstatic joy, all we can think of is dullness and misery.

Maharishi used to say that you know you have a good pot if you throw it and it doesn't break. We are defined not in the moments in which we sit on a pedestal in pristine beauty but by the moments we are thrown—against a wall, against a floor, or out the door. What do you do at that moment? Do you start from where you are, broken as you may feel?

My advice is yes, start there. Start with what you've got. Start as slowly as you need but take a step and start.

You don't have to know how you will reach your goal. You can have no idea. You can be totally unqualified. Depending on the situation, that might be better. Start with innocence. That doesn't mean that you will always achieve your impossible goal—but if you start from where you are with a pure desire, you will accomplish something great.

Think of Something Great To Do

I learned this quote from Maharishi that I have always felt deeply inside: *"Think of something great and do it. Never think of failure at all, for what you think is what you get."* This is a best-case scenario. If you can do this, do it. Set your eyes on the prize and go for it.

Imagine runners in a sprint. They don't have time to look left or right. They don't have time to do anything but sprint. The split second they would lose in checking out their opponents could cost them the race.

If you can, be like a sprinter. Don't look left or right. What anyone and everyone is doing or thinks about you is irrelevant. Walk your own path. Run your own race. Choose your own goal.

Be Open to Change

Remember also that everything passes. How do we know what we want? Remember that just as cherished items become stuff (think of that old iPhone), cherished goals become neutral memories— or are even forgotten! Think of what you've wanted to accomplish that is now a memory: degrees, events, even love.

That means in setting goals, be open to change. Keep them broad. What you think you want now might not be what you want next week, next year, or in 10 years. With every day on the path, we are changing and growing. The nature of life is for more and more. What seemed right might become a distant memory.

The best path is the one you are on, with your whole force and being. Where that path takes you is in God's hands—and yours.

The Story of the Thai Monk

While I was traveling in Thailand for the first time, I had the opportunity to meet a famous Thai monk. Thailand is unique in its tradition that "everyone should be a monk for at least a day." That means that all boys spend at least one day of their lives living as monks—and many of the girls also spend at least a day as Buddhist nuns.

This monk was famous because when he was still a junior monk in his teenage years, he developed a keen intuition. He discovered he was able to accurately predict lottery numbers. At first, he did it for himself. Then he started doing it for anyone who asked. Naturally, he became famous and highly sought-after.

His skill at predicting lottery numbers was causing such a circus that the senior monks encouraged him to take his full vows as a monk. This included giving up gambling. He would have to stop predicting the lottery. He did this happily because he was, in reality, an aspiring monk. He viewed his ability to predict lottery numbers as a distraction from real spiritual pursuits.

With the money he had earned from his lottery winnings, he built a giant jade temple of Lord Buddha and took his vows as a monk.

When I met him, many years later, he and I were both about 25 years old. His face radiated great bliss. When I entered the room, I was wearing some jewelry given to me by Maharishi after I had some experiences of enlightenment. I felt it was a blessing and a sort of symbol of accomplishment.

This Thai monk took one look at the jewelry I was proudly wearing, heard the others explaining it was a great honor, and started to laugh. He kept laughing until I asked what was so funny.

He explained that jewelry or other gifts given by a master in that way are to keep a disciple on the path. "You wear it with pride," he said, "but it is like a carrot for a donkey, goading it on." He went on to explain that for various reasons, disciples can be discouraged; and just like every other area of life, a reward system for steps of accomplishment keeps motivation higher.

At first, I was a little bit insulted and shocked, but then I realized he was right. The jewelry was a symbol of something inside— something that only Maharishi could see. I didn't need the jewelry. Although I'd convinced myself it was blessed by Maharishi, the blessing was also on the inside.

I was blessed by Maharishi, not the jewelry. The jewelry was a means, not the end. But the monk's words resonated because up, until that point, I'd thought of myself as totally dedicated. I didn't need a carrot like a donkey!

That day I realized another simple truth: without steady encouragement, love, and inspiration, even the most dedicated devotees and aspirants can lose inspiration and motivation.

Like seedlings growing, without water and sunlight, we dry up. Even the best seeds, without the right soil and nourishment, will not grow. The bigger the goal, the more important the start and the constant nourishment. A master knows that nourishment is not for weakness but for strength.

The need for encouragement on the path is not a sign of weakness but a sign one is still on the path. Without being on the path, no encouragement is needed. It is when we must continue through the dark, or grow from nothing, that we need the support and light of possibilities.

So whatever carrots come your way on the path—whether it is a kind word, an inspiring quote, a gift from a teacher, or anything else—take it with pride and keep believing in your goal. You deserve the carrot—and you deserve the goal.

Keep striving and keep laughing. Like the Thai monk, while striving for your goal, remember not to take yourself, or anyone else, too seriously.

आनन्दमयोऽभ्यासात्
"Bliss becomes blissful through practice."
or
"Brahman becomes blissful through practice."
~ Brahma Sutra 1.1.12

This Vedic expression summarizes this chapter for me. Practice. Practice means to continue, step by step, from wherever you are. Isn't bliss, by name and definition, blissful? Yes and no. The nature of life is bliss. We are consciousness, which in its nature, is bliss. But we may not experience that all the time. We may have forgotten.

That is why bliss becomes blissful through practice. It is already blissful. Only we have forgotten the essential nature of bliss and started to believe that life is anything other than blissful.

Practice, the experience of our essential nature as bliss, makes the experience of the joy of life more rich, full, practical, and evident. We take one step and then another. We continue the path of right action even when we don't see results.

When you enter a cave, it is filled with darkness. There is nothing to see. As your eyes adjust, you might find some shafts of light. As time passes, you might be able to make out shapes, patterns, or structures within the cave. This is like the experience of meditation and the experience of bliss.

While the nature of life is bliss, you might not notice it right away. But with time and dedicated practice, the nature of life, bliss, zooms forth. Bliss cannot resist expressing itself. Bliss becomes blissful through practice and the fullness of life re-emerges. No matter how far away you feel, start from where you are; and with simple, effortless practice, bliss will find you.

The Seagull Story

There is a story Maharishi used to tell from the Upanishads of a mother seagull as a reminder to start from where you are and keep believing, no matter how impossible the goal is. This story is the expression of the idea that it is the purity of the heart and not the means of action necessary to accomplish the goal. Here is the seagull story:

One day, a mother seagull lay her eggs on the beach. During a mighty storm, the ocean rose much higher than usual and washed her eggs away. Devastated by the loss and furious, the mother seagull asked the ocean to bring her eggs back. "No," the ocean replied, "they are gone." She pleaded, but the ocean ignored her cries.

"Fine," replied the mother seagull, "then I shall drink the ocean dry." The mother seagull went to all the other birds and asked them to help her bring her eggs back. No one wanted to help. She pleaded, but still, all the birds said it was impossible to drink the mighty ocean dry.

So the mother bird alone flew out to the ocean and brought back as much water as she could hold in her beak. She did it over and over again, drop by drop. She thought only of her goal to bring her children back as days passed.

Slowly, the other birds noticed and began to join her. As more seagulls joined her, the message reached the king of the birds, mighty Garuda. Hearing of the determination of the seagull, Garuda went to speak to the sea.

"Please return this mother's eggs, or I shall myself drink you dry in one gulp," Garuda told the ocean. The ocean churned, considering, and then, with the power of Garuda and his blessings, the ocean returned the mother seagull's eggs to the shore.

The seagull story is a reminder that if one mother can set out to drink the ocean dry to protect her children, we all can set and achieve impossible goals. Think not of all the steps. Set the goal from the purity of heart and act. Like the mother seagull, when we move with focus and determination, our purest desires and goals will gain extra support. The appearance of Garuda, king of the birds, is a reminder that nature has millions of ways to manifest support even in the most impossible situations.

What goal do you want to achieve? What is your first drop or first step?

Action Steps

Here are some reflections, ideas, and actions to absorb and experience this thread of wisdom:

1. Break Boundaries. What is something that you have been avoiding or that seems scary? Just take a step. It can be a tiny step. Take a tiny step or action every day for a week. How does it feel? Consider any progress, no matter how small, good progress.

2. Set Goals. Set some big goals for one to three years from now. Then set the smallest goal toward those that you can do right now. Do that. Every time you do it, think

that you're working toward your big goal. Like the seagull, what is the first step you can take?

3. Remember Bliss. How do you see bliss becoming
blissful in your life? Reflect or write on the growth of
happiness and how bliss has grown for you. When was a
moment when something that didn't start out as happy
became a source of happiness for you?

4. Power of Purity. *"The success of action depends not on
the means of action but on the purity of the heart of the
actor."* What are the moments of greatest purity, innocence, and naturalness that have brought you great
success? Can you see a pattern in your life when this
happens, compared to other times when you are trying to
control the outcome rather than allow pure consciousness
to organize the outcome?

5. Well Begun is Half Done. What were the moments
when you had a clear resolution, took action, and had
great progress? Do you see the relation to *"well begun is
half done"* in your resolution and results?

6. Set Goals. Think of the main resolutions you would
like to accomplish, regardless of the means to accomplish
them. Any initial step you can take in that direction?
How will achieving these resolutions change your life
forever?

7. Remember. *"Established in Being, perform action."*
Transcend and then start the action of your resolutions.
See how transcendence helps you to fulfill your resolutions by following the opportunities presented on the
basis of resolution and transcending. What progress has
this brought in your life?

8. Reflect and Write. Consider two modes of yourself to accomplish a goal. One, you have a perfect plan but something doesn't go the way you intended and it doesn't happen. Or, a second mode, in which you make a resolution of what you want, you transcend, and start more dynamic action to accomplish it using the principle of *"well begun is half done."* In this second mode, with your resolution in mind, keep on watching and being alert to details, indications, or signals that nature is giving you, even if they were not in your plan. Compare these experiences and their results.

Awakened inner magnificence reveals unbounded mighty self-vibrant oasis manifesting peace.

Thread 13: Love is the Best Gift

"I seem to have loved you in numberless forms, numberless times...
In life after life, in age after age, forever.
My spellbound heart has made and remade the necklace of songs,
That you take as a gift, wear round your neck in your many forms,
In life after life, in age after age, forever..."
~ Rabindranath Tagore

I have loved you in numberless forms—for, in whatever form, we are essentially consciousness, playing through our own love. In life after life, age after age, forever, we appear and reappear. We evolve, but the thread we carry with us is the fullness of love. Love is the greatest gift we can give ourselves and others. Maharishi, echoing these words of Tagore, says, *"Have my love and enjoy."* This is the essence of love overflowing in any form throughout eternity.

What beauty is love? It is not a one-time present but an eternal reality of giving. What we are today in love can become even more tomorrow. To love is to dance with eternity. It is beyond form or time. It can take any expression. It is a gift and an offering that can be given and re-given forever.

With such a precious gift of life, blossoming in the heart of all, life is a journey of creation through love.

How strange, then, that love has taken on an almost commercial quality in common understanding. It is easy to get caught up in the need for material giving—comparing what you have to others and to feel pressure—especially around holidays or birthdays, to give. This desire to give is followed by the search for the perfect gift. And yet, as Tagore describes, the perfect gift is love—love woven into a song, a necklace, a poem, or just in Being. Love opens the doors to infinity. Love shines light in a tunnel of darkness. Love melts stones and hearts long frozen.

Whether it is a child, a spouse, or a friend, love is the gift that transforms life. And to give love is to give from within, from yourself and your Being. Sometimes the expression of love will also involve a material gift. But it is never about the thing. It is about the impulse of love that finds fruition in giving.

At the beginning of this book, we talked about my frustration with material gifts. How they can never capture the infinity of heart or mind. Beyond that, material gifts are occasional, saved for holidays, birthdays, graduations, or other special occasions. The gift of love can be given every day, in packages large and small, woven into words and feelings, reaching through the void we sometimes find ourselves facing, even if we are right next to someone.

To love is to reach beyond into infinity and to bring forth the essence of life. To love is to bridge a gap of any size between two hearts and two beings. To love is to give new life where there was none and to transform the purpose of life on earth. To love is both most simple and most profound.

When a child comes into this world, it has one basic need: love. With love comes care, protection, and fulfillment of survival needs like food and safety. In the busy society we live in, it is easy to forget that our one basic need never actually changes. No matter how many tests we pass, degrees and promotions we receive, money we earn, or accolades we gain, our one basic need remains love.

To receive love gives life, and to give love restores life. The flow of both is essential to living. There is no secret and no cure. Real love is felt. It resonates from heart to heart. It breathes life and gives breath. When you love, you give the best of yourself, but you are never depleted. The act of love is an act of regeneration.

We were each born with a purpose, a goal, and a path. What we all have in common is our need to feel and give love. Love is the bridge between human and divine. Love takes life in its daily monotony and makes it something inspirational. Love transforms a city street or falling snow into a beautiful escape. With love, everything is possible.

How to Find Love

Most people think of love as happening based on life's circumstances. You "fall" in love if you are lucky. But love is created from within. Love doesn't depend on the outside—it depends on the inside.

How does that happen? The deepest quality of every person's consciousness is love. Love is, at the deepest essence, who we all are. When we touch on and generate love within, it radiates outside.

Love can be like a small pond—limited yet refreshing. But love is a mighty ocean, waiting to be discovered. In the small pond, there are small waves of love, ripples of refreshment. In the ocean of love, there are tidal waves, one after the other filling life with an infinity of love. Whether we're in the small pond or the mighty ocean does not depend on who we love or what happens on the outside—it depends on inner reality.

Love is not based on luck. It is based on inner transformation. The essence of love in its fullness is already available within each of us. It is already there, we only need a way to systematically taste it.

Transcendental Meditation is one effective means to reach a reservoir of love within yourself. Others may have other paths that they find to reach the ocean of love within themselves. However you choose, to reach the ocean of love is the nectar of life. To live it, even for moments, makes life infinitely sweeter.

Speaking of unbounded love, I heard Maharishi say that the devotee finds love in the chamber of her heart and opens it from there, lighting up everything outside. When we tickle love, all expressions of love open from the outside. It starts with a gentle, inner impulse.

The idea that love requires commitment, or that love is in any way conditional, takes away from the very nature of love. To love is to give on an unbounded scale, without limitations, and without thought of return. Love blossoms in the most surprising places, like a flower blooming from the cracks in the sidewalk.

There are an infinite number of flavors of love. One can love a child, a spouse, a parent, a friend, the divine, or anyone else. While each type of love and expression of love is different, the essence of flow in the heart remains the same. When we love, we fulfill our essential destiny. Love makes us strong and gives us the courage to accomplish the impossible.

In the words of Lao Tzu, *"Being deeply loved by someone gives you strength while loving someone deeply gives you courage."*

There have been countless fortunate days in my life where love and kindness were delivered with such care, such attention, on the eve or near major events. Compared to the events—graduations, birthdays, holidays, major losses—the love shines as the singular event. It stands in my memory, my body, my soul. Love can change us in so many ways.

Events are convenient to make lists. This happened, then this happened. But when love is the gift, its rippling effects reach far beyond one day, one hour, or even one week. Sometimes we see the effects of love blossoming even years later. To give and receive love is the nectar of life.

And yet, in a book "filled with stories, I struggle to find a story to tell you that I can pin down and mark as "the story" of love. Because to describe love is to describe the unbounded. To share love is to melt into unity, infinity. This chapter, in many words, is part of a picture of love I want to paint, to open my heart and show you this is it. And yet, the words, descriptions, and events still only express a few degrees of the vista; they all fail to capture the essence of love.

Love in its essence is eternal happiness. Love is unity and unifying, giving and receiving at once. Love is, in its existence, discovering an ever more magnificent field of love. Perhaps this thread is a signpost for others that there is a unique gift of love waiting for each of us. There are not enough words to capture or stories to tell the song of the soul that flows in love and sees love blossoming all around. It is not only for the fortunate—love is the destiny already waiting within each of us.

No Drop of Love is Ever Wasted

To love is to flow from the heart and attract all good to us. To love is to be. In his book *Love and God*, Maharishi explains, *"No drop of love is ever wasted. For every drop of love, the angels in Heaven run down to keep count. Such is the power of love."* Such is the power of love that the almighty divine in any form should take notice.

So many feel that love is given for something in return. But love is never wasted. It moves an ocean from a drop and touches the feet of God. To love is to bring the divine into daily living.

To love is automatic. The only choice is to allow yourself to be innocent to experience it. Many tend to block love with stress or intellectual ideas: "She did this or he did that, therefore I cannot love." Love is not about the beloved and is not conditional on performance. Love is a flow of the heart that moves regardless of outside conditions.

The process of loving is a process of refinement. All the divine realms described in various traditions have a quality of love—from the Angels in Heaven, to the Devatas, to the Bodhisattvas. From a fully-developed heart, love flows naturally. There is no restriction and no limit. It is for this reason that saints are often described as having unbounded love. The quality of love is the Divine moving in each of us.

The Path and the Goal

Love is both a symptom of a full heart overflowing and a path of self-refinement. Love is both the path and the goal. To love is to purify oneself. To love is to bring a higher purpose into vision. To love is to allow yourself to be what you already are—divine, all-powerful, and all-loving.

To be in love and live in love is the birthright of every human being. It cannot be stopped and will always flow, regardless of changes in politics, culture, religion, or beliefs. To love is the essence of Being, and to Be is the fullness of love living.

If you feel love, cultivate that love in your heart and encourage it with wonder. Love that beautiful quality rising in you. With every drop of love, with every move of an overflowing heart, you regenerate yourself and the world regains its balance.

What we feel inside, what we are inside, radiates out into the environment. Love is the power to restore humanity, to bring light into the darkness. Hearts full of love can change destiny to a new world based on the power of love, not the power of might. It is already dawning.

Wisdom from El Parque del Amor

El Parque del Amor is a beautiful garden—it exists between houses, surrounded by hibiscus, jasmine, and flor de la noche. All rich tropical fruits blossom in El Parque del Amor: mango, pomegranate, papaya, banana, guanabana, cherries, and more. Cool turquoise waters like the Caribbean lap at the white sands nearby. Colorful parrots chatter with crows as hawks soar overhead and colorful chickadees dart between trees. The sun dances with the leaves and warms the skin but never burns. It is a tropical paradise but does not exist in the tropics.

El Parque del Amor is a reality seen in the eyes of the beloved, felt in the heart, tickling the skin, and reverberating to the depths of the soul. The light of the sun tells its story, but it is stronger than the sun's rays. The breeze whispers of el amor, but the touch of love is softer than the sweetest breeze. The odor of the earth, rich and pungent, breathes with love; but no smell is as sweet or as rich.

The entrance to El Parque del Amor is like the entrance to a secret garden: it requires a key and searching, as the vines and brambles that have grown over it mean it is impossible to find with the eyes. It must be felt with the heart.

While two may enter the park, there is only ever one. To step into El Parque del Amor is to become one in heart, body, and soul. The pull is incredible, powerful, and soft, while also patient, kind, insistent, and demanding.

The wisdom of El Parque del Amor is softly spoken in the birds and the trees, the sun, and the flowers, but it is not even these whispers that contain true wisdom. The real wisdom blossoms in the heart. It is not known by the intellect or the mind. No amount of study or trying will ever open the door.

The wisdom of El Parque del Amor comes in surrender to the river of love, like opening arms wide and falling backward into a vast unknown and being caught at once by the beloved. To enter this park, you must cross through the heart and allow another to become one with you. That, my friend, is when the magic happens.

And what will you find? That is for you to see, but here is a whisper, a hint of the vision: the wisdom of El Parque del Amor is that more love is always possible. To fall in love means unity. To be in love is not a destination but a beginning. And with every beginning, a new circle of completion. Love is the destination and the goal, but it also opens new paths and new beginnings. Love is all possibilities.

The wisdom of love is ever-changing. It takes an infinite number of forms. Sometimes soft, sometimes hard, but always dancing with the new hope of rebirth in the glory of love anew.

———

The whisper of El Parque del Amor is the reminder to dance, to sing at the top of your lungs, and most importantly, to let love into your soul. Because without love in the soul there is no El Parque del Amor. Love is the water and sunshine that makes the garden of love at the deepest level of who we all are come alive and breathe with the reality of, "I am you, my love. I love you."

Beyond even El Parque del Amor is the love and unity with the master. In the Vedic literature, it says:

त्वदीयं वस्तु गोविन्द तुभ्यमेव समर्पये
"Thy gift, my Lord, I offer to Thee."

This expression takes love to another level—to that of the Master and the disciple. It is an expression of pure love encapsulating the reality that love is the best gift. This expression of gratitude acknowledges that the teaching, the wisdom, and techniques to open a student's full potential come from their teacher or Guru.

From these teachings, the student grows, developing capabilities and outer success, as well as inner wisdom and enlightenment. Whatever the student can become is based on the teaching of the Master. The Master, or Guru, is the guide. They point the way. The student follows the path.

And upon discovering she was more than she could ever imagine, in humility and love, in recognition of the greatness of the teacher, the student acknowledges all that she has become is, in reality, the gift of the Guru.

This is not a superficial level of Guru like a "Yoga Guru" or a "DIY Guru." This is a Guru in the purest sense. "Guru" means one who removes darkness or ignorance—who can see the reality and teach the reality to others. This expression of love to a Guru is the expression of adoration for the fullness of life that blossoms through the teaching of truth and techniques for self-realization —realization of the inner power of consciousness.

This expression of love is like a mango tree that was patiently tended from a small sprout by a gardener. When it is large and mature and the fruits are ripe, it bows in humility to offer the fruit to the gardener. It was the gardener who tended and protected the tree, ensuring its growth, and the tree then offers the ripe fruits back to the one who helped it blossom.

Thy gifts, I offer to Thee, is an expression of the fullness of love, expressed to itself, which continues time after time, age after age, generation after generation.

Action Steps

Here are some reflections, ideas, and actions to absorb and experience this thread of wisdom:

1. Love. Love yourself, love your friends, love your family. Let your heart be open to love, and whenever you feel a prick, choose love. Every day for a week go out of your way to show some extra love to those around you. This can be a genuine compliment or point of admiration, a hug, spending extra time together, or anything else that the other will feel your love.

2. Make Space in your day for love to grow. Rushing down a to-do list and checking boxes leaves little time for the heart to flow. Make time for the heart, and the rest of your life will flourish, too. Think of a loving moment in the last week. How did it make you feel? How did even that moment change your day?

3. Reflect and Write. When have you felt the gift of love in your life? How did it make you feel? How did you change with that love?

4. Remember. When have you given the gift of love to others this week or this month? How did you feel during and after? How did loving change you?

Now absolute reality as you awakens new awareness of love within.

Thread 14: Become a Successful Traveler of Life

"A good traveler has no fixed plans and is not intent on arriving."
~ Lao Tzu

The cliche is true: life is a journey. We are all travelers of life. We come here for some time, and then we go. No one stays here forever. This thread is about making the journey of life successful. We've all experienced Lao Tzu's words. Even if we think we have fixed plans, life often has other plans.

But let's talk for a moment about shorter journeys. Travel holds an undeniable appeal. Everyone loves to travel. You might love the idea of travel, the process of traveling or being in new places.

Travel has always been a part of my life. From childhood vacations to adult adventures farther afield, I am fortunate that I could travel often. That has become easier to do with family and friends who are savvy at saving and multiplying hotel and airline points. What would have once been an exotic and expensive holiday is now achievable for more people.

In fact, I am writing this from a small cottage on the Côte de Rose (roughly, the pink rocks coast) of Brittany, France. I drove here for a change of scenery and culture. I can hear the ocean roaring outside my window and during the day look at its turquoise expanse. I never realized how milky and turquoise the English Channel is!

Why talk about travel in a book about inner discovery? Because travel puts that same self in a different light. A journey brings out parts of ourselves that get hidden or lost in the mundane routine of life. When we are stuck in a rut—emotionally, professionally, or personally—a change of scenery can bring a new perspective. And with a new perspective comes both clarity and gratitude. It doesn't have to be a long trip. It can be an afternoon spent one town over. Whether you love long trips or have never traveled, please take the journey of this chapter with me.

Potential Like a Diamond

Imagine that our human potential is like a diamond—a giant diamond necklace. Suppose you have been wearing the necklace for a long time and that over time the diamond has become caked with dirt and has lost its luster. You start to feel its weight around your neck. It may start to rub and feel uncomfortable. You stop seeing its beauty and start to see it as a nuisance.

The diamond in this analogy is our human potential. If we forget our potential and fail to take care of ourselves, then each daily task becomes one more burden of responsibility. It no longer seems like a beautiful treasure but starts to feel like it all rubs the wrong way. We feel unhappy, discontent, and frustrated with our lives.

The same is true for our environment. Take another analogy. When you get into a warm bath, you notice its soothing warmth. It feels soft and relaxing—wonderful on your skin. But over time, even if you manage to keep the bath water at the same temperature, it begins to feel a bit chilly, uncomfortable, or like nothing at all. You stop noticing the warm, soothing quality of the bath. Instead, it feels wet and a bit clammy. But when you move your arms in the water, you feel warmth again.

The bath in this analogy is our environment. We might have a beautiful home in an ideal location and a great community, but with time, we stop feeling it. We stop appreciating the warmth of the blessings in our life. Like moving our arms in the warm bath, sometimes we need to stir the environment to experience all that we have.

For me, travel is like stirring the bath. It brings three main benefits: creativity, self-discovery, and gratitude. Culture or experiences are almost an automatic part of the package, especially if you are in a foreign country. However, the benefit is not in the cultural experience itself; it is in the creativity, understanding, and gratitude it inspires and the new understanding and capabilities that it opens.

Gratitude comes from the qualities cultivated on the journey. This includes the most fundamental, essential qualities of who we are. Love, compassion, patience, intelligence, creativity, and grit get strengthened with the challenges of travel. It is with these qualities that, with nothing else, we can create something. It is the power of who we are as individuals that, in turn, can shape our reality.

This gratitude extends to family and friends because the larger body of who we are reaches to include everyone we hold close. Their strengths become our strengths, and ours become theirs.

When faced with a journey, these essential qualities often come to the forefront. It pulls out of each of us the ability to adapt, be creative, think on our feet, use intelligence, and connect to other humans through love, compassion, and humility—sometimes across language barriers.

To be a successful traveler in life means more than packing your suitcase and going somewhere. It means recognizing that we are all already on a journey. The destination is perfection—enlightenment—but every step along the way is its own destination.

Using Intuition

Without knowing where we are going or how we will get there, the usual tools of a journey—a compass, a map, or a GPS—are useless. The tool of the spiritual traveler to find the path is intuition. Intuition gives us the capacity to naturally react and make better use of outer circumstances.

On a journey, especially the journey of life, we rarely have all the information about the path or how the journey will go. In these circumstances, intuition knows faster than the intellect the best path. Intuition breaks down the barriers between the past, present, and future. It stands on the threshold of consciousness which knows only the truth. It establishes, on the level of our conscious awareness—the infinity of all possibilities designed into one best course of action.

Intuition, when connected to pure consciousness, guides choices for the best direction for each of us. Just as nature knows the path of minimum effort, intuition knows the best path for the next steps on an unfathomable journey.

How do we know we are going in the right direction? Growing bliss and happiness are an indication of evolution in life.

Enjoying the Fruit of the Goal

I learned from Maharishi that at every step along the path, you enjoy the fruit of the goal. Every step along the journey is its own goal. It is its own end and destination. Then there is no need to worry about where the final goal is because our destination of today is enough.

We are already enough. We are already "there." Could it be that simple? Could this truth, whispered through the ages, be it? Could the answer to "Is this it?" be our last destination—and our next? It is such a simple truth, and yet, there it is. We are all travelers on the path of life, and our next destination, wherever that may be, is our goal—at least for that moment.

It is said in the Vedic Tradition that no two people are ever in the same state of consciousness at the exact same time. We each perceive the world from our own unique perspective and grow with those perspectives toward our next goal. It is an ever-evolving process. For that reason, no two people will ever see the world exactly the same. Nor will two people ever have exactly the same destination.

Think of the famous Shibuya crossing of Tokyo, or the thousands of bikers commuting in Amsterdam, with masses of people moving past each other, each focused on their own destination. We are all like that when we move through life. We are not going to work or school but to the destiny of this life—and all lives before us. We are destined for greatness, and we are already travelers on the path.

Sometimes we forget that we are supposed to be moving. We get comfortable sitting on a bench and prefer to remain there in security rather than move on to something greater. But we may find that after sitting on the bench for a while, a bear starts getting too close or storm clouds roll in. Life has a way of pushing us on the journey even when we would rather stay still.

The real stillness is in the absolute, unchanging nature of life. Everything else is always changing. Nature, the universe—whatever you want to call it—will push you on to the next destination, the next goal. It can be tempting to resist, and resistance may seem to work for some time. But even like a toddler throwing a temper tantrum, nature will be like a patient mother, picking us up and driving us to where we need to go.

We are all like rivers running to the sea. Until we have merged with the unbounded, until we have reached our ultimate goal, we will keep moving. And even upon reaching that goal, the ocean itself moves with the tides and the currents, swirling within itself.

Life is a giant journey—from a drop of water joining a mighty river and flowing to the ocean, and then, as the ocean, moving within itself. Each step of the journey is a destination and a goal. Each destination is both natural and significant. The whole process is automatic and deliberate.

What an incredible journey is the process of life! We travel as individuals. We believe we leave one place or one destiny behind and pick up the next. In reality, all that we have been and all that we have experienced are woven into the fabric of who we are.

With the internet and technology, we can see almost anywhere in the world as though we have visited that place. And yet, it does not feel the same. To breathe in the sea air is not the same as watching the waves crash on a computer screen. To feel the tightly-woven wool in a Tibetan tent and smell the overpowering aroma of butter tea is not the same as watching someone else do it through a GoPro.

When we travel and experience a place, that place is woven into our physiology and consciousness. It is not only the sensory perceptions of the place that we miss through a computer screen but the laws of nature. The way the ocean moves, the trees grow, the winds change, how the sun feels; how the people live, what makes them smile, and how they form communities and support structures. All of that is unique to a place. Most of it cannot be learned in a book or in a video. It is a feeling that is absorbed in our consciousness.

A World of Diversity in Unity

The geographic and climatic conditions of any specific area are an expression of the laws of nature of that area. The way people live in that area—their culture, religion, clothing, customs, and food —are all a reflection of the laws of nature there. The world is more than mountains, oceans, and even cultures. It is natural law that builds up and governs these different realities.

The source of all these laws of nature—all these diverse ways of living and value systems—is the same unified level of consciousness. By experiencing different parts of the world, we are experiencing different expressions of the most fundamental and powerful level of ourselves. Consciousness is a holistic level of awareness that is the source of our individual thoughts.

You don't have to go far to experience these different laws of nature. Sometimes, even from one town to the next, there are subtle differences. Within most countries, there are major differences not only in the climate but in the way people dress, eat, think, speak, and what they value. We are a world of diversity.

That world of diversity, with all its cultures springing from the laws of nature, is at the same time a world of unity. On the deepest level, there is no separation between the person in India eating kitchari and the person in Argentina eating empanadas. There is no separation between the American eating tex-mex and the African eating bunny chow. We are one world family. Diversity is our beauty.

Like a garden filled with a variety of beautiful flowers, the different laws of nature that make up the world create a world of differences on the basis of unity. A garden only filled with roses is beautiful, but a garden overflowing in different parts with thousands of different flowers and plants is spectacular.

Our strength is in our diversity within unity. Without unity, the diversity is scattered and leads to disagreements and a feeling of "otherness." Without diversity, the world would be homogeneous, boring, and much less beautiful. Unity with diversity creates a world of differences united at the deepest level.

These days, as the differences of opinions get amplified on social media, it is easy to get caught up in the differences or to be upset by others' opinions. It is too easy to forget that diversity is what makes our togetherness—our fundamental unity—so powerful and unique.

To travel the road of life and find unity in diversity is to find that the drop in the river did, in fact, come from the ocean. We take different shapes in different phases of life. Through the process of traveling, we come home to ourselves.

Of all the places I've ever been, the most beautiful is within myself. Sometimes I glimpse that beauty from the ocean in Bali, the plateaus of Tibet, or the mountains of France; but always, wherever I go, that glimmer of unity, of my inner self, is the indication that I have come home.

There is the old saying, "Home is where the heart is." I would say, "Home is wherever we experience the unity of all we are." Because in the end, unity, too, is the expression of love. To travel is to find unity, peace, and love already living within each of us.

The Story of Angelica

I met Angelica in the ocean off the northern coast of the Dominican Republic. She is the only person I have ever met *in* the ocean and remembered later. But even as I write this 24 hours later, her perspicacity, her smile, and the brightness in her eyes stay with me. Angelica was nine years old when we met on Easter weekend, both of us splashing in what was for me waist-deep turquoise water as the waves rolled in around us.

For Angelica, the water was up to her chin. She was swimming in circles around a young black man—her father, I assumed—hanging on to his arm to rest from time to time.

Angelica had her hair in neat braids, each one adorned with dark pink beads. Her eyes were striking in brightness. Our eyes met from quite some distance, and she caught my attention. She had a smile that could light up any room, or in this case, the ocean.

I was taking my afternoon swim. I would swim out until I started to worry that a boat might hit me, then back to the shore, and out again. The ocean was rolling that day, and I ducked under waves at regular intervals as I continued, out and back.

After a while, I gave up swimming and rolled onto my back to float. When I rolled back over, I saw Angelica near me, looking intently, the man in tow. "Hola! Eres escritora?" (Hi! Are you a writer?) she asked. I was taken aback by her directness, her accuracy, and her smile.

"Si," I replied. Yes.

She proceeded to ask if I could understand her, and it was with both relief and happiness that I confirmed I could. "Then you are a writer?" she asked again.

"Yes," I confirmed.

"I knew it!" she exclaimed.

There was something about the fact that she could look at me and see that, and her enthusiasm to come and meet me, that was touching. In my basic Spanish, I thought of a few things to ask, including her name, age, grade in school, and about the man she was with. It turned out the man was her older brother, and she was hoping I would date him.

He had her same bright smile but was shyer and reserved. I told them I was happy to meet them, and after some time went on my way, walking along the golden sand and looking out at the turquoise water. What I didn't expect is that I would keep thinking about Angelica.

She was so innocent, and joyful! What eyes and perspicacity! How could she know I was a writer? Was she used to seeing bloggers? Could I really say I was a writer? Yes, I write, but does that make me a writer? All those thoughts ran through my mind as I walked.

And now, Angelica is here because she is the embodiment of becoming a traveler of life. She seized the moment, trusted her intuition, and plunged in with joy. How many of us would have done the same at nine years old? I would guess that at that age, many of us would have been more fearless than we are today.

I'm not sure I would have been as bold as Angelica, but I was always making new friends close to my age. Every swimming pool or playground was a place to find new friends.

As we get older, we stop trusting our impulses, stop believing in the power of our smiles, and forget that there is a friend waiting around every corner. Angelica is the reminder to believe the voice inside of us that can see through a person or situation. She is a reminder that with a friendly smile, we can make a new friend and that as travelers of life, every day is a day to renew ourselves. With a smile and kindness, we, too, can light up the world.

Each of us has an innate ability to connect and uplift others. The power of our consciousness amplifies this. Using this ability each day can make the days a little softer and brighter for someone else, as well as for ourselves.

Angelica is a reminder that one doesn't have to be an ancient sage, saint, or goddess to make a difference. She is the reminder that each of us could plunge in with intuition and heart and explore beautiful, unexpected adventures every day.

Maybe she was an angel who came to life as her name implies. All of us are surrounded by angels all the time. They turn up in the most unexpected places, like floating in the ocean off the coast of the Dominican Republic.

In reality, what we see far from us and what we see within are interconnected. This is expressed in the Rk Veda:

दूरेदृशं गृहपतिमथर्युम्

"Far, far away, the indweller of the house is seen reverberating."
~ Rk Veda 7.1.1

This verse describes the deep unity of life in which, even far away, in the field of diversity, unity with oneself is seen. Even the most diverse cultures, lifestyles, and people can be found, in the deepest essence, within ourselves. In this case, nothing remains separate. It is the goal of the traveler of life to experience the vast field of the diversity of cultures, climates, religions, beliefs, and realities of life as unified.

Then the differences are not a threat to one's point of view, beliefs, or way of living. From the field of unity, all diversity can grow and flourish. We can be travelers of life and through the journey find the ultimate unity within ourselves.

Far or near, great or small, the highest unity is within us all. The only thing that remains is for us to awaken to it and remember who we are. We are an ocean of power, an ocean of peace, an ocean of happiness, and an ocean of joy. Why not live that oceanic joy and celebrate every drop?

Mount Kailash

Mount Kailash in Tibet is considered the holiest mountain in four religions: Buddhism, Hinduism, Jainism, and Bon. While it was not something Maharishi often talked about publicly, he did mention in private the significance of this mountain in creating a new destiny for the world. It is a point of great spiritual power— where heaven and earth meet. I had wanted to visit Mount Kailash since I heard about it in 2006. That desire came true a decade later but not as I imagined.

I had envisioned my visit to Mount Kailash as a crowning moment of enlightenment—when everything was in place for fortunate outer circumstances and all-time inner bliss. When I went to Kailash, I was feeling the opposite. I was discouraged by many outside circumstances: organizational politics that I found disappointing, loss of friends and people close to me, and a feeling that I hadn't found my place or role and wasn't doing what I envisioned for Maharishi. In a word, I felt lost.

There is a saying in India and Tibet that you can only visit Kailash when the mountain calls you—and once it calls you, you go. I waited for what felt like an eternity, until September of 2016, to visit the holy Mount Kailash.

Tibet is the most starkly beautiful place I have ever been to. The high plateaus are often like moonscapes interspersed with lakes the color of the Caribbean Sea, reflecting snow-capped mountains.

Visiting Mount Kailash was an experience of opposites. We crossed one of the highest mountain passes in the world at 18,500 feet. We spent more than a week living at over 14,000 feet. To put that in perspective, Denver is 5,280 feet and many people experience altitude sickness when they arrive.

On the physical level, it was a challenge. We took medication to improve breathing, but getting enough oxygen still felt like a conscious effort. You had to think about every breath. As we climbed higher, each step was more challenging.

The trek around Kailash is about 52 kilometers (32.3 miles) and takes three days. We took an additional day to hike up toward the north face during the second day and stayed an extra night there. The path around Kailash followed a stream part of the way. There were ancient monasteries located where we stayed on the first and last nights.

On the third day, we awoke before dawn and started off in the dark in case it took more than 12 hours to cross Dolma La pass at 18,500 feet. I rode a donkey as I wanted to be able to cross the pass and not get caught in the thin air. Yes, I could have walked, but it was my first time at this altitude and thought safety first was a better plan.

We each had a local guide who walked with us at whatever speed we chose. As we made our way step by slow step (even the donkey kept stopping to catch its breath), we watched the sunrise as it touched the mountains and made them glow like golden flames.

When you reach the pass, the tradition is to throw something, symbolizing the departure from old karma or past limitations and the start of a new life. I threw a hat knitted by my mother. Someone could collect and use it or perhaps it would become part of the hills of ice. In any case, it was something precious that I had for years that I left as an offering to the local tradition and the mountain.

The air was so thin that my guide, a man named Arjuna, rushed me not to linger up there and take in the feeling. "Go down quickly before you lose your breath!" he urged as he took a bottle I was carrying to fill with sacred water from Gauri Kund, a small high-altitude lake.

He sent me to start walking while he scampered down the bank. The donkey and his tender also carefully picked their way down the rocky, steep descent.

As we reached the bottom after about an hour, we came to several large tents with wood-burning stoves inside and cushioned benches lining the walls. I asked if I could lie down on the bench. The owner of one of the tents kindly let me rest there, and I slept for almost two hours before the rest of my group arrived. They had walked the whole way—one breathless step at a time.

We continued together to the cave of Milarepa and a monastery next to the cave where we would spend the night. That monastery had a front room made of glass that was so warm with the sun that it felt like an oven. Coming from the frigid high mountain pass, it felt like a warm bath.

The fourth and final day was the easiest physically. Along the way, there were many rocks with lines where the original writing of Dhanvantari, the first physician, was said to be written. The water that drips from those rocks is said to cure any disease.

I completed the Kailash kora around the third week of September 2016. It was a trek, but it was something more. It sent ripples that gradually softened my heart, eased my worries, and helped me see new paths and opportunities when I had been frozen.

Various traditions have different interpretations of the significance of the Kailash kora (walking or riding a donkey around Mount Kailash). These usually involve clearing lifetimes of past karma or creating new lifetimes of better karma. For me, the new lifetime began at the moment of completion. One time ended and a new time began.

That new lifetime wasn't immediately evident outside. It took time to build strength, skill, and new form. There was a strength, solidity, and conviction different than before—it was more self-reliant.

Sometimes certain journeys can transform outer circumstances. Sometimes it happens right away. Or, like me, it can happen over time, gently easing into a new reality and new possibilities.

Since visiting Kailash, I can see the mountain inside me, not as a memory of my mind but more of a memory of my body and soul. I can feel the freshness of the air, the softness even in the hard mountain environment. I think a part of my heart is still in Kailash, and a part of Kailash is with me. I will probably never know all the blessings I received from the mountains or the ways they changed my path. But I know the joy they brought continues to build to this day.

The Technology of More than We Deserve

There is a system in the Vedic tradition called Yagya. We discussed it in Thread 10 in the section on the compassion of life. But it is worth mentioning here again. To become a successful traveler of life does not mean the path is without obstacles. It also does not mean that we have to struggle to overcome every obstacle.

The technology of Yagya allows you to receive more than you deserve. Done properly, it lifts the weight from the traveler's shoulders so they can see light in a new path or new opportunity. Yagya can avert the danger before it arises. This is one more vital tool in the traveler's hands that can make at least some of the difficulties easier.

Armed with intuition, our own pure consciousness, and technologies to clear the path and avert danger, the path and the journey find a new purpose. The travelers of life find that impossible destinations can already be available within. Traveling toward bliss, love, fulfillment, and peace without knowing the path or the goal—we find them already within each of us.

Action Steps

Here are some reflections, ideas, and actions to absorb and experience this thread of wisdom:

1. Find an Adventure. Take the opportunity for a change of scenery at least once a month. This can be a trip or just a short outing from home. Get out to see something different, ideally in nature. It is good for perspective and resetting balance. When you come back, notice how you feel. How did your perspective change?

2. Perspective. Take a few minutes each day this week to see the world through another person's eyes, culture, or desires. How do they see the same situation totally differently? Why is their view so important to them? Allow their diversity to be integrated into your view and who you are.

3. Reach Out. Do something each day that you wouldn't

normally do to touch someone else's life. After you do it, notice how you feel. How did your perspective change?

4. Reflect and Write. What was your most memorable travel experience? How did it impact or change you? How did that affect your spiritual growth or worldview?

5. Draw. Evolution is circular from one fullness to another. Draw those circles of fullness in your life. Within the circles, mark in your life the fullness or points of confluence, like a circular journey. Or draw a design of events of your life. See when one phase of the journey reaches a new fullness and when a new cycle of fullness begins. How did these cycles affect your life?

Seeing holistic reality, expanding experiences manifest perspective, healing and triumph.

Thread 15: Failing Leads to Greater Strength

"Life isn't about finding yourself. Life is about creating yourself."
~ George Bernard Shaw

The process of finding ourselves leads us to renew ourselves over and over again. Each renewal is like a re-birth, each failure like its own death. Sometimes we mourn the loss of love; sometimes we mourn the loss of a loved one; sometimes we mourn the loss of an idea or vision; sometimes we mourn the loss of ourselves.

In Chinese, the word for crisis or failing means opportunity. Every situation that brings a challenge also brings hidden wisdom or an opportunity to build steps of progress in life. Every failure is an opportunity for growth.

To be the creators of our own destiny does not mean a life without failure. Although the result—enlightenment—is said to be a "mistake-free life," the process of arriving there can feel like one great big series of mistakes and failures.

That is an important distinction. Because the very, very rare individual who is enlightened may live a life free from mistakes doesn't mean our path to get there is to try to be "perfect."

To try at anything is a trap. As soon as you introduce the word try, or trying, you have lost the innocence and power to accomplish. Think about it. In your moments of power, all your attention and energy was on the process of accomplishing—looking to the goal. As soon as you try, you introduce doubt into your mind and divert your attention from the goal to the process of doubting.

In the words of Yoda, *"Do or do not. There is no try."*

But doing often means to fall short, and to get up, over and over again. Remember the clay pot? You know you have a good clay pot if you throw it and it doesn't break. Life is often throwing us like a clay pot. Breaking and building the resilience to persevere even after life has knocked us down is a part of the path. Every fall is a part of the process. Every setback is a part of the process.

We are building strength, resilience, grit, wisdom, compassion, patience, and so much more. Think of life as applying glazes— each coating creates more gloss and more perfection. The process of evolution is in and of itself a process of "failing" to build up a permanent reality.

When the mind and body experience Transcendental Consciousness, it leads to total brain functioning. That subjective glimpse of transcendence might only last a second or a minute. But every time it is experienced and lost, it trains the mind and body to maintain a highly-integrated state.

The process of losing holistic functioning is a step to regaining and establishing more permanent holistic functioning. The process of using the full brain, then returning to limitations, or of experiencing unboundedness and limitations in alternation serves to establish the habit in the nervous system to maintain holistic functioning.

The same can be said for many other types of training. After strength training, the muscles have tiny tears that need to be rebuilt to be stronger. Failing is not failure but a process of building a new reality of our full potential of which we might not even be aware.

Life's setbacks can be big or small. Little failures can erode our confidence. These can be anything from forgetting to pack your child's lunch, to getting into arguments, making a business presentation that is a flop, "failing" on a diet, or divorce.

The idea that the path to perfection is perfection is a myth. It is like a Chinese finger trap. The more you pull and try to reach perfection, the further you get from ever achieving real freedom.

Another Perspective on Mistakes and Failure

We've described the law of karma, of action and reaction, in Thread 3. In the Vedic tradition, those who deliver karma, or past actions, are called *grahas* in Vedic astrology. Maharishi has explained that the concept of punishing someone for a mistake or failure doesn't make sense since everyone's actions are under the influence of the grahas. It is like a double punishment.

First, they made a mistake because of some influence on their mind and thought, and then they were punished after having done so. There is no guarantee that will change or improve future actions.

The graha that stands out on this thread of learning from mistakes is *Shani* (Saturn). Shani represents learning from difficult situations. Suffering comes from wrong action, violation of natural law. When we can do right spontaneously, actions have the support of natural law. In this case, everything feels easier. We are in a sort of flow. But even when there is suffering or failure, there is an opportunity for wisdom or evolution. From this perspective, we can use the wisdom of the grahas so that all failures in life are opportunities.

Every person is born with the best conditions for evolution in this life. Circumstances and events are automatically calculated and prepared for each person to use all that life brings for maximum evolution. Looking like this, everything happens for good.

People often wish they had been born under different circumstances. We all think someone else has it better. In reality, within each person's nervous system, nature has provided the best way to promote evolution in our living conditions.

There are landmarks waiting for each of us with birth. Sometimes those landmarks involve challenges or opportunities that we call failing. Every failure is an opportunity for wisdom. From that perspective, we could say that we are all living a mistake-free life.

Every person inside has the intelligence for perfection from birth, even in the most challenging situations. The feature that is most powerful in each of us is that we are born with all the intelligence necessary to move through these situations successfully. We are all born to succeed. Everyone is born for perfection. Association with our own inner intelligence is the basis to connect with our own wisdom of life. That will allow any person to go through whatever situations life brings.

Everyone, in their deepest intuition, knows if something they are doing is right or wrong. Again, intuition becomes important for right or wrong.

Be Yourself

To reach perfection is to be completely ourselves—not the people we think we are supposed to be and not the way we think enlightened people act. To reach perfection is to be authentically, wholly, and totally ourselves.

For that, we need to discover who we are. From the time we are young, we try on different hats to make us feel like we fit into society. As children, we classify ourselves by our interests or talents—athletes, artists, nerds, gamers, musicians, theater kids, "popular," etc.

As adults, we classify ourselves by our careers, our political or religious beliefs, our families, and our accomplishments. What we do is who we are. But how many of us are doing what we believe, in the depth of our souls, we are meant to be doing? A lucky few. But many, most, are doing something to get by.

We deny our soul's longings. We deny the whispers in our hearts. We trade life and living for a stable income or societal norms. Instead of being free, we become the servants of our bosses or the servants of our businesses. Our time is not free. It is tied up in meetings, deadlines, and value propositions.

But what about the value of human life? How can we go on to discover who we really, truly are within these boundaries of 60-hour workweeks, 9-5 days, jobs that leave us feeling lifeless, or relationships that define us?

The only way to feel freedom is in unboundedness. As long as there are boundaries, there are limits to growth. Only in unboundedness can complete freedom be gained. It is for this reason that the path to life in perfection is first to experience, even for a split second, unboundedness. Allow your mind to go beyond its own limitations. Reach beyond all that can or should be—transcend limitations and reach for all possibilities.

Having glimpsed infinity, anything becomes possible. The unbounded can be experienced within the boundaries of life as we live it. A dream of a thousand lifetimes is a dream of the moment. To be, know, and achieve any dream can be within reach.

Find Your Callings

The next step is to start to listen. Listen to your heart and your gut and observe your feelings. What brings you moments of ecstasy or joy? What makes you feel so fulfilled that you could do it day after day? Where is your bliss? These are your callings. They could be life callings or callings for now. There is no need to make any absolute decisions. Take a direction and start to move.

Some people already feel they have found their life calling. They are doctors, lawyers, writers, humanitarians, artists, or other professionals who love what they do. That is one part of life's calling.

But the highest part of life's calling is to reach complete happiness, to go beyond the limitations of life's ups and downs to reach a state of eternal freedom. That makes everything in life richer. It is like seeing the strokes of a painting and the vision of the artist, rather than glancing at the artwork.

But like the artist who had to re-do, erase, or re-define the artwork, the process of life is a process of re-doing and re-defining. I have experienced countless failures in my life. Some seemed devastating at the time. All of them, with time and perspective, made me more resilient, patient, and compassionate.

Talk to Your Future Self

One interesting trick to try during failure is to talk to yourself in the future. You are not looking for an outside guide but guidance from your own older, wiser self. It is something that was advised to me by a wise friend and proved to be both useful and surprising. Here is how you do it:

— Sit quietly and close your eyes for about a minute. Imagine yourself as you are now, approaching yourself of 5, 10, or even 15 years in the future.

— Ask that future self about the current failure or disappointment and any advice she/he/they have.

— Listen and be patient. Give yourself time to absorb the wisdom, advice, and perspective.

You may be surprised by how much that different angle and perspective brings peace in the moment of failure or heartbreak.

You can use this with a broken heart, a business failure, an injury, or any other disappointment in life. The ability to remove yourself from the pain of the moment and ask yourself how you will feel about it in some years will be refreshing—and often surprising. This is not an exercise of the intellect. If you go through the exercise, you might find it engages feelings you didn't realize were there, your emotions, and the depth of your heart.

You can even build on this with your creativity. See the person of 5, 10, or 15 years from now. Where are they? Because it is the wisest version of yourself, maybe you see them in a cave or other natural place that is holy or sacred to you. This is not an exercise of the imagination. Nor are you going to project what you think should happen. The key is innocence. See what comes. Be innocent. Having observed, accept the peace that follows.

This exercise is not to give you a definitive answer or predict the future. It is a way to connect with your higher wisdom and higher self for guidance. Instead of waiting for the voice in your head to push you in a direction, you seek your own inner wisdom.

Stepping Stones to Unboundedness

When you experience unboundedness through Transcendental Meditation, that inner guidance becomes more available. Connecting with your higher self, the failures will start to feel like stepping stones for growth rather than catastrophes. It will not remove the sting but will at least provide a path through and a light at the end of the tunnel.

When I've encountered someone particularly rude or abrasive, I've sat afterward and asked my older, wiser self what I am supposed to learn from this person. Why did they come to me? Usually, that person highlights a weakness in myself or a place I can grow. And because what we put our attention on grows, by seeing the weakness and how I want to grow, progress starts.

The other times I talked to my older, wiser self was during heart-break. In that time—which stretched on for months—I would from time to time sit and ask my older self of five or seven years in the future how I felt about the present time. The answer was always the same—it would be a phase and a memory—without any of the sting. It would become something on the path of growth, like a bus stop on a journey.

At first, this perspective was shocking and infuriating to me. Something that was so important was going to become trivial. But with time, that prediction of my future self came to be. While the warmth of the heart can always love, the cracks of heartbreak build new life and new love.

We are each on our own journey, but we often forget that we have built-in wisdom to guide us. The threads of wisdom shared here are already within each of us. The innate understanding of who we are and who we are destined to be will pull the strings even while we resist. Of course, there is a limit to the pulling and the pressure, as our own free will comes into play.

Seeing the Good

But no matter the failure, there is always something good. Maharishi tells a story that a great leader can find and focus on a good quality in any person. He explains that a man might have 100 bad qualities, but a true leader will find his one good quality and focus on that. As soon as the man hears the praise for his one admirable quality, it will transform his attitude about himself and his relationship with the world. Other good qualities will start to emerge.

When you practice kindness and find one good quality, others will start to appear. What you put your attention on grows stronger in your life.

Related to this principle, there is a story in the Vedic Literature that Maharishi was fond of telling. It illustrates the wisdom in finding the good in any situation. It is a reminder that even in extreme, difficult situations, there is always something good. Here is the story of the pearly white teeth:

> There was a saint who had a reputation for seeing good in every situation. No matter what people brought to him, he could find something good in it. One day, to test the saint, a man asked him to come with him. The man planned to take the saint into a dirty, rat-infested alley where a cat had been run over by a car. He thought that surely in such a disgusting and dirty situation, the saint would not be able to find anything good.
>
> When they arrived in the alley, the man pointed out the run-over dead cat, saying, "Look how disgusting!"
>
> The saint replied, "Oh, but look at those pearly white teeth."

The moral of this story is that no matter how bad a situation appears, there is always something good and beautiful in it. Look for the pearly white teeth. Likewise, no matter how many undesirable qualities a person has, there is always something good and beautiful. Find the good, find the beautiful, and express it to amplify it through kindness.

> *"Love watches for any sign of strength. It sees how far each one has come*
> *and not how far he has to go."*
> ~ Maharishi Mahesh Yogi

This is true for others, and it is equally true for how we should treat ourselves. Watch for any sign of strength. See how far you've come, not how far you have to go.

The Nature of Life is Bliss

The nature of life is for more and more—more happiness, more creativity, more power, more love, more peace, more intelligence, and more affluence. Even in moments of failure, nature, God, or the Almighty are pushing us toward more. We can create and re-create our own lives over and over again.

This is encapsulated in the following Upanishads verse:

पूर्णमदः पूर्णमिदं पूर्णात्पूर्णमुदच्यते
पूर्णस्य पूर्णमादाय पूर्णमेवावशिष्यते

Translated by Maharishi as:

> *"That is full; this is full.*
> *From fullness, fullness comes out.*
> *Taking fullness from fullness, what remains is fullness."*
> ~ Shāntipātha, Ishā Upanishad

This verse takes the idea of "failing leads to greater strength" to an even greater degree. Let's look at it line by line:

"*That is full; this is full.*" Expresses the reality of life that we are all already created from a state of fulfillment. Whether that fulfillment is perceived as empty or full, it remains a state of fulfillment. Another way to say this is that when we think we are failing, falling back, or losing our path, many times something is being taken away so that we can realize the fullness that we are. It is a cosmic re-adjustment. From a higher perspective, it is saying that even if we appear to have forgotten, we are all already, in our deepest nature, the fulfillment that we seek.

"*From fullness, fullness comes out.*" This can be visualized as a mother giving birth. A mother is a complete person, full in her own right. The child is also complete and full in his or her right. One fullness creates another fullness. This expression describes the reality of creative possibility on the level of consciousness in which there is no limit to the state of fulfillment. It also expresses that fulfillment is a creative state, not a static state.

You don't just arrive. You keep on creating and growing. Something being full or complete does not mean it is stagnant. It is always changing, growing, and evolving. The process of fullness creating is the nature of fullness.

In the same way, a fulfilled human life is not stagnant. You don't become full and then stop. Fullness is ever-evolving and ever-creating. The nature of being full, of being fullness, is to create more fullness. But it can still fluctuate. You can take fullness OUT of fullness.

"*Taking fullness from fullness, what remains is fullness.*" In the cosmic sense, this gives expression to the reality that when something is full, it can never be depleted. You cannot exhaust or use up fullness. Fullness, totality, is infinite. This is a level of consciousness available to all of us, and some of the many qualities of consciousness include happiness, intelligence, creativity, and all possibilities.

From a personal perspective, this means that any failure, short-coming, or faltering cannot take away from or deplete the deepest fullness of who we all are. Tapping into this level, your resources for happiness, intelligence, and creativity are unlimited. You open the door to all possibilities. This is so important for every person seeking to be able to give their best selves and to be their best. Only from a level that is infinite, that can never be depleted, can we truly give and grow.

Taken together, these expressions describe the reality that consciousness, being awareness, is a field for practical life. The expressions describe unmanifest consciousness creating itself. But they also describe the possibility of living that reality in daily, normal life and existence.

They offer a simple solution to the age-old problem of failure or feelings of not being able to do, be, or give enough. Consciousness, or Being, is not something outside. It doesn't require a pill, a course, a degree, or even belief. It is the latent power and deepest nature of each of us—waiting to be accessed and utilized for fulfillment—the fullness of life.

The Blessing of Departure

This is a story that is more recent, and rawer, but so important to share. We all face loss, which can also sometimes feel like failure. While finishing this book, I had one of the greatest losses of my life. Here is the story of how even in that loss, there is a blessing.

I have noticed, throughout my life, that when someone central to my life leaves, some great new, unrelated blessing enters my life after some time. It is a small, mundane version of *"taking fullness from fullness, what remains is fullness."* Put another way, nature fills a void. If you are left alone, without, or in a sudden change, nature won't let it stay that way forever.

I first noticed this when my best friend at boarding school, with whom I spent every waking moment, decided to return home. For some time, there was a void. I missed her so much. But after some time, I decided to write the letter to Maharishi described at the beginning of this book.

I was so happy with my friend that had she stayed at school, I might never have felt the dissatisfaction and longing that led me to reach out to Maharishi, which, in turn, changed the course of my life. If she had remained at school at that time, I would not be the person I am or where I am today. Even in her departure, she gave me a gift.

And that departure from my life was temporary. Twenty-five years later, she is still one of my closest friends. The fullness we had in our friendship became a new fullness as we both grew in many ways. But before that, there was the power of the void.

I've seen that several more times with people who were close to me. When they suddenly left, for some time there was a void. And then, as if by Grace, nature filled that void with inspiration, knowledge, love, or a new focus and understanding. Without the emptiness of the departure, the new blessing would not come in the same way.

It is not that one should wish for a departure or a void. But there is relief in knowing that when it comes, nature always fills the emptiness with fullness again. Nothing empty lasts forever. Nature likes fullness to become more fullness.

I am experiencing that in the most personal way right now. My mother departed unexpectedly in August of 2021. She didn't leave for another state or even another country. She left the earth with little warning, full of life only a day before.

While this was an enormous loss to me, the blessing I received was immense. It feels almost too tender and sacred to put into words. There was a moment of shock, a void, and weeks of processing. I felt like the wind got knocked out of me—and it took about a month to catch my breath.

But then, I began to feel her in a new way. I felt her happiness and joy. I felt her power and peace. I felt all the best of her without any of the suffering, physical discomfort, or moodiness that can make up mundane daily life. In essence, I felt her more with me than ever before. And I feel her free.

I started to see how much of my thinking was shaped by her voice and her guidance and how much of herself she had already put into me. I remembered also how my own voice is identical to hers and how my fingerprints were formed with her, moving in her womb.

And now, in carrying her in my heart, she is driving me more than ever to be the fullness of who I can be. I am shy about writing it because it is so fresh. But I feel her with me, not as a person, but as an essence of love and goodness so powerful that nothing can extinguish it. That is another very real, very tangible level of *"from fullness, fullness comes out."*

Every departure brings a gift, even if some are so shocking or difficult that it can be hard to see. But just as failure leads to greater strength, departure leads to new blessings.

Life on the outside is always changing. Although the eternity of existence is non-changing, everything else is a field of change. We can fail, be left, or succeed. Whatever the situation, eventually it will change. The secret is in finding the fullness, even when fullness is taken away.

This is the essence of this thread. As I have seen with my mother, how in taking away the fullness she had in her life on earth—the beauty of all she radiated—a greater fullness was created. When we take away from fullness, we end up with even more fullness.

Whether you lose someone through departure, divorce, a move, or any other circumstance, remember this: nature always fills a void. It feels like its own type of failure, but this too will lead to greater strength. We never wish for emptiness, but even in that, nature always finds a way to make emptiness full again.

That being said, the thread of the compassion of life continues as there are performances and means to bless and uplift those who have moved on. Maharishi describes it as such:

> *Departed souls, where ever they are on their path of evolution, the blessing of a Yagya will always reach them, even if they have passed away a long, long time ago.*

> *Also, any already re-incarnated soul will benefit from the blessings created for them through a Yagya. Time does not matter, living or departed souls do not matter. A Yagya blessing is never lost, it will find the owner of the blessings.*

> *Every Yagya performed is supporting the evolution of the soul. Also, the person ordering the Yagya for a departed soul will receive some blessings through a departed Yagya since he is mentioned as yajaman in that Yagya.*

> *Even if some soul has been killed in the war and passed away a short or long time back, the blessings created through a departed Yagya now will be received by his soul.*

We think we are separate, or they are gone, but the interconnection of life is that they can always be reached, and more good can always be created.

Action Steps

Here are some reflections, ideas, and actions to absorb and experience this thread of wisdom:

1. Find the Good. Don't dwell on what went wrong in the past. Don't beat yourself up about failures. The nature of life is to grow. Progress is the path of evolution. Every time you start to feel bad about a failure, think of one good new thing that came out of it.

2. Reconsider. Pick a failure that was devastating to you. Now think of 10-20 good things that came out of the same failure. How did your life change for the better as a result of that event?

3. Find the Fullness in Emptiness. In the case of loss, when something appears empty, find the good in that situation. Think of a recent loss in your life. What new good came into your life after loss? Note in a journal, or share with a friend, moments when after a loss your life took on new fullness or happiness.

4. Reflect. Talk to your older, wiser self. Approach her, him, or them with respect and see what guidance is offered about a situation that is now frustrating, challenging, or feels like failure.

5. Reflect and Write. Remember a failure or loss from long ago that no longer stings. Do you notice a point of failure or loss in your life that turned out, with perspective, to be for the best?

6. Waves of Life. If a wave settles in the ocean, we see it as a loss. But the loss of one wave is just preparing for a new wave. The pathways of these waves, their rising and falling, describe what can appear as failure and success. Take your life as a series of waves. Observe both the peak moments and the falls. See if there is wisdom or a common current that guides you through all these phases of evolution.

Absolute intelligence manifests self-referral, already unbounded, harmonious, kind love expressing eternal melting.

Thread 16: Life is in Moments— Not in Days

"Eternity (is) always in the hands of the present. It only needs to be appreciated.
The present holds the master key to unlock the treasures of eternity.
Every moment of our life is supplemented with the eternity of the bygone past
and that which awaits us in the moments to come.
Eternal existence of the unlimited Cosmos is available to us for our own power."
~ Maharishi Mahesh Yogi (1967)

This vast scope of the eternity of life is the vision of all possibilities at every moment. It is why we start with the idea that life is in moments and not in days. We connect to the past and the future through the present. The phrase *"Eternal existence of the unlimited Cosmos available to us for our own power"* is a way to say that unlimited power of consciousness is already available, in every moment, within all of us. Power, in this sense, is not a superficial power but the ability to fulfill our desires. It can be the power of love, the power of peace, the power of compassion, the power of forgiveness, the power of light, or the power of good in any and all its forms.

This idea of using the moment is also reflected in a famous verse from the Yoga Sutras.

हेयं दुःखमनागतम्
"Avert the danger that has not yet come."
~ Yoga Sutra 2.16

Averting the danger before it arises is essential for life and evolution in terms of using the moment and guidance on wise living. Don't do what you know to be wrong. Don't do what you know will cause harm. Don't do what will later become a problem. It is the simplest advice yet one of the most important: avert the danger before it arises. This can be done at any and every moment.

This act to avert the danger that has not yet come is rarely a single large act but, more often, the culmination of many small actions, thoughts, decisions, and intentions. Life is the culmination of many tiny moments rather than one large act. Life is a flow of moments. People think they can have success by doing something great. In reality, it is all the little moments that lead up to the one that really makes a difference.

There are levels of this. The most profound is on the level of consciousness. When you transcend, the almighty power of consciousness can help to solve problems and avert danger before it arises. In the Science of Creative Intelligence, Maharishi gives a principle for this: *"The field of all possibilities is the source of all solutions."*

By reaching a level beyond the limitations of thinking and environment, solutions to intractable problems are found. Danger can be averted before you are even aware of it. This is the most important level of the Yoga Sutra verse: *"Avert the danger that has not yet come."*

On a more surface level, we can avert the danger that has not yet come by not doing what we know to be wrong. If saying something unkind will hurt someone else—don't say it. If taking a trip brings some exceptional risk—avoid it. If you aren't sure if your action is right—wait and see if it becomes clearer.

To avert the danger that has not yet come is rarely about one big, valiant moment. More often, it is about the little moments—the daily choices of thoughts, behavior, company, routine, diet, and other factors that, over time, help to avert the danger.

Little Moments Make a Day

The big moments of life are not what are important. The graduations, marriages, new houses, new cars, vacations, and other highlights are landmarks. Instead, the big moments are the outer facts —like the clothes we wear to cover the inner reality. What happens between those big moments and leading up to them build a life and changes the course of destiny.

The moments that matter are the little ones: the ones that are wrinkly, raw, beautiful, and yes, sometimes shocking or ugly. These moments can be a kind smile, a held door, a brush of the hand, or loving encouragement.

Or it can be our own omission or failure. How often do we let one little moment color our whole day? Perhaps it was forgetting to do something we promised, an unkind word, or a lack of attention. Those simple slip-ups, in moments, can change the direction of the whole day. The moments that have the deepest impact are often unplanned and unexpected, and yet their repercussions ripple through our lives.

The power of these moments is amplified when we are under duress. This can be stress in our environment from work, family, health, emotional or financial pressures, or it can be internal pressures.

Of course, there are ways to manage stress—from Transcendental Meditation to various forms of therapy, counseling, supplements, and medication. All of these can, and do, help. But what about looking at it from the other perspective?

How to Use Little Moments

If one 2-minute episode can color our whole day, what about using a 2-minute episode to color our whole day for good? What about using small moments to build up ourselves and everyone around us?

Small moments of kindness to ourselves and others can have an incredible impact on well-being and overall happiness. By taking the time to offer moments of love, compassion, and kindness to others, we start to feel better about ourselves.

Science says that our brain chemistry changes when we smile. The physical act of smiling changes our mood and emotions. Therefore, just the simple act of smiling at a stranger will have a positive effect.

I sometimes challenge myself to smile at, and make eye contact with, every person I pass in a day. I really want to see each person and connect, even for a moment. That can be a challenge, but it pulls me out of my shell and it can do the same for you. Try it and see how you feel.

Moments make a life. They are the time we take to help our children with their homework or throw a baseball with them after work. They are the time when we cuddle with our partners rather than staring at our phones.

We cannot control most moments; we can only respond. If we are judging in any way, good or bad, we are not responding to the moment. In that brief period of time, when we are truly present, we are not thinking of the past or hoping for the future. There is only the reality being lived in that moment.

The response we have comes from the heart. When the heart is full, the response is full of love without judgment. The heart seeks to unify and protect. There is no space for criticism or judgment. The ultimate "safe space" is a loving heart. A loving heart, a heart full of love, can find only the ability to love more. The response to any moment is love.

Unconditional love opens the door to happiness and peace. Lasting happiness and peace are found in the unbounded field of consciousness. They are the deepest essence of who we all are and who we are born to become. When we are settled and full of love, we automatically respond to the moment with the kindest and most loving part of ourselves.

Life-changing Moments

Another life-changing and perspective-changing moment came just last year. I sat to meditate, innocently, not expecting anything. Suddenly, I observed from inside the top of my head an opening to see stars, planets, and even galaxies. I felt so much bliss. There was a feeling of something soothing and powerful pouring on my head—almost like a river of water. In that moment, I saw my small, individual body and the universe melt together, taking different forms of Divine Beings. There was one in particular that I recognized. But the power of this unity, this form, was so overwhelming. I felt—not even saw, but experienced—"I am the universe."

My whole perspective changed in a moment. The experience was so simple and so powerful that it left me with a feeling of happiness—bliss—that carried over through that day and into the next. It was a concrete reminder that life can change for the better in a moment.

Whether you've had a life-changing experience or not, these flashes of our true nature can happen at any moment. You do not have to wait for something outside. It is the inner Being, our own inner intelligence, there, ready to awaken at any moment. Life is not just in chronological days; it is to use every moment for the best. What we do with the little moments becomes life.

When you use the power of small moments, the power of now, these moments can become something great. Indeed, many people experience big or "a-ha!" moments in their lives.

In those moments, the full potential of the mind is used. Meditation can connect you to a level where you find more peak experiences—more moments of "a-ha!" For everyone, those moments of revelation can occur. The opportunities for the expression of life are waiting to be seen and experienced, at every moment.

The Magician

Long ago, in ancient Persia, there was a skilled magician. With the simplest props, he could perform fantastic magic tricks like making people appear to levitate or pulling a bouquet of flowers from his sleeve. He could even appear to bring on storms and change the weather.

The magician was so skilled that kings and farmers sought him out, asking him to fix their problems. Some would ask for wealth or fame, while others would ask for rain to come onto their parched lands or happiness to come into the hearts of their people.

Sometimes, the magician would grant the wish, but most of the time, he would ask the person to go home. He would direct them to sit in a certain spot, at a certain time, and think about their wish. Then he would ask them to imagine it being fulfilled. He asked them to forget their worry and for ten minutes a day to be unabashedly happy.

The people said, "We cannot do that. That is too much time. That is too difficult."

"Do you want your wish?" the magician would ask. "Then that is my price."

Some went away assuming the magician was a crazy old man. But some decided to try. After all, what did they have to lose?

Those people would come back to the magician later in amazement as they found their wishes came true. They found paths to happiness, wealth, fame, or all they desired.

"How did you do it?" They would push the magician to answer. "We want to know your trick!"

"Ah," the magician would say, "but you already know it. It was not I who changed your destiny, but you."

"But you perform magic, we've seen you!" cried the people.

"Yes," the magician would reply. "I do perform magic tricks. But the real magic is in the moment. The real magic is in your mind. The price I asked you to pay, of belief and happiness, tipped the scale. Moments of genuine happiness always do. This is the real magic and the real secret I have now taught you."

The people would leave in disbelief. How could it be so simple and so obvious? But for the fortunate few who learned to use even a few moments each day for happiness, the magic was real.

The magician is one great teacher of living in the moment. He is a reminder that everyday happiness is its own kind of miracle. The difference between a happy life and an unhappy life has nothing to do with riches, fame, the weather, or any other outer circumstance—it comes from inside. We all, within ourselves, have with time and attention the power to make that inner happiness blossom into a field of beauty.

Another story of living in the moment comes from India and the great King Janak.

The Rishi-King

A Rishi is a seer, one who sees the ultimate reality. A Rishi-King is a ruler who sees the ultimate reality and rules established in universal wisdom. This is someone who embodies the highest ideals of bringing good to all people. The phrase Maharishi used for a Rishi-King is someone who is able to bring all good to everyone.

King Janak, a great king in the Vedic tradition, is known as a Rishi-King. King Janak was famous for his just and wise rule and for being the father of Sita, the embodiment of divine feminine power.

One day, a young sage called Shukadeva appeared at the doors of the palace asking for King Janak's blessings for enlightenment. King Janak gazed into his eyes, heart, and mind and told Shukadeva that he would give him enlightenment.

But first, King Janak explained, "I will take you on a tour of the castle. I want to show you all the rooms throughout the palace. Please hold this ghee lamp—a small candle made of oil—and make sure the flame does not go out. Some of the rooms have big drafts; please make sure the lamp stays lit."

And with that, King Janak began to lead Shukadeva around the castle. He described the rooms and their history, their spiritual power, and their great opulence. King Janak and Shukadeva moved from room to room for hours, with Shukadeva always minding the ghee lamp.

At the end of the tour, back in the entry hall, King Janak turned to Shukadeva and asked, "Did you enjoy the tour?"

"To be honest," replied Shukadeva, "I couldn't see much because I was so focused on this ghee lamp. It took all of my attention to make sure it didn't go out."

"Ah," replied King Janak, "then you did enjoy the tour. You learned the lesson I was teaching you. You asked me for enlightenment. There is no secret to enlightenment, just a one-pointed focus on the master's directions. Just as you have been focusing on this lamp, live each moment focused on your path. With the blessings of your master and your unwavering focus, you will find your goal."

And with that, King Janak sent Shukadeva on his way.

We are, in many ways, like a small part of Shukadeva searching for enlightenment. We say we want one goal or another but become so distracted that we cannot focus on it. Our attention wavers, but unlike a ghee lamp, we don't see our goals being snuffed out. Shukadeva was successful because he gave every second his full attention. Full attention in the moment builds momentum enabling one to take advantage of opportunities and attain success.

Setting Goals

Especially as women, with our skill of multitasking, it can be easy to juggle so many balls in the air that nothing ever gets our full attention. Take time, slow down, and focus on what you want. Devote your full attention to it even for just a few minutes.

Almost all goals can be achieved with consistency. You can reach a very high level through sheer persistence. If you want to lose weight, get healthy, secure a better job, be a more present parent, run a marathon, write a book, sail around the world, or any other goal, you can achieve it. Break it into small steps and then act.

People will tell you to set SMART goals—goals that are specific, measurable, attainable, realistic, and time-based. If that works for you, great! But if that seems overwhelming, take just the time-based aspect and make it realistic. Here are some examples (choose any goal that works for you as this is merely to get you started):

- Set a goal to meditate for 20 minutes twice a day. This will make all your other goals easier.
- Set a goal to have a deep conversation or connect with a loved one for even 15 minutes a day.
- Set a goal to exercise three times a week and mark it in your calendar.
- Set a goal to write in a journal for even a few minutes daily.
- Set a goal to read a book for 30 minutes daily instead of watching TV.

Whatever goal you choose, give it a timeframe that is small enough to be attainable most of the time, and then don't beat yourself up if you fall short. Get up and start again.

The idea is to take a few moments each day and focus on the direction of the future you envision. Maybe you don't know what that is. See what ideas and inspiration come. The secret of this thread is both focused attention and space. Because the moments pass us by so quickly, it takes time to cultivate our consciousness, heart, and mind to respond to the moment with the profundity of wisdom and joy that will change any circumstance.

At the same time, we can use moments to create patterns that will lead to greater opportunities. The two go hand in hand.

Just as Maharishi has stated that it is a pathless path, he also said, *"God helps those who help themselves."* Be on the path, experience the unexpected possibilities of every day, and cultivate your greater ability to respond to those moments. Start moving from consciousness and from conscious action toward the future and moments you desire.

Like the magician sending people away to create magic, we all have the power to create magic in moments from our own happiness, and ultimately, the depth of consciousness that can unfold all possibilities and make all that we want a reality.

Action Steps

Here are some reflections, ideas, and actions to absorb and experience this thread of wisdom:

1. **Ask Yourself.** When in the last few months did a moment or a few minutes change your day for the better or for worse? When has one of those moments had longer-reaching impacts on your life? How did it make you feel in the moment? How do you see that pivotal moment after some time?

2. **Reflect and Write.** Have you had a chance (intentionally or unintentionally) to change someone else's life in a moment? How did that feel? How could you make it better?

3. **Remember.** Think of five "a-ha" moments or peak experiences in your life. How was that moment, which could have been an instant or a few minutes, significant for your whole life? Do you realize it was more of your full being present in that moment that brought the difference?

When you have the habit of transcending, any moment of your day after transcendence could become a peak moment because your full creative potential is more available in your daily life.

4. Reflect. How do you see the two messages, "stay focused on your path" and "live each moment," combining in the life of someone you admire? How can they work together in your own life?

Now already ready as yourself, awaken new absolute totality.

Thread 17: You Already Know the Answer

Even in a book filled with advice and spiritual observations and in a world where everyone is always looking outside for answers, you already know the answer.

While this is a glib statement and it might appear to not always be true, it is. You do already know the answer—in your deepest, wisest, most settled level of yourself. Maybe it was that deepest, wisest self that suggested you pick up this book to remind you of that!

Very near the level of pure, unbounded consciousness within each of us, there is an expressed level of intelligence that knows everything. Maharishi expressed this as *Ritam Bhara Pragya,* or *"a state of intelligence which knows everything and which registers only the truth."* It is the name given to the innate wisdom within each of us.

This level of intelligence, which knows only the truth, is a lively field of all possibilities. In knowing and seeing the truth, we can use it in daily life. Many people will interpret the term *Ritam Bhara Pragya* as the ability to fulfill desires. This is also the right interpretation. When we connect to the level that knows the truth, where we already know the answer, nature works to support the fulfillment of all evolutionary desires.

Listen to Your Intuition

When you transcend, intuition grows. To say that you already know the answer doesn't mean the logic or reasoning you've built to ignore that answer is right. It means that truth lives in each of us, and only by allowing ourselves to listen will we hear the answer. We can all be like an inattentive spouse to inner wisdom. It is there speaking all the time, only we have become accustomed to tuning it out.

This thread of wisdom is especially important for me, as there have been times in my life when not listening to my inner voice put someone I love in danger. One time, someone close to me was out walking, slipped on some leaves, and fell headfirst off an embankment in an area without cell phone service.

Something felt wrong, but my logic reasoned that he must have received an important call and would phone me later. Still, I called and called, trying to get through, but got no response. *Oh, well*, I thought, *he will call when he can*. Over an hour later, I started to worry. So I took my bike out into the forest looking for him. I found him, barely able to walk, with bruised ribs. He had been walking alone in the cold for almost two hours, having extracted himself from the dangerous embankment with no one to help.

If I had listened to my intuition, I could have found him in a short time. Instead, he was alone and afraid, unable to even call the emergency services. I felt responsible because I hasn't listened to what my intuition was telling me.

The moral of this story is that you already know the answer. You know what is right in the deepest recesses of your intuition and Being. Don't let your intellect run circles around you or convince you to avoid what you should do.

Using Intuition

Maharishi has said that *"the field of all possibilities is the source of all solutions"* and that has been my experience. Many times, when I have a problem or something worrying me, I sit to meditate and forget everything. After meditation, an idea or solution will come to me. It is so easy and automatic. For big problems, sometimes it takes a few days, but a solution always comes.

A flashier example of "you already know the answer" happened to me when I was a university undergraduate. We were required to take standardized tests for the university's accreditation. One of the standardized tests was trigonometry. While I always wished I'd taken trig, I never actually had. In other words, objectively, I really didn't know the answers. So I decided to test my intuition. It helped that most of the questions were multiple choice.

When the standardized test results came back, I discovered that I did exceptionally well. I don't remember the exact score now, but I believe it was in the 95th percentile or better. I was so excited, not because of the good score that (should have) proven my skills in trigonometry, but because it demonstrated the skill of my intuition. I didn't try to understand the problems, I just went with my inner vision.

While that was a dramatic example, there are countless others that occur day-to-day. I choose this thread both because of its deep truth and as a reminder to myself. We all need regular reminders that we are never lost at sea without a compass. We do, in fact, already know the answer. We are the source of all solutions.

I often feel that knowing intelligence as a nudge inside. Something that says, "That is it!" Usually, I don't understand the logic. But with time I'm getting better at listening when my inner wisdom suggests a direction.

How to See What Is Right

I like to use a simple test to see whether I am listening to my intuition or building logic that "seems" right. If I am doing mental gymnastics to justify something, I know I am avoiding the truth. The truth is clear, simple, and direct. It is already there. That truth can also be a decision on what is right or wrong. If you have a thought that at the moment seems illogical but feels right, often that is also the truth.

In my time helping other people take direction in their lives, I have heard countless people explain in detail the pros and cons of various options. In the end, they usually choose what they had in mind all along. When we are debating in mental turmoil, it is usually because what we want appears to conflict with what we think we should do. The two appear mutually exclusive.

When we really listen to the answer we already know within ourselves, it all becomes obvious. The simplest answer is almost always the right answer. This is true in art, science, and every area of life.

When we look closely and listen, it is usually the intellect choosing to make complications out of simplicity. Truth is simple and elegant. How many times, in all areas of life, have we proclaimed that we thought it couldn't be that simple? It is that simple. You already know the answer.

The ability to reach the answer comes back to unfolding full human potential. When we access the field of consciousness and awaken our full brain potential, we access more subtle, powerful, and refined levels of thinking. That which previously seemed difficult becomes easy. The simple and elegant truth becomes obvious.

What is the practical application of this chapter? It is two-fold. First, transcend. Experience the finer levels of thought. Access your full mental potential. Begin to train your brain and utilize its vast potential.

Second, begin to listen. Listen to the voice of your intuition. Listen to the voice of self-doubt or worry and ask what it is really trying to tell you. Listen to your gut feeling telling you to do something—or not.

The habit of checking in to listen, even for a moment, along with the ability to open your full mental potential, will open new doors and worlds. The answers were never missing. Now you can begin to access them.

This thread of wisdom comes with a warning about humility. Your inner wisdom may be telling you one thing, while your partner or child's inner wisdom is saying another. In many cases, they are both right. The humility to listen means not only giving yourself the grace to see the answer but also respecting the answers and wisdom that are coming to you from the environment.

It is not an exclusive telephone line to wisdom in your brain. We are all connected. Your brain and my brain can reach the same level of intuition. Nature can speak to you in an infinite number of ways.

Listen to the messages nature is giving you through all sources and situations. They are not judgments or dictates but whispers of guidance and support. The path is often obscure; the answer can be even more unclear. But those willing to listen will find the answer is already there.

In the Vedic tradition, there is a science called Nimita that shows the connection of apparently disconnected events. Nimita looks at how these events, like the landing of a crow or a change in the direction of the wind, connect or give hints about what is to come. By simple movements and events, those with an understanding of Nimita can derive a lot of information.

Nimita has been used for thousands of years. It is outer whispers from nature to confirm inner intuition or guidance. I've often used the simplest values of Nimita (like the direction of an animal crossing my path) to guide decisions and have seen repeatedly that nature knows, and speaks, what I had not anticipated with my intellect. Wise scholars use Nimita for everything from agriculture and understanding how a growing season will turn out to predicting the health and well-being of both people and pets or livestock.

The Antidote Always Grows Near

To give an analogy, in herbalism they say that the antidote to any poisonous plant is found growing near it. Nature provides the poison and the cure. In the same way, the answer to any question is found growing near it. Nature provides the question and the answer.

In all natural medicines, and especially in Ayurveda, it is said that a vaidya (an ayurvedic doctor) can see the plants growing in an area and know the diseases of the people living there. That is because nature provides the cure for the disease in the area where the people are afflicted. A plant that reduces blood pressure may grow in an area where that is a problem, while another plant that increases fertility may grow where some people are struggling to have children.

These examples of ancient wisdom all reflect the reality that we know the answer in our deepest intuition, and nature also provides clues and hints outside if we start to look and listen. The key to finding the answer, like finding the correct antidote, is alertness and the ability to listen. Observe and be present. Accept what comes not as judgment but as a gift of guidance.

At first, it may seem unnatural. You may only do it for a few minutes each day. But what you put your attention on grows.

With attention, the answers will become more obvious. Like those optical illusions that you can only see after staring for some time, looking deeply into your heart and mind for what you are creating or seeking will reveal answers you asked for—and those that you didn't.

How is this possible? It is possible because of the power of consciousness within each of us. This universal level of power and intelligence within us knows the answer and is always ready to provide it. Maharishi has also called it the "cosmic computer." It is a level of intelligence in nature that can keep billions of planets in millions of galaxies spinning in perfect balance while also ensuring the delicate balance of millions of species here on earth—and the harmonious existence of every other planet and galaxy.

It is the same intelligence of nature, encoded in our DNA, that takes us from a tiny zygote to a fully-formed human being who cannot only think and act independently but can tap into this universal source of power within.

Chiti Shakti Riti

In the Yoga Sutras (4.34) it says:

$$\text{चितिशक्तिरिति}$$

"Power of Consciousness Alone Is."

I capitalized each word for emphasis. Power of consciousness is the power of the universe, the power of the multitude of universes that exist. It is the driving force beyond space, time, and causation. And it is the power that ensures that every apple seed grows into an apple tree, that Earth continues to orbit around the sun and the moon around the Earth, and that billions of galaxies remain in perfect precision while the universe continues to expand.

That is the power that "alone is." And this power of consciousness, this infinite magnitude of intelligence that calculates everything automatically and instantaneously is embedded in each of us—it is the depth of who we are. All that we think of as our unique characteristics are expressions of this power of consciousness.

From the way we look, to the way we act, think, feel, who we love, or where we live, the underlying reality of all of this is the power of consciousness. It is not something else. It is not something outside. It is the deepest reality of who we all are. The power of consciousness, the deepest, wisest level of our own selves, is the reason you already know the answer.

Almost everyone at certain moments of life will have flashes of intuition or perception that allows them to better understand what they have to do. That wisdom is already inside you. The ability to choose the right path can be made more accessible with the habit of experiencing the settled state of consciousness and dipping into the source of all intuition.

The answer to your current question, and all others, is already within you. The power of consciousness is there, waiting to be accessed, waiting to be seen, heard, and realized. And from there, you already know, and will always know, the answer to any and every question.

The Story of Ilia Teresa

The story of Ilia Teresa is a reminder to listen to your intuition and believe what you hear. Ilia Teresa was an ancient Kogi medicine woman, a rare female visionary of the high Sierra Nevada Mountains of Northern Colombia. The Kogi people have lived there for thousands of years. They say their record goes back "to the beginning of time."

Their way of life has been unchanged for many thousands of years. Each generation is born and learns to live in harmony with nature. They see Mother Nature as the divine mother nourishing all. They learn these rhythms and see themselves as the protectors of all. They are the Elder Brothers of the world—and the elder sisters. Their mountain home, known to them as Gonawindua, is called the heart of the world.

From the heart of the world, they are protectors of us all and of mother earth. We, the rest of the world, are the Younger Brothers and Sisters, sent away from the heart of the world. It is their role to guide and protect humanity from its heart.

While the medicine healers and seers are traditionally men, the supreme figure in their tradition is female—the great mother or Aluna. The great mother is the creator and force of life in every animate and inanimate object.

They have a special tradition to bring out the inner vision of those entrusted with guiding the tribe. To become a spiritual healer or Mamo, at birth these children are put into a dark cave where they are given food and water but no light until their inner vision dawns. This can take eight or more years. Once they can see from the inside, they are trained to guide and protect the community and the whole world. This training is the ultimate "believe in yourself and your intuition."

Although boys are normally selected for this role, there are times when girls are chosen before birth. Ilia Teresa was one such girl, born about a hundred years ago. This is her story.

When my mother, herself a girl of about 18 cycles around the sun, fell pregnant with me in the second month after the harvest moon, Itepo, the Mamo for our village, and by that time an aged man of about 75 cycles of the sun, saw something with his inner vision. He felt an aura of light and a child appear.

"I am Aluna," the child said. "Now I am taking this form to bring a new time for our people. They are being pulled by the machines and comforts of the Younger Brother. They are being taken from the heart of the world. They need to stay and protect the world from ignorance. I will come as a girl child. I will be the Mamo you train. I am both your Aluna and your disciple. I will be born to Anali in 10 moons, on the full moon day after the equinox. You will call me Ilia, with the 'I' of your name and the 'A' of her mother. She is the child to save the heart of the world."

With both fear and lightness in his heart, Itepo moved with slow, heavy steps toward my mother's hut. He found her outside, sitting by the fire and tending to the food. He told her of his vision and began to make preparations for the special Mamo hut that would be used after my birth.

And so I came into the world out of darkness into darkness. The hut was warm and full of soft scents wafting through. Sometimes I smelled something sweet and other times something thick and darker, what you would call smoke. I felt the cool breezes in the evening, and each day, Itepo would come to guide me.

By the age of three, I understood the deep meditation and began to connect with Aluna. It was brief at first and usually completely dark. But I continued, for there was nothing else to do. One day I saw a flash of light as I sat there. It was golden, brilliant, and streaking. What was that?

The cycles of warmer and cooler, outer light and dark continued, but I mostly saw only the inner darkness. I knew not of the prophecy or the guidance Itepo had received, only the world of the small cave, all in the dark.

By the time I was seven years old, as you would count, I still saw nothing. Darkness surrounded me day and night. I had learned the routine of when the food would arrive and when Itepo would come to check on me. I slept more and more because the heaviness of sitting to practice seemed to be too much.

By this time, most Mamo boys start to have visions. It builds gradually for them. But other than that early flash, I had seen nothing. Itepo went to Aluna and prayed, concerned he had made the wrong choice. By this time, he was a very old man, much older than most Mamo when they returned to Aluna. He didn't have time to train another, and yet I saw nothing.

Aluna replied to the prayers and offerings of Itepo, appearing as the same child he had seen eight years before. "You have asked, and now I will be awakened. The child has the character of deepest peace. In that darkness, every fiber of her heart is filled with my love and peace. Now when she sees, she will see all."

At that moment, I was lying in my cave, but I became overtaken by light. There was so much brilliance. So many variations of colors. The colors spoke, danced, and made new formations. I could see so many forms of creatures all speaking. And I could see the great Aluna guiding the world.

I felt no more a child in a cave. I became one with the rainbow of colors, of beings, of destinies moving together in Aluna. I felt the ecstasy of bliss like I could not imagine. And I felt so much love for this Aluna. I felt I had been hidden so I would bloom at this moment.

The power rose within me, and I became Aluna. That, I realized, was my real initiation. I was no longer Ilia, but Ilia with Aluna within her. It was then, from the time of awakening, that it was time to leave my cave and serve my tribe and the heart of the world. I would guide the Elder Brothers of the World to protect the world.

From that moment, the inner vision became more powerful, more tangible, and real than the outer vision. When my people were looking for where to plant the seeds, I would guide them to where Aluna told me they would grow best. When my people needed fish, I would ask Aluna and we would choose the spot that would not harm but would bring all that was needed.

When it was time to support the Younger Brother and protect Mother Earth, I returned to my childhood cave, and awakened day and night for a year, took the power of Aluna to bless the world.

Like that my life passed, and Aluna took a new form. A new Mamo joined the tribe, gifted from Aluna. The child I trained stayed in the dark, as I had before him, until the inner vision dawned.

You say to trust your intuition or listen to your inner voice. My story is a reminder that intuition or inner voice is the real vision. Just as the earth has layers you know about—from the surface crust to the molten center—and layers within the land—from the highest point of the mountain peaks to the depths of the ocean— life has layers you can see and layers you cannot see.

What you think is real is but a small whisper of reality, like a leaf dancing on the wind, telling neither the story of the tree at its source nor the wind carrying it to its goal. Your intuition is where you remember Aluna. Your inner vision is where the Little Brothers and Sisters can become the Big Brothers and Sisters and guide the world. We are all one. We are all one family. See this vision and be one with us. You already know the answer.

I share the story of Ilia Teresa because we are all as if in a cave of darkness without our intuition. But the light of intuition is there, waiting to shine. Maybe it will take only a moment and a flash, or perhaps it can take years to see it clearly. But the power of consciousness is already awake, already lively, waiting for us to see, experience, and realize our own inner vision and our power to create from there.

Ritam Bhara Pragya and *Chiti Shakti Riti* are, in reality, two sides of one coin with one eternal message. The power of consciousness alone is moving and guiding each of us. The level of intelligence which knows only the truth is our own inner intelligence—this same consciousness reflected in its finest expressions. How we use it and when we choose to listen is up to us. But it is already there.

In the words of Lao Tzu, *"At the center of your Being, you have the answer; you know who you are and you know what you want."*

We know it inside. And for hints, nature is already telling you the answers if you can read the signs. Inner guidance and outer guidance are, in fact, one reality of wisdom. The supreme wisdom of the ancient sages is not far—it is within you if only you have the ability and patience to listen.

Action Steps

Here are some reflections, ideas, and actions to absorb and experience this thread of wisdom:

1. Consider. Whenever you notice a thought that seems out of place or illogical, instead of ignoring it, consider it and listen. Just innocently have the intention to listen to your intuition and the answers it gives you.

2. Reflect and Write. When in the last month have you felt or seen an answer in advance? When did you feel guided from within in a specific direction? How has your intuition helped you in your life?

3. Remember. Have you experienced guidance coming from someone in your environment? How did you respond in the moment? How would you guide yourself at that time to respond with the perspective you have now?

4. Reflect. Mark five moments in your life, in any area of interest, where you did something not based on your reasoning but on an impulse that turned out to be very successful. Do you notice that when you were more peaceful and restful you were able to listen more to yourself?

5. All-knowing Moments. There is a place in our own Being that knows everything. Have you ever experienced that and known that what you understood, concluded, or saw was correct? When was this and what happened to you when you allowed it? We can call these the all-knowing moments of life.

6. Reflect and Write. On what occasions in your life was the same thing (guidance, suggestion, an offer, etc.) brought to you a few times from apparently unconnected sources? In those moments, could you understand it as a message from nature? Did you recognize it? From this, do you feel more clearly that there is something inside you that can know everything needed for your evolution?

Having revealed enlightened eternity, manifest all that you can be.

Thread 18: Even the Hardest Rocks Melt with Love

"Don't forget love;
It will bring all the madness you need to unfurl yourself across the
universe."
~ Mirabai

The final thread of wisdom comes back to love. The power of love is like the ocean, moving, flowing, peaceful, and yet powerful. The heart, with its peace, can reach where the mind and intellect can only fathom. This oceanic power of love can gently, gradually melt even the hardest rocks.

Why can love melt rocks? In the words of Lao Tzu, *"The softest things in the world overcome the hardest things in the world."* Also, *"Water is the softest thing, yet it can penetrate mountains and earth. This shows clearly the principle of softness overcoming hardness."*

Nearly nothing in the world is as soft and fluid as water. And yet, for dissolving hard and inflexible rock, nothing surpasses it. In the same way, only love can be so gentle and simultaneously strong. Only love has the power to withstand the hurricane of life and the gentle touch to make the flower of the heart blossom. Only love can heal the unhealable. Love can melt the hardest rocks and create miracles.

Simultaneous gentleness and strength is the unique miracle of love. Love, by its very being, reminds us constantly that we are always open, soft, and gentle but also possess incredible strength. We have the resilience to overcome whatever life may bring, no matter how difficult. To live in love is to overcome the hard rocks of our hearts. By conquering ourselves in love, we conquer the universe.

From where does such a tremendous, unfathomable power of love grow? It grows in the heart of the seeker of good. Love grows in the heart of the adorer of life. Love grows with reverence and humility. Humility is like fertilizer to love. And love, for its part, can grow from tiny cracks in the most inhospitable hearts where it appears to have no hope. Love is invincible.

It is the gentleness and humility of love that makes it invincible. Love is without ego. There is no need to want or declare. Love is unity. Love is the joy of surrendering and finding, whatever is there, is full of love. When love flows, life flows. Humility is the quality that allows us to develop more love. It is only by holding something, or someone, as greater than oneself that the fullness of love can flow.

In this, the ego is like a trap or tripwire. The ego declares its beauty, its power, and its accomplishments. The ego separates and divides. Love flows and unifies. From a humble heart, the ego is pacified. Then love conquers all. Even the trap of the ego is enveloped in the soft embrace of love.

The intellect can also challenge love. It will ask what have you done? What is your position, degree, or title? Who are you? Love doesn't ask, love sees. Love knows that it is not what one has done but what one is and how much one has loved that matters in this life.

All the money, power, and accomplishments in the world mean nothing in the eyes of the divine if a person cannot stand with an open heart and say, I have fully loved. I gave my best to live in love.

It is to love and not to have loved because love is not a destination and has no end. Love can blossom, but pure love never ends, not in this life or the next, not because of wrong actions or wrong intentions. Circumstances change, relationships change, but love never ends.

Who we are is far more important than what we do. The purity of the heart is more powerful than the strength of the mind. To live a life with a full heart—with abundant inner life, in giving the best to life—is to have lived in love. No caste, no wealth, no status, or diploma can confer the richness of the inner life in love.

Each of these threads is important to my life, but this is, in some ways, the most important. The hardest rocks I am referring to are hearts hardened and covered by intellects, egos, or goals that don't allow love to flow. My heart, 15 years ago, was one such heart. I was so focused on accomplishing my goals that I didn't yet see how integrating love was the greatest power of all. Just as the sea can erode solid rock, so love can dissolve the obstacles we have within ourselves that we cannot see.

I was focused on my intellect and memory, appearances, lectures, accomplishments, and even the rigidity of my daily routine—all the outer paraphernalia that I thought would help me reach my goal—enlightenment. To be sure, many of those qualities helped me tremendously. Focus on routine, desire to learn, and the wish to understand and attune to the Master's thinking are precious tools on the path.

But without the sweetness of love, it was like trying to build the Garden of Eden in the Sahara Desert. The fullness of love is not the flower. Life itself is the flower that blooms with love. Because of love, the desert of the pursuit of enlightenment becomes a verdant oasis of beauty unfolding itself. This is the final thread of wisdom and the deepest and most important secret of all. I am writing about something that is so enormous, so tender, and so beautiful that it is beyond words.

Our greatest strength is our greatest tenderness. Our beauty is in what we give and what we radiate. It happens spontaneously. All we have to do is not chase the purity of love away by intellect, agenda, or routine so that infinity blossoms. The solution, as with so much in life, is to take it as it comes and enjoy what comes our way.

The Rishi Recognized

There are countless stories in the Vedic tradition of wise teachers or seers, called Rishi, disguising themselves as ordinary people. In one such story, the wise teacher took the form of a beggar from the lowest social class. He went onto the streets to ask the people to help him, thus testing the purity of their hearts.

Many people passed him by, put off by his dirty, bedraggled appearance. But one young woman took pity and felt love in her heart. She brought him food and offered him a place to stay with her family.

The Rishi, seeing the purity of her heart, appeared in his true form and blessed her with wisdom and enlightenment. This story is a reminder that an open, humble heart creates the receptivity and possibilities for all good in life.

All religions and spiritual paths have their own variation of this concept: help those who are less fortunate, keep an open heart, and unexpected blessings will come to you. Sometimes the benefit is not so obvious. It can appear later in life. But the purity to give love with an open heart is a blessing that brings more blessings. For this reason, love—the process of being humble and loving in and of itself—is a process of transformation.

Love Changes

The heart melts when it flows in love. When consciousness expands, and with it the depth and power of thinking and feeling expand, love also expands. The two go hand in hand. Like the mind, reaching its unbounded depths, a heart unable to reach the infinite is bound. Caught in boundaries, love appears like a superficial quality.

That is where the ideas of falling in and out of love, or that love changes, come from. Love, in its essential nature, is unbounded. The heart, in its purity, is unlimited. It is stress and strain, limitations and conditioning that leads us to believe that which is unbounded can be confined within limits.

When unbounded love gets caught in boundaries without the humility to go beyond those boundaries, the love appears to stop. But the essence and power of love can never be stopped.

When the awareness becomes unbounded and unlimited, the flow of love is unbounded and unlimited. The gatekeepers of the heart, asleep from lack of use, are awakened as the floodgates of love are thrown open. Unbounded heart and unbounded consciousness —one opens the door for the other.

Like two sides of the same coin or two directions of the same path, love expands consciousness and consciousness expands the heart to love. Higher consciousness can be reached without love, but it is very dry, like a desert of infinity. Emptiness. Love floods the desert with the nectar of life, making the hard ground blossom. Love takes the desert blooms and scatters their fragrance on the wind. Love is, and becomes, more and more each day.

There is no end to love, as there is no beginning to consciousness. One becomes the other in a continuous circle of connection. To expand consciousness is to reach all possibilities. To love, and to be loved, is to melt the rocks in the hardened heart and live those possibilities full of indescribable joy.

That is why Rumi says that *"through the heart, you can touch the sky."* The heart opens doors we didn't know existed. The process of loving lifts you up, elevating happiness, hope, purity, and passion.

Before, we were only trying to accomplish a goal or to get through the day. Now, love shows us new layers and dimensions of ourselves previously undiscovered. Through love, you can reach beyond whatever you thought you were to something greater and, in a sense, touch the sky.

For many people, this is far from their current reality. Caught in a cycle of physical need, passion, or dependence, love immediately gets captured by small boundaries. But even in the smallest of boundaries or tightest of places, given the water and fertilizer of attention, love can begin to grow.

This thread of wisdom is true whether you are divorced, separated, single, or married. It is true regardless of sexual orientation, gender, or cultural ideals. The purity of love is not dependent on outward expressions. Who you choose to love and how you choose to love them is deeply personal.

The process of loving is an internal process of the person loving. In a way, it is private even from those you love. Physical or emotional separation cannot stop love. Outward status does not determine love. Only you determine the quality of your love.

Love is the most intimate expression of your heart flowing and taking new dimensions. It moves and flows. No one else can say what is right or wrong, who you should love, or how. The heart can continue to grow along any path it is given.

Once again, it is up to each of us to write our own paths. If you had a relationship end and don't feel love, you have new opportunities to open your heart and experience the petals of your love unfolding with others. There are always paths, new opportunities, and fertile soil for the tender petals of the heart to unfold.

Love is Unbounded

In the biggest sense we've been discussing, the nature of love is unbounded. This type of love is without boundaries and without judgment. All the traditional cultural norms and requirements do not exist here. All the outer paraphernalia of expressing love does not justify or intensify love. Love can be shown in a million ways, big and small. The secret of love remains in the heart. When you love, you choose how to express it. You choose how and when you can touch the sky.

The path is to look around. See those in your life who bring you joy. See those in your life that you love. Once you see, let your love flow. Rather than an attitude of indifference or trying to hide away the flow of love out of self-protection, protect the self with a flowing heart.

Quietly love from wherever you are, whatever your relationship, and watch how you change—and how your life blossoms. Like many things in life, love exists with opposites. On the one hand, we're saying to choose love. On the other hand, love is not a choice and is not something that can be controlled. Love chooses those it deems worthy. To be worthy is to have a receptive heart.

In the words of Khalil Gibran, *"And think not you can direct the course of love, for love, if it finds you worthy, directs your course."*

Love becoming the director of your course means that love takes over your thinking, feeling, and Being. It touches the core of who you are and transforms you in unexpected ways. Love does not take; love always gives.

While this reality is beautiful and powerful beyond words, that does not mean the path of love is always clear. It is often rocky and difficult. To receive a supreme gift often comes with its extreme challenges. Every rose has thorns. Usually, the bigger the rose, the bigger the thorns.

This is one of the lessons of love. In directing your course, you find not only the miracle of love but the patience and strength to bear all that may come with it. It doesn't mean that love always brings difficulties. But there is a principle in nature: when light or purity rises, darkness or ignorance rises up to meet it.

As love increases in your life, the power of the purity of love will often bring with it other, unexpected events. When there is light, darkness tries to remove it.

The answer to this whispered through the corridors of time and amplified now by Maharishi is, *"Truth alone triumphs."*

That which is pure, that which reflects truth, will ultimately arise victorious and protected. Light will win over darkness. In the end, the power of purity, the power of love, can conquer any obstacle.

In the book, *Love and God*, Maharishi explains, *"The strength of love makes one tender and firm, makes one weak in wrong and powerful in right, brings forgiveness in authority and grace of fields of life. And this is the destiny of the fortunate. Love is the fortune of the fortunate. Abundance of love is the goal of all destiny."*

This is the destiny of us all. To love and flow in love. To be powerful is right and compassionate in moments of authority. To naturally live a life of Grace.

Maharishi continues, *"Fortunate are those, whose hearts flow in love. A loving heart, a heart full of love, is the precious essence of human life. And that when it flows in abundance, when it flows in unbounded tidal waves of bliss, it is the glory of the Supreme, the blessing of Mother Divine and the grace of God..."*

In this, Maharishi takes love on a path directly to the divine. To live in love is to have a higher power, a divine reality. To be alive in love is to bring the divine to earth. This is the message of this thread. Nothing is impossible through love. The power of love is infinite, and the power of transformation through love is also unlimited.

The Story of Laila and Majnu

The story of Laila and Majnu is a tender reminder that love can make the impossible possible and melt stubborn hearts and resistances. It has been told by Swami Rama, Swami Muktananda, and other wise seers. Here is the story of Laila and Majnu:

> *Laila was a princess; Majnu was the son of a laborer. They lived in a remote Himalayan kingdom of ancient India. Their union was forbidden, and yet neither could think of anything but each other. Their love was an impossibility.*
>
> *Majnu wandered the streets, unable to think of anything but Laila. Laila's father tried everything to dissuade her from her love of Majnu. He brought in doctors, counselors, astrologers, and more; but no one could convince her to change. He offered to take her on trips to beautiful places with cool breezes and the most exquisite scenery.*
>
> *With every offer, she would sigh and reply, "Will Majnu be there? If not, I cannot be there without him."*
>
> *Finally, to fulfill his daughter, the compassionate king offered food, clothing, and anything else needed for Majnu. He sent out an official proclamation that all shopkeepers should give Majnu whatever he needed and send the bills to the palace.*
>
> *The real Majnu took no heed, still thinking only of Laila. But thousands of others who did not want to work decided to take*

advantage of the generous king, appearing in shops across the city claiming to be Majnu.

The king, realizing what must have happened, asked his trusted minister what to do. The minister assured the king that he would take care of the situation, issuing a new proclamation: Majnu had broken the law by loving the princess. He was to be executed at the palace in the following days.

Suddenly, all those pretending to be Majnu fled the city, forgetting their new goods. Only the real Majnu appeared at the palace, so filled with his love of Laila that he could not even be bothered to fear his own death.

Laila and Majnu were so absorbed in love for each other, so deeply united, that even impossible circumstances could not keep them apart. Their attention and love were unwavering; their minds unshakeable. It was from this basis that they were able to achieve what should have been impossible and win over the king and the kingdom in their love. They were already united as one.

Love is not love for its own sake; it is a process of transformation to weave the Divine into every breath of life. Attention is a power for infinite transformation. Melted with love, purity, and deepest intention, it can move mountains and create miracles.

What impossibility do you have in your own life? What dreams are waiting, shut away? Now find the power of Majnu and Laila within you: think not in what you believe you can be but in the truth you see in your heart. Truth alone triumphs. The power to revive and renew happens at every moment with the miracle of love. Unity can be achieved not by searching outside, but by hearing the truth already spoken inside. Your love can melt any rock.

To acknowledge the creative power within your ability to love is to step onto the path of the creator and become, from today, one with the creation. As the ocean erodes granite with millennia, love in the heart can melt even the hardest rocks. Never forget the power of your love.

Miracles in Colombia

A more recent demonstration of the power of love is in the work being done in Colombia by a famous priest, Father Gabriel Mejia. Father Mejia has dedicated his life to saving more than 100,000 children from the streets and the most difficult conditions in life. The children who came to him were guerrillas in a brutal civil war; they were prostitutes, drug addicts, or living alone on the streets before they were teenagers. And their lives were transformed with the power of his love.

Father Mejia says that love is the imperial medicine to heal all the damage of life and restore all the beauty in everyone to bring each person to their real power. To accomplish that, we open the inner treasury of love. This is waiting for everyone through Transcendental Meditation.

With that, the process of loving is facilitated because the love grows from within. When the children discover the love within, it transforms their lives. The inner love and outer loving environment can transform any life. That is why Father Mejia says at the end of our life we will be judged by how much we loved.

One poignant example of this was the child guerilla brought to Father Mejia at just ten years old. He bragged that he was adept at carrying two guns or automatic rifles and shooting them at the same time. He had killed many people. As a child, he knew only war and killing. In other countries, he may have been locked up for decades or life.

Father Mejia took this boy into his rehabilitation facility where the primary process of rehabilitation is love. He provides the children a secure place and a loving environment and teaches them to find the unboundedness within through Transcendental Meditation and its advanced programs.

That child is now grown and is Father Mejia's close assistant, working with him daily to help transform the lives of thousands of others. Trust and love built a new life for the boy carrying two guns. Now he carries the tools of love and transcendence to help others. This is a demonstration of the power of love to make a person invincible. The impossible becomes possible through the power of love.

An additional element of Father Mejia's process of healing involves collective group meditation. This is something Maharishi has spoken about since the late 1960s, when he predicted that even a small percentage of the population practicing Transcendental Meditation in a group would have a positive effect on the whole society. This was first demonstrated in 1975 with cities where 1% of the population was practicing TM. It was later demonstrated that it only takes the square root of 1% of the population practicing the advanced programs of TM to have a similar positive effect on societal trends.

Since then, over 53 peer-reviewed scientific research studies have confirmed what is now called the Maharishi Effect. When people practice Transcendental Meditation and its advanced program in groups, accidents, hospitalizations, and crime decrease, while positive trends and economic growth factors improve.

The first beneficiaries, as was seen in Father Mejia's centers, are the participants themselves. But the benefits extend to those in the surrounding area. Depending on the size of the group, this positive effect extends to the country or the world.

These collective groups are another way to express love to the larger community. In Maharishi's words, *"Silence that flows is love."* By participating in the groups, the children of Father Mejia's center have the opportunity to do good beyond themselves. They can express love as silence flowing to the whole community. Love from this level can create world coherence for all. Love flowing can be the flow of peace.

This opportunity is not limited to the children of Colombia. The ability to express love as silence flowing is open to everyone, anywhere in the world, by joining the group practice of Transcendental Meditation and its advanced programs. When peace is there, the silent power of love to create peace is expressed from within. The power of love, while sounding miraculous, rooted in silence can create peace.

Whether you choose to love to melt your own heart or to create peace for the world, the words of Rumi ring true just the same: *"Only from the heart can you touch the sky."* Love and unfurl yourself across the universe. Love and touch the sky.

Soar, my dear friends. Soar seekers of truth. Soar choosers of love. Touch the sky and paint it brilliant with your light. Be the truth that you are. In the end, the happiness you radiate in love will transform you—and your world—more than you could ever imagine.

Action Steps

Here are some reflections, ideas, and actions to absorb and experience this thread of wisdom:

1. Be Open to Love. Wherever your attention goes in love, allow it to be. This can be any type of love: love of a partner, love of a child, love of parents, love of a friend, love of a teacher. There are an infinite number of paths for love to flow.

2. Remember. When has love helped you change a situation? When has someone loving you made you a better person? How did you grow with the experience of love? How did your ability to love grow as you were loved?

3. Reflect and Write. Think of a situation in your life that was very difficult, but you persisted by being warm and loving, and finally, the door opened. Compare that to situations where you were not so patient and nurturing. How did the outcomes differ?

4. Find the Source of Love. Usually, we believe that love depends on others, that someone will come and make us feel love. But in reality, love is a quality of our own Being. Examine the most glorious moments of love in your life and note how much love was not what the other person was doing but a quality of your own self. Realize that love is your own resolution, and a strong resolution can melt any rock.

5. Look and See. In some ancient cultures, love means looking at things in a special way. The physical process of attention going to a point can better create a positive, loving effect. What you put your attention on grows. Can you reflect on the best moments of love and compare them to your ability to watch lovingly? How does it make you feel that love is just your decision to put your attention on someone or something?

6. Imagine. Imagine you have lived a life and are writing an autobiography. Evaluate its quality from the level of your ability to love: what you did and what could you have done better. Do you realize that love depends on you and not how the others deal with you? If you were to rate your loving ability, what would your mark be at this moment, and what could you do to make it better?

Self-healing recognizes every experience manifesting phases of absolute happiness within our lives and for others.

Go for the Highest

If all the lessons of this book could be summarized in one phrase, this would be it: Go for the highest first. Whatever you desire— peace, happiness, love, family, money, fame, success, or accomplishments will follow.

Capture the fort. Don't be like the man in his small hut afraid to leave to take ownership of the castle. Go for the castle. The castle is not something that can be seen or touched—the castle is the wisdom, happiness, intelligence, love, creativity, and bliss inherent within each of us. Go for the real castle from which everything can be achieved.

That doesn't mean it will be easy or that you will accomplish everything you set out to. It can be overwhelming. You might feel like you're succeeding in one area and slipping in another. Just because I've written these words of the highest inspiration doesn't mean I don't also slip, fall, mess up, and get up and start all over again. But as long as there is life, there is hope and the power to transform at every moment.

You can take one thread that particularly resonates and focus on that. Or there is a workbook to use as a guide week by week. As we said in some of the later threads:

- Start where you are but see the goal.
- Failure leads to greater strength.
- Life is in the moments.
- And with love, anything is possible. You can be invincible.

Your guideposts on the path are woven into the chapters; but more importantly, the path is already woven within you.

Maharishi was fond of the saying, "*Seek the highest first.*" And this is just what it means—gain enlightenment, or at least step onto the path to enlightenment, and see all the wondrous new opportunities that come to you. Take this with you in your heart. Each day requires courage and strength. I believe you are brave because even in moments of feeling hopeless I've found a way to be brave. And I know you can, too.

There is nothing to lose and everything to gain. Whether you start at point one, point fifty, or point ten thousand doesn't matter. The point is to start. And to start means to search for—and find —greater happiness, greater peace, better health, and a more fulfilling life.

You are unique and you are powerful. Even when it doesn't feel like it, your brilliant potential is there, not waiting to be developed but already fully awakened. Find yourself. Be yourself. And be more than you ever imagined. It starts with one step, one day, or one moment.

In the words of Rk Veda (10.191.2-4):

समानी व आकूतिः समाना हृदयानि वः
समानमस्तु वो मनो यथा वः सुसहासति ॥
*"United be your purpose, harmonious be your feelings, in the same
way as all the various aspects of the universe exist in togetherness,
wholeness of life."*

My hand is here to hold you as we share this path. May the sweet
fragrance of the goal tickle your nose and fill your heart, wherever
you may be. I admire your bravery and respect your unique journey. May we all together rise higher than we ever thought possible.
May we fill the world with love and create real, lasting peace.

Practical Application

If you've been following along with the action points at the end of each chapter, you have already integrated a lot into your life. This section is a short summary of the practical application included in each of the chapters to remind you of the simple ways you can take steps on a daily basis to improve your happiness, fulfillment, and contentment.

Whether you are seeking wealth, fame, love, romance, happiness, peace, stability, success, or anything else, these simple steps will take you closer to your goals, day by day.

1. Follow Your Path

Whether this is your religious teachings, a spiritual advisor, or something else, if you were already seeking and have found something that brought value and greater meaning into your life—do that. Everything mentioned here can be applied to enrich any spiritual path.

People of all religious faiths have found that the other practical techniques mentioned in this book, especially Transcendental

Meditation, enrich their lives and bring greater meaning to their spiritual path and understanding.

Likewise, people who have found benefit or relief through other forms of meditation, breathing exercises, yoga, or self-development practices should continue to learn through those channels. The first and most important principle is that when knowledge is true and pure, there is always more to learn and more to absorb and live for the practical benefit of your life.

Because knowledge is different in different states of consciousness, the same truth that resonated with you in the past may resonate for a new reason later as you see it in a deeper light. The truth and goodness you have found in your life, if it is based on absolute truth, will only continue to bring more truth and goodness. Of course, if you no longer find value, it may be time to let it go. That is for you to decide. Listen, observe, and see what new meaning and depth you find within your path of knowledge and understanding.

2. Learn Transcendental Meditation

As you've seen, I personally have witnessed the power of Transcendental Meditation in so many people's lives. It offers a platform on which all the exercises in this book have greater meaning. When I talk about the power of consciousness, I'm talking about the experience that comes more and more with this effortless practice.

Transcendental Meditation (TM) and the Advanced Techniques are the most simple and automatic way to start to experience the source of your own thinking process. It requires no belief or lifestyle change. Millions of people of all religions, races, cultures, and socioeconomic backgrounds from all countries around the world practice the Transcendental Meditation technique and experience benefits in their daily lives.

Anyone who can think a thought can practice Transcendental Meditation. Children as young as four years old can learn the children's "word of wisdom." It is easy, effortless, and simple. Transcendental Meditation uses the nature of the mind to always search for more and more happiness. Like diving below the rough surf of the ocean to experience its silent depth, the Transcendental Meditation technique leads from the surface chaos of daily thinking and obligations to a level of inner peace.

The benefits of this experience have been documented in more than 700 published scientific research studies as well as the personal experiences of millions of people worldwide.

When the mind settles down, the body settles down as well and gains deep rest. The benefit for the body is the release of deeply-rooted stresses for better health. The benefits for the mind include increased creativity, intelligence, learning ability, and clarity of thought.

An analogy to explain this is like a bow and arrow. The technique to allow the arrow to fly far is to draw it back on the bow. The technique to increase human creativity, intelligence, and even happiness is to draw it back to the source of thought. From there, it can reach farther and achieve more.

Without the experience of the settled state of your own mind through Transcendental Meditation, the benefits of the exercises in this book will remain limited. There are still benefits, but when combined with the ability to take your mind beyond boundaries to a field of unbounded peace and happiness, the benefits are multiplied.

If you would like to learn Transcendental Meditation, you can visit TM.org or TM-women.org to find a TM center near you. There are flexible payment plans for those who cannot afford to learn, and scholarships are available for the lowest income categories. If someone really wants to learn and cannot make it happen, please visit www.bemorehappy.com and contact us. We will help you to find a way to learn TM. Even if you already practice TM or just want to reach out, please contact us at www.bemorehappy.com and share your experience!

More on Meditation

The ancient practice of nearly every world religion—meditation —has become a worldwide phenomenon in the last 20 years or so. Growing up in rural Iowa in the '80s and '90s, meditation was seen as abnormal and mystifying. Some people even said we were worshiping the devil. Now there is a yoga studio on every street corner, and everyone from fitness trainers to celebrities to political and religious leaders is touting the benefits of meditation.

There is no doubt that every type of meditation brings results. Some bring more results, some bring less, but all are training the mind. Meditation can build creativity, intelligence, and peace. Just like the diverse people who practice meditation, the benefits gained are diverse. One person may sleep better while another finds they need less sleep. Another person may experience reduced blood pressure, and yet another increases their fitness performance. People meditate for all different reasons, and they are getting results.

When I refer to meditation here in this book, I am referring to Transcendental Meditation as taught by Maharishi Mahesh Yogi. What makes Transcendental Meditation (TM) unique is that it is completely effortless. Anyone who can think a thought can practice TM. Children as young as four can practice the children's technique. It requires no concentration, no contemplation, and no effort.

Yes, it is effortless. Even if you don't believe in it, it will work. It is automatic.

How can it be effortless? Transcendental Meditation uses the nature of the mind to experience finer and finer layers of thought. The mind is always looking for more and more, especially more happiness. If you hear your favorite song playing nearby, your attention will be drawn there. The nature of the mind is to go to a place of greater charm.

Remember all the times you've sat in a meeting, lecture, or other event as the speaker prattled on for too long? Your mind started to wander—to what you had to do, what you were planning to have for dinner, or something interesting you'd seen earlier in the day. That wandering quality is the nature of the mind to search for more and more happiness.

You will hear meditation teachers refer to it as the "monkey mind." Just like a monkey jumps from branch to branch looking for the best fruits or leaves, our minds keep jumping looking for greater charm and greater happiness.

While many forms of meditation will ask you to try to control or calm this monkey mind, Transcendental Meditation uses the very nature of the mind searching for more and more happiness to lead it to a more settled state automatically. In Transcendental Meditation, the mind is lively but undirected. And naturally, the mind reaches for subtler and subtler states of thought.

What are subtler layers of thought? Think about the most outward expression of thought as speaking—you voice the thoughts in your head. Finer than that is whispering softly. Finer than that is thinking loudly—perhaps when you're upset or over-whelmed. We can call this mentally yelling.

Subtler than that is regular thinking, and still subtler is thinking very softly, almost a whisper of a thought. More subtle than that is the level of intuition. This can be called a gut feeling, something in your heart, or a soft whisper guiding you inside. This is a very fine, almost non-expressed thought.

More subtle even than that is the source of thought. This is the field of infinite creativity, power, and intelligence. This is where the magic happens. It is where the strokes of genius come from; what you tap into when you have an "a-ha" moment, a brilliant inspiration, or excel beyond what you thought possible.

It is always available because it is just that—the source of all thinking and action. But stress, tensions, and limiting beliefs all hold us back from accessing this reservoir of power and creativity within us. It is always there, waiting, and yet out of reach.

This difficulty has been expressed by philosophers and spiritual teachers throughout the ages who said it was very difficult to achieve or that it required years of dedicated practice. Without a shortcut, that is true. Someone could spend their whole life looking for a glimpse they once had of the source of thought. In fact, many of the great modern poets and philosophers describe moments of transcendent inspiration, only to spend years or decades searching to repeat that experience.

The shortcut, as you guessed, is Transcendental Meditation. It uses the nature of the mind to go to the source of thought, which is also a field of infinite happiness. In just a few minutes of this experience in the morning and evening, the mind is recharged with the power of that creativity and intelligence. What was difficult becomes easy. What looked impossible becomes possible simply by turning on the innate power of the human mind.

The greatest resource available in the world is sitting, unused, within each of us. What a difference it would make for billions of people to be able to contact the source of thought for even a few minutes each day.

One of the ways TM achieves this so effectively is because as the mind settles down to finer levels of thought, the body settles down. Just as in sleep, when the body rests it starts to restore and rejuvenate itself. Unlike sleep, when the body settles down during

Transcendental Meditation, the mind remains awake and alert. The body gains rest deeper than deep sleep while the mind is wakeful. This unique combination of inner wakefulness with deep rest restores and rejuvenates the body—allowing you to throw off not only surface fatigue but also deep-rooted stress.

The benefits of removing stress and fatigue are wide-ranging. It explains why one person practicing TM may have lower blood pressure, while others experience better sleep, less anxiety, or better memory. When stress and fatigue are removed, the body can start to heal itself.

Some doctors say that up to 70% of disease is psychosomatic, or stress related. With a systematic way of gaining deep rest and releasing stress, it can be expected that people will see improvements in a variety of health conditions.

The research backs this up. From hospitalization rate to heart health, from anxiety to insomnia to memory, Transcendental Meditation provides a missing crucial element that allows people to throw off stress for better health. It is worth sharing this technique with anyone suffering from the debilitating effects of stress so rampant in the modern world.

There have been over 700 scientific research studies conducted at more than 200 universities and research institutes in 50 countries around the world verifying the powerful effect of Transcendental Meditation on mind, body, behavior, and environment.

Because it requires no belief and is automatic, it is used as a tool for those looking to manage or cure chronic health conditions. People learn Transcendental Meditation for all different reasons, but they get a wide variety of benefits. While they may only start to control their blood pressure, suddenly they find more creative inspiration or happiness in their life.

As the saying goes, "You pull one leg of the table and the whole table comes with it." Whatever the reason a person chooses to start, the wide-ranging effects of TM will benefit many areas of their life.

Children especially take to meditation like fish to water. I learned the children's technique at age 4 and have memories of walking the hallways of our school, 20 or so children per class, all quietly practicing the children's walking technique. For older children, sitting quietly in meditation becomes a refuge during the day.

Transcendental Meditation is so powerful in transforming lives that if you were to give a child only one gift in a lifetime, it could be this. There is the saying, "Give a man a fish, and he eats for a day. Teach a man to fish, and he eats for a lifetime." I would extend that to say: teach a child to meditate, and they will have a resource to navigate life and open possibilities to achieve their dreams.

A Word About Cost

Yes, you can get a meditation app for $10 these days, but the adage holds true: you get what you pay for. There is no technique in the world that has the far-reaching and all-encompassing universal benefit that has been shown by Transcendental Meditation for more than 60 years.

There is no price that is enough for the benefits of unfolding your full human potential. Whatever price you pay is more like a symbolic offering for something that can add years to your life and increase your well-being by adding more value to each day. If you only take one action after reading this book, please learn TM.

3. Write About Your Experience

What you put your attention on grows stronger in your life. When you give something attention, like watering a plant, it begins to grow and flourish. Now is not the time to rate your experiences as good or bad. Check judgment at the door. Simply record what happened along with any insights you might have had.

When writing your experience consider recording:

- An experience in meditation that stood out to you.
- An insight that was either brought on by some piece of knowledge or through a spontaneous "a-ha!" moment.
- Any moment of learning in your day.
- An experience that stretched you as a person.
- A moment of great happiness: elaborate on those feelings.
- A moment of peace: what made it peaceful? How did you feel?
- A moment of love: what did it feel like?
- A moment of gratitude: what made you grateful?
- Anything else that seems important or that you want to remember. This is a record for you.

The habit of writing down your experiences will naturally build its own momentum. As you do it, you will want to do it more. Bringing your attention daily to the good in your life has been shown to increase happiness and well-being. And because what you put your attention on grows stronger in your life, regularly focusing on the good will bring more into your life.

4. LEARN ADVANCED PROGRAMS

Transcendental Meditation is the primary technique to experience the settled state of the human mind. The benefits are so enormous and life-transforming that many people think that is it. But that is just the beginning. After you've been practicing TM for a few months, you can start to learn the advanced programs.

Maharishi brought out Transcendental Meditation in the late 1950s as the "basic" program for those who had no experience with meditation or even necessarily interest in spiritual development. The advanced programs were brought out later, in the 1970s, and are called Advanced Techniques including the TM-Sidhi program.

The Advanced Techniques accelerate the benefits gained through the TM technique. With TM, you experience the source of thought. Advanced programs, such as the TM-Sidhi program, train the mind to think and act from this settled level of awareness. Think of TM as training the mind to dive into the peaceful depths of the ocean—you take the correct angle and the rest is automatic. The Advanced Techniques train you to stay at the bottom of the ocean, swim around, and explore.

If you learn TM and find it enriches your life, you will find that the Advanced Techniques do even more.

5. Find Ways to Reach Beyond Yourself

While going beyond yourself can be a simple act of kindness when you would rather just go home, it can also be a regular activity. Think of something that would make a big difference for another person that you would not otherwise do.

This can be an extra hour weekly playing with a child; time spent visiting an elderly home; making your family's favorite meal when you would rather order takeout; planting spring bulbs throughout your neighborhood for everyone to enjoy; taking a page from "The Lupine Lady" and planting lupines in nearby empty fields; teaching a younger person a skill you have; spending time with older people in your life and just listening; volunteering for a cause important to you; explaining an important cause in a way that makes sense to people who don't understand; planning a special day for your partner; the list goes on.

There is no way for anyone else to tell you what is reaching beyond yourself. Look inside, and then look out and see what you can do that would help someone else. It is not about changing their view; it is about making their life happier or richer.

For this, you don't need to give money, although you can. This is about giving of yourself. You will be amazed at how much you transform when instead of looking in—you look out.

In Spanish, there is an idiom about someone being too busy looking at his or her own navel to see anything else. This is the opposite of that—get out of your own navel and create good for someone else.

6. Practice Gratitude

Social and psychological sciences have started to show just how important gratitude is for mental health. The practice of gratitude alone makes you happier with what you have and draws good to you. Like attracts like. Gratitude attracts more to be grateful for.

You can practice gratitude through writing, speaking, or simply mentally noting all that you are grateful for. One way to do this is to give yourself five minutes at the beginning and end of each day. If five minutes is too much, take 30 seconds and list things that you are especially grateful for. These can be big things like health, family, and a comfortable standard of living, but it's good to also get into the specifics. Here are a few examples to get you started:

- "I am grateful that I was inspired to finish my paper yesterday."
- "I'm grateful for the yummy cookie from the school bake sale."
- "I am grateful for wonderful friends who make me smile hours after we get off the phone."

- "I'm grateful for the new beautiful houseplants I got that add so much to my home."
- "I'm grateful for the sunshine and warm weather—and that I got outside for a walk."
- "I'm grateful for the delicious dinner made by my spouse."
- "I'm grateful that I saw my kids doing something kind for each other."
- "I'm grateful that my house is clean."
- "I'm grateful that people value my opinion and want me to participate in this board or committee."

You will see that many of these examples would have an opposite, ungrateful perspective, such as:

- "This board or committee takes so much of my free time."
- "Why do my kids always fight?"
- "I only got a 20-minute walk in the sunshine when I wanted to go for an hour."

The idea is to bring your attention to the positive in a situation. Start with as many things in your daily life as possible that make you grateful. Repeated practice at locating points of gratitude will make it easier. When you note something that you are genuinely grateful for, notice the welling up of peace you feel inside.

7. Practice Kindness

Kindness is one of the most powerful tools to transform yourself and others. This is related to doing for others, as well as gratitude, but is a separate activity.

The best way to practice kindness is to start on yourself. We are often more critical of ourselves than we would ever be of a friend or someone we love. Find something to appreciate about yourself. When you are tired, give yourself a chance to rest or carve out some time to do something on your own.

Kindness is not about big, grand gestures; it is about the little moments. When your pants are too tight, instead of declaring yourself fat and ugly, try another pair and comment on how gorgeous you look in those. Or keep the pants and feast on the beauty of your eyes, your hair, and your smile.

When you are feeling down, smile at yourself in the mirror. It is not just the big or life-transforming moments; it is about picking out the good in any moment.

Remember the story of the pearly white teeth (Thread 15). Watch for the good in yourself and others.

> *"Love watches for any sign of strength.*
> *It sees how far each one has come and not how far he has to go."*
> ~ Maharishi Mahesh Yogi

8. Practice Generosity

True generosity means giving without any expectation of return. It is not an investment for the future or a sort of trade. Generosity is another way to go beyond yourself. Generosity is giving for the sake of giving. It can be giving when you believe in something or someone, and it can also be giving when you don't believe they deserve it.

Sometimes generosity at an undeserved moment can change a person's life. Whether this is a rebellious teenager or an adult who finds themself in a difficult situation, giving out of love, compassion, and generosity of spirit can be life-transforming.

The secret of generosity is that when it is done in its pure form, it may or may not transform the receiver, but it will always transform the giver. It is a way to reach beyond. Teaching is one form of generosity, which is why the saying *"The teacher always gains more than the student"* makes so much sense. Giving from a full heart without expectation of return will transform you in ways you cannot imagine.

If you are not in the habit of giving like this—if you normally give presents to family and friends out of obligation and don't think much beyond that—then generosity will take some creativity and thought at first. You can brainstorm the people in your life who you would like to give to and then start thinking of what would be wonderful and unexpected for them.

Generosity is another way of reaching beyond yourself. You can also choose to be generous to people you don't know. You can volunteer at a shelter or food bank, donate food or other items, give $20 to children in need, or choose causes that speak to you and volunteer or make regular donations.

9. Talk to Your Older, Wiser Self

Just sit quietly for a few minutes and see an older, wiser version of yourself. This can be you in 5 years, 10 years, or 50 years—it is up to you. After respectfully approaching the older, wiser version of yourself, begin to ask your questions. This can be whatever is concerning you—relationships or breakups, job or career choices, wealth, children or family, friends, home, or anything else.

After each question, sit quietly and listen to the answer. Take the time to really listen. This is not you speaking today. This is you of the future. If you suspend your immediate reactions and listen, you will be amazed by the simple truth that has unfolded.

You can ask yourself anything. You can ask how you will feel toward someone that broke up with you five years from now. You can ask yourself if you should pivot in your career. You can ask both general and specific questions.

- A general question might be: "Should I consider other directions for my career?"
- A specific question would be: "Should I become an investment banker instead of a teacher?"
- Another important question might be: "Should I worry about (child name)'s current behavior?"
- Or the question might be guidance: "How can I reach (person's name) or make that person feel loved?"

Pause and take time to listen. When it is a big decision or emotionally charged important life moment, you can visit your older, wiser self more than once. You can do it every few days or once a week. The important thing is not to try to change the answers you receive. You are listening and observing.

This simple practice is a way to make use of the latent wisdom and deep all-knowing quality within each of us. Make your older, wiser self the guide. With years of experience and the advantage of perspective, it can help you navigate unclear situations in life. This is a way to reach the level of you that already knows the answer.

There is no requirement for regular visits. You can speak to your older, wiser self once a year or once in a lifetime. When you feel lost, confused, unsure, or heartbroken, you can always take recourse to your own latent wisdom.

10. CREATE A GROUP

When we gather, we are stronger. Bring others together for a higher purpose. This can be for discussion and inspiration—but even better if it also includes practice. Most ancient spiritual traditions include some form of group practice.

Research has shown that when groups practice Transcendental Meditation and the advanced programs together, the effect is more powerful for the individuals in the group—and for the people in the surrounding area.

One way this was demonstrated was by measuring brainwave or EEG coherence. What researchers found was that not only did those practicing the techniques exhibit increased brainwave coherence, but during and after the practice the measurements of EEG coherence of people on the street also increased. These people on the street didn't do anything different—and yet their clarity of thinking and ability to use their full mental potential increased. What a powerful tool to change society for the better. (See Thread 18 and the story of Father Mejia in Colombia for more on this).

If there is already a group practicing TM and advanced TM techniques together in your area, you can join them. If not, be a community organizer and bring family and friends together. While the group practice can be daily, organize special events such as a weekend picnic, an evening knowledge and inspiration session with an interesting speaker, or other community events. Make it about coming together. Adding the power of consciousness to the joy of human gathering can change the life of a whole community and beyond.

Footnotes

[1] The Science of Creative Intelligence

The Science of Creative Intelligence was an early expression of the theoretical knowledge of consciousness created by Maharishi. It is still used to teach children or as introductory material to understand how we relate to the world and how consciousness is the basis of life. Transcendental Meditation and its Advanced programs are the practical aspect of the Science of Creative Intelligence that makes this theory a living reality.

[2] Yoga

Sutras Verse 1: अथ योगानुशासनम्

"Now begins the teaching of Yoga."

Yoga is now taught in studios across the world. Some teachers attend a four-week training; others go to India or Nepal for an authentic experience. But almost always, yoga in the western world means exercise. Yoga as an exercise is fantastic for health, flexibility, and overall wellness. But to say yoga is just exercise is to put it into far too small of a box.

Maybe your teacher mentions nirvana and uses the Sanskrit names for the poses. Do they talk about the eight-fold path? The eight-fold path of yoga is described by Patanjali, the great Rishi, or seer, whose cognition and teachings form the basis of modern yoga.

Yoga means "union" or "unifying" and the purpose of yoga is to unify the individual with the cosmic reality so that they are no longer bound by small limitations. The purpose of yoga is to create freedom from limitations on all levels of life.

Most modern teachers who talk about the eight-fold path of yoga describe it as a sequential path. In reality, it is a simultaneous path, where the highest level of yoga can be experienced from the very beginning.

The eight limbs of yoga are:

1. Yama: the observances that connect the individual life in harmony with the entire field of creation. These include qualities like truthfulness, non-violence, and non-covetousness.

2. Niyama: the five rules of life that bring balance to the individual body. These are: purification, contentment, austerity, study, and devotion to God.

3. Asana: the postures we associate with yoga. The goal is to create perfect functioning of the limbs of the body in coordination with each other.

. . .

4. Pranayama: the individual breathing. You will hear of teachers offering different pranayama breathing exercises.

5. Pratyahara: what lies between the objects of senses and the perceiver. This takes yoga into the more subtle fields of life.

6. Dharana: the field of life between the senses and the mind. The purpose of Dharana is to create a steady state of the mind where it is no longer drawn to the senses.

7. Dhyan: the field of life between the senses and Being. Another word for Dhyan is Transcendental Meditation. Dhyan covers the process of the refinement of the mind to experience its purest state, Being, or pure consciousness.

8. Samadhi: the transcendental state of Being, the source of thought, the most settled and powerful level of existence. This is also called pure consciousness, the source of thinking, creativity, and Being.

Commonly misinterpreted as the end goal of the previous seven limbs of yoga, Samadhi can be experienced from the very beginning of the path through Transcendental Meditation or other practices. The goal can be experienced from the start.

Yoga is not just exercise. It is also not only for those who are willing to live in the Himalayas with an enlightened master. The path of yoga is a practical path of daily living. It is a way to open the unlimited potential of every individual. Yoga is the path and the means to know, do, and achieve anything.

[3] Scientific Research

Over 700 scientific research studies, conducted at 200 universities and research institutes in more than 40 countries around the world, verify the profound benefits of Transcendental Meditation, its advanced programs, and practice in groups. The benefits are seen for the mind, body, behavior, environment, and society, improving life as a whole.

A sample of the research includes:

Reduced Stress and Anxiety:

• Alexander C.N., et al. Effects of the Transcendental Meditation program on stress reduction, health, and employee development: A prospective study in two occupational settings. Anxiety, Stress and Coping: An International Journal 6: 245-262, 1993.

• Barnes V. A., et al. Impact of Transcendental Meditation on cardiovascular function at rest and during acute stress in adolescents with high normal blood pressure. Journal of Psychosomatic Research 51, 597-605, 2001.

• Barnes V. A., et al. Stress, stress reduction, and hypertension in African Americans. Journal of the National Medical Association, 89, 464-476, 1997.

• Brooks J.S. and Scarano T. Transcendental Meditation in the treatment of post-Vietnam adjustment. Journal of Counseling and Development 64: 212-215, 1985.

Decreased Depression:

• Brooks J.S., et al. Transcendental Meditation in the treatment of post-Vietnam adjustment. Journal of Counseling and Development, 64:212–215, 1985.

• Kniffki C. Tranzendentale Meditation und Autogenes Training. Ein Vergleich (Transcendental Meditation and Autogenic Training: A Comparison). Munich: Kindler Verlag Geist und Psyche, 1979.

• Ferguson P.C., et al. Psychological Findings on Transcendental Meditation. Journal of Humanistic Psychology 16:483-488, 1976.

Reduced Insomnia:

• Haratani T., et al. Effects of Transcendental Meditation (TM) on the health behavior of industrial workers. Japanese Journal of Public Health 37 (10 Suppl.): 729, 1990.

• Ljunggren G. Inflytandet av Transcendental Meditation pa neuroticism, medicinbruk och sömnproblem. Läkartidningen 74(47): 4212–4214, 1977.

• Lovell-Smith H. D. Transcendental Meditation—treating the patient as well as the disease. The New Zealand Family Physician 9: 62–65, April 1982.

• Orme-Johnson D. W., et al. Meditation in the treatment of chronic pain and insomnia. In National Institutes of Health Technology Assessment Conference on Integration of Behavioral and Relaxation Approaches into the Treatment of Chronic Pain and Insomnia, Bethesda Maryland: National Institutes of Health, 1995.

Increased Longevity:

• Alexander C.N., et al. Transcendental Meditation, mindfulness, and longevity. Journal of Personality and Social Psychology 57: 950-964, 1989.

• Alexander C. N., et al. The effects of Transcendental Meditation compared to other methods of relaxation in reducing risk factors, morbidity, and mortality. Homeostasis 35, 243-264, 1994.

• Barnes V. A., et al. Impact of Transcendental Meditation on mortality in older African Americans—eight year follow-up. Journal of Social Behavior and Personality 17(1) 201-216, 2005.

• Glaser J. L., et al. Elevated serum dehydroepiandrosterone sulfate levels in practitioners of the Transcendental Meditation (TM) and TM-Sidhi programs. Journal of Behavioral Medicine 15: 327-341, 1992.

• Schneider R. H., et al. The Transcendental Meditation program: reducing the risk of heart disease and mortality and improving quality of life in African Americans. Ethnicity and Disease 11; 159-60, 2001.

You can see more scientific research on Transcendental Meditation and its advanced programs at https://www.tm.org/research-on-meditation

[4] Seven States of Consciousness

Maharishi explains that there are seven states of consciousness, each with a unique style of functioning of mind and body.

There are three states of consciousness we are all familiar with:

1. The state of being awake as we go about daily activity (waking state of consciousness).

2. The state of being asleep (deep sleep state of consciousness).

3. The state of dreaming that is physiologically different

from deep sleep (dreaming state of consciousness).

Each of these three states of consciousness has unique physiological and mental characteristics. How our bodies and minds function when we are awake is completely different from when we are dreaming.

Our perception is also different in different states of consciousness. While dreaming, we might be chased by a tiger. When we wake up, we find we are in bed, and it is morning. While we were dreaming, the tiger seemed real. Once we wake up, the tiger seems like an illusion, and our pillows seem more real.

The bridge to experiencing higher states of consciousness is through the universal consciousness we were discussing. When we experience, even momentarily, this vast field of consciousness—a level beyond limitations, ideas, or beliefs—it is life-transforming. This level of consciousness is pure Being, pure awareness, pure intelligence, creativity, and power, and also has the qualities of happiness and bliss. It is as if a light is switched on. It is called the 4th state of consciousness—transcendental consciousness.

Experiencing this 4th state of consciousness, the latent potential is awakened, even momentarily. It is a key to many locks and a solution to many intractable problems. It is light in perpetual darkness and opens the possibility for higher states of consciousness.

Higher states of consciousness are as real and as practical as what we experience as reality right now. Transcendental consciousness is both our inner latent secret and the bridge to higher truth. It is so universal that it is at once the source, course, and goal of evolution. From the perspective of this level of consciousness, it is true that we are all already at the goal. Now to discover it!

The best way to know more about higher states of consciousness is to experience them directly. How could you understand a strawberry, no matter how detailed the description, if you had never tasted any fruit? The taste is in eating. The reality of higher states of consciousness is in experience. And that is where the fun begins because each person will see and experience all higher states of consciousness through their own view or lens of reality.

Higher States of Consciousness

What are these higher states of consciousness? Perhaps you think of altered states caused by drugs or delusions. But higher states of consciousness are not drug-induced. They are not abnormal functions of the nervous system. Higher states of consciousness can be experienced when we use the normal—full potential—state of the nervous system.

Quite simply, higher states of consciousness are experienced when you use more of the nervous system. If you were using 10% of your full brain potential and you start using 15%, it will seem like you are in a higher state of consciousness—a greater range of functioning. While any ability to use a greater percentage of our nervous system could be considered higher, Maharishi defined specific landmarks of each of the seven states of consciousness. Every state of consciousness has unique characteristics of the functioning of the mind and body.

These are like signposts on the way. But unlike a linear path, you can glimpse any higher state of consciousness at any moment. It can be sequential, but it can also be simultaneous.

The first three states of consciousness are ordinary states of consciousness. Everyone experiences waking, dreaming, and deep sleep states of consciousness. Here are the different physiological and mental styles of functioning in these first three states of consciousness:

• In waking state of consciousness, the mind is alert and able to perceive what is around us. The body is also awake and not resting.

• In dreaming state of consciousness, the mind is in a delusion or dream world; it does not see reality. The body is gaining rest.

• In deep sleep state of consciousness, the mind is completely inactive to outside perception, as if in a state of blackness. The body is gaining an even deeper state of rest.

We all dream, sleep, and wake up daily. What comes next? The 4th state of consciousness, called Transcendental Consciousness by Maharishi. In the Vedic Tradition, it is called *Atma Chetana*. In Buddhism, it is called *Nirvana*. It can also be called *Samadhi* and many other names in various traditions.

What makes Transcendental Consciousness different from waking, dreaming, and sleeping states of consciousness is that unique combination of the function of mind and body. Like the waking state of consciousness, in Transcendental Consciousness, the mind is awake and alert; but instead of being alert to outside perceptions, it is awake within itself. At the same time, the body gains deep rest, like that of deep sleep, but often even deeper. This is the hallmark of Transcendental Consciousness or Turiya Chetana: inner wakefulness of the mind and deep rest for the body.

Beyond Transcendental Consciousness, there is still more. There is the possibility to train the nervous system to maintain the restful-alert quality of Transcendental Consciousness even while waking, dreaming, and sleeping. This means the unique activity of the nervous system to promote Transcendental Consciousness is not lost when you are moving about during the day. This is called Cosmic Consciousness.

In Cosmic Consciousness, the mind is fully developed. That means the nervous system is able to maintain the fully-integrated functioning of higher states of consciousness all the time. It sounds like this is the pinnacle of human achievement, but it is still the beginning.

Beyond Cosmic Consciousness is God Consciousness. The path to God Consciousness is through the development of the heart. The heart flows in waves of love and devotion, melting in love to God until everything in the creation becomes as dear as the creator. In God Consciousness, one can perceive all the finer levels of creation. Here you can perceive, through all senses, the worlds of angels, devatas, and other light beings. God Consciousness is the world of heavenly God—the worlds of the celestial and the divine.

It can be tempting to stay millions of years in the many exquisite worlds of God Consciousness, but the force of evolution propels the seeker of supreme truth onward. There is no path from God Consciousness to Unity Consciousness; the process of evolution is through time. Time takes the fullness of the celestial and a universe of devotion and love to God and transforms it into Unity Consciousness.

Unity Consciousness is the 7th state of consciousness. In Unity Consciousness, gradually all the diverse qualities and attributes of the universe begin to be experienced as a part of myself. There is no more "I" and "mine" because everything becomes "I." In Unity Consciousness, you don't lose your sense of identity by becoming one with everything. All that you were before you still will be. It is just that starting with what is closest and expanding out, unity predominates, and differences become secondary.

[5] Develop Your Total Potential

As it turns out, humans use a very small percentage of their full mental potential. Some say 10%, some say 17%. Whatever the percentage, that leaves a huge percentage of human potential untapped.

When I was asking, "Is this it?" I probably should have been asking, "Is this all that I am?" And the answer would have been, "No—there is so much more potential and so much more that you are." That is true of every person, from every country, culture, race, religion, gender, sexual orientation, belief system, or socioeconomic background.

In the western world, parents fight for every advantage for their children, often submitting applications to the best kindergarten shortly after birth. The pressure continues throughout childhood with the need for the best schools, academics, and extracurricular activities to give the children every possible advantage for the best university education, and thus, the best life.

The irony in this is that nearly 18 years of fighting to give children the best advantage does not increase the children's ability to learn. Nor does it connect the children to the subjects they are learning about or to their higher purpose. Parents fight for their children to have the best in life in hopes that it will make them happy— and this often makes both themselves and the children unhappy in the process.

The simple experience of the source of thought through Transcendental Meditation opens a whole new dimension in education. It is a hidden treasure for parents to truly equip their children with the best advantage in life. It is a gift for parents and children to take recourse to greater potential.

The whole process of conventional education is focused on remembering facts. Those who do well in a classroom are good at retaining information and re-formulating it in tests and presentations. We can say that good students are good at filling their brains. But what about increasing the capacity of the brain?

Let's think of the brain as a bowl, like a fishbowl. The bowl can retain a certain amount of knowledge, just like a small fishbowl might hold one gallon of water while a large fishbowl could hold ten gallons or more. Every day when students go to learn, they place chemistry, math, literature, and history into their bowl of knowledge. Good students are good at placing and keeping information in their bowl of knowledge. What happens when the bowl is full?

What if they were able to expand their capacity for knowledge? What if, instead of having a fishbowl to fill with facts, they had an Olympic-sized swimming pool? Their capacity to learn and retain knowledge would increase dramatically.

This is what happens with the practice of the Transcendental Meditation technique. During meditation, the total potential of the brain is used. It is an automatic process. Even when someone feels like they are not settled, much of the total potential of the brain is enlivened.

This is measured as maximum EEG coherence between all the hemispheres and lobes (i.e. different areas of the brain). It can measure 80% or 90% or, at moments, even 100% coherence during TM. This trains the brain to use its full potential. Like any other practice, as someone becomes accustomed to using more of their full brain potential, they can use more of that full potential in daily life automatically.

Use Your Full Potential

Athletes say it. Dentists say it. Doctors say it: use it or lose it. Train to gain. That is the principle of brain potential, as well. If you don't use it, you lose its ability to help you. When you train your brain to use its full potential, you are tapping into the ultimate advantage in life.

People who train their minds to use their full potential reap the benefits a million-fold. Arguably, people who train their bodies to be physically strong and attractive receive opportunities and benefits. At the very least, they reap the rewards of good health, good sleep, good digestion, etc. But that is a small advantage compared to harnessing the untapped power of the human mind.

The power of the mind opens all possibilities. Time and again, when faced with an intractable problem, after meditation a simple win-win solution is clear. Where there had been no answer, the solution suddenly appears.

Sometimes circumstances occur to make this happen, such as someone changing their mind, a change in scheduling, or some other outer change. Other times, the solution was there all along, only it was not obvious or the problem had been viewed in a different way. Meditation opens new doors of opportunity through new perspectives and with greater support from the environment.

Here is a simple analogy: think of going about your life with the use of only one finger out of ten. Think of how difficult or impossible it would be to perform simple tasks—from picking up an object to using your cell phone to taking a shower.

In the same way, by failing to develop the full potential of the mind, we are choosing to handicap ourselves in life. It is like going about your day with one finger. A task that should only take a few seconds could take hours.

If there is one most important point to take away from this book, it is that you need to develop your full potential. You are giving away too much precious time and opportunity from your life.

You simply cannot afford to continue using only a small percentage of your brain.

This is not to say you will instantly become a genius or never make mistakes. But you will start to find that life gets easier: insights come at important moments, difficult tasks get easier, or stressful situations affect you less. All of these are signs that you are tapping into your full potential and starting to use it to fulfill your desires and achieve all of your goals.

It is easy to step into the trap of thinking that because someone meditates they are automatically perfect. This could not be further from the truth. The choice to step onto the path brings incredible blessings and unexpected gifts, enriching the person's life in so many ways. However, it does not make them perfect.

Everyone is on their own path, at their own stage. Someone who is already a very kind and loving person could learn TM and find that these qualities grow. Someone else could learn TM while suffering from past trauma or anger and find that while their pain lessens, they are often still angry. While they will both benefit, neither person is prepared to advise or guide someone else on their path.

It is impossible to judge the state of consciousness of another person. We are only fully aware of ourselves. The power of TM is that you are completely self-sufficient. You don't depend on anyone else to guide you after you learn. You are the guide of your own destiny.

Never imitate or assume that another person is better than you or has authority over you. The length of time they have been on a spiritual path does not make them an authority. You are the best guide on your own path—always. While you can certainly learn from, be enriched by, and grow from the contact and inspiration of others, believe always in your own truth, your own experience, and your own place on this path. There truly is no one just like you.

About the Author

Dr. Alison Plaut has been studying and applying Maharishi Mahesh Yogi's principles for the past 35 years. At the age of 24, Maharishi honored her with the title of "Raj Rajeshwari" for her research on consciousness in relation to the unfolding of full human potential.

Alison holds a PhD in Political Science from Maharishi University of World Peace, a Master's in Business Administration with an emphasis on Sustainability from Maharishi International University, and a Masters in Maharishi Vedic Science from Maharishi University of Enlightenment.

She has worked on projects promoting the development of consciousness across the world, from New Zealand to Brazil and

Guyana to India. Through these projects, she has helped thousands of people to start unfolding their full potential and get more happiness, success, and fulfillment out of each day.

Acknowledgments

While the dedication was already made to Maharishi, I have to first acknowledge that it is Maharishi's revival of the ancient wisdom from the Vedic Tradition that is expressed in modern language throughout this book. It is not my knowledge or contribution: I am simply a more modern, familiar voice of ancient wisdom carefully restored and revitalized by Maharishi.

Next I want to thank my parents, whose love of a higher purpose and dedication to creating a peaceful world planted the seeds in me from an earliest age that anything is possible. They have built my confidence and enthusiasm for life, and most of all been a source of great love and support. Thank you for who you are, for giving me the best you see in life, and for letting me find my way.

Thank you to the early readers, who endured some fairly annoying typos, gave heartening encouragement, and pointed out where a section needed revision. Each of you brought many unique contributions to this book, and your comments often kept me playing for days.

Thank you to Lynn Owens, Carol Banka, Joelle James, Jennie Rothenberg Gritz, Channing Swanson Dragas, Lynne McMahan, Trevor McMahan, Ed and Teresa Frease, and a few others.

A special thank you to an anonymous early reader who suggested adding stories and experiences and kept suggesting refinements that improved it so much. And thank you to Julie Preminger for her artistic vision (and patience) on the cover design!

Thank you to the Red Penguin Books team. Stephanie Larkin brought so much enthusiasm and insight throughout this process. She was ready to say "yes and..." on many occasions, which led to not only this book but two others. Stephanie, it is a joy working with you. And thank you to the editors, especially Janet Larkin, for your flexibility, patience, and precision.

I have been fortunate to be in the company of many wise people over the years whose example has added richness to life. Thank you to all the friends, colleagues, and champions for peace, including members of the Mother Divine program, who I have found on this path. And thank you to my friends who are like family; you are always in my heart.

Finally, I feel to thank the beautiful enlightened living around the world. Your presence on this earth is a source of great comfort and inspiration.

As it's clear from the above, this book is a blend of the hearts and souls of so many. It is the echo of many voices speaking and sharing from their own experience. And most of all, it is the fruit of over 35 years of learning from Maharishi. May we do justice to this knowledge to make everyone happy.